Anja-Katrin Ehrich '93

Anja-Katrin Ehrich '93

von GERKAN · MARG & PARTNERS

von GERKAN · MARG & PARTNERS

Meinhard von Gerkan

ACADEMY EDITIONS ERNST & SOHN

ACKNOWLEDGMENT

I should like to express my gratitude to all those who have worked on the projects presented in this book, to my partners Volkwin Marg, Klaus Staratzke and Rolf Niedballa for their important contribution to the joint achievement of gmp, and to the photographers for permission to reproduce their work. The designs and buildings discussed in detail in this book date mainly from the last four to five years. Many people have been involved – members of our architectural staff, engineers, clients and representatives of public authorities. As the architecture is a collective work, the product of many minds, our warmest thanks go to all who played their part in the creation of the whole. I am especially grateful to my publisher, Andreas Papadakis, for making this book a reality.
Meinhard von Gerkan

Jacket: Multi-storey Car Park, Hamburg Airport;
p2 Jumbo Shed and Workshops for Lufthansa, Hamburg;
p3 Stuttgart Airport;
p4 Architect's House (Interior)

Edited and designed by
ANDREAS PAPADAKIS LTD

Translated from the German by Eileen Martin

First published in Great Britain in 1993 by
ACADEMY EDITIONS
An imprint of the Academy Group Ltd
42 Leinster Gardens London W2 3AN
and
ERNST & SOHN
Hohenzollerndamm 170, 1000 Berlin 31
Members of the VCH Publishing Group

ISBN 1 85490 166 4

Distributed to the trade in the United States of America by
ST MARTIN'S PRESS
175 Fifth Avenue, New York, NY 10010

Printed and bound in Singapore

CONTENTS

INTRODUCTION

by Ken Powell

Sheer productivity alone would mark out the practice founded in 1965 by Meinhard von Gerkan (born 1935 in the Baltic city of Riga) and Volkwin Marg (born 1936 in East Prussia) as a considerable force in contemporary German (and hence European) architecture. It has built in most of the major German cities and now has offices in Brunswick, Aachen and Berlin as well as in its home base of Hamburg, where von Gerkan lives in a stunning, humanely modern house, next to the office, overlooking the harbour. In the field of airport design alone, the firm has to be considered alongside such international masters as Norman Foster and Helmut Jahn. It is undertaking large scale masterplanning exercises and building on a small scale in the countryside. Von Gerkan, Marg & Partners is a very large operation. But there is more to it than size.

It is the versatility and range of the practice's work which impresses most. It is tempting to see an inherent pluralism to its work, since, whatever it does, it does with real conviction. A Rossi-esque parking garage in Bremen, a psychiatric clinic in Rickling which has an almost Krieresque vernacular directness, an airport which takes the language of High Tech and gives it a new complexity and eloquence: all exhibit a quality of total commitment and integrity. Yet this is not merely a matter of stylistic diversity. The style is not the point. Materials and manners derive from the brief and from the needs of the client. The practice's breadth of approach is not a self-conscious attempt at clever versatility. It reflects a belief in diversity in design related to the diversity of human life and a refusal to accept that one way of building can meet every need.

The fact that von Gerkan, Marg & Partners' architecture has, so far, been insufficiently known and acclaimed internationally reflects the relative isolation of German architects on the world scene. German architecture in the post-war era passed steadily into an arid sterility from which it was rescued by historicist and post-modernist influences which became prominent in the late seventies. Gottfried Böhm, O.M. Ungers and Josef P. Kleihues have been amongst the leading proponents of an expressive, rationalist historicism which has produced some powerful and memorable buildings. Kleihues directed the IBA project

Hanse Viertel, Hamburg: Arcade intersection, 1980

DAL offices, Mainz, 1984

Above: Grindelallee 100, Hamburg, 1987
Opposite: Stuttgart Airport, 1980-1991

9

Berlin-Tegel Airport: Noise insulation hangar, 1975

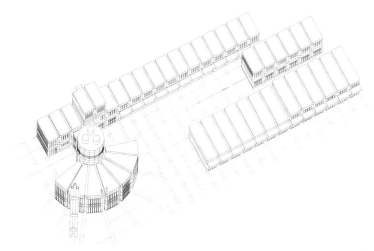

Berlin-Tegel Airport: Workshops and plant station, 1975

Stuttgart Airport: Departure hall, 1980-1991

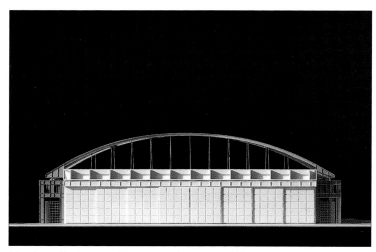

Hamburg-Fuhlsbüttel Airport: Jumbo shed, 1989-1992

which strengthened the hold of Post-Modernism and Italian-style Rationalism on Germany. This school has taken on the role of an "establishment" in German architecture, but it is not unchallenged and the new modernism (in which Günter Behnisch is a leading light) is a resurgent force. Younger architects like Daniel Libeskind, Eisele & Fritz and the Austrian-born Christoph Langhoff are pursuing an expressive, liberated Modernism. The nature of the debate in current German architecture is epitomised by the controversy over the redevelopment of the Potsdamerplatz quarter of Berlin, where Hilmer & Sattler's officially approved masterplan - thoroughly rationalist and broadly in line with the urbanism of Rob and Leon Krier - has been denounced in some quarters as scandalously reactionary and a throwback to the aesthetics of Speer.

It is in this lively context, with German architecture once more on the move (at a time, moreover, of intense activity on the development scene) that von Gerkan, Marg & Partners' architecture has to be judged. In the seventies, it was building large and glossy curtain-walled office slabs. By 1980, with the Hanse Viertel development in Hamburg, the firm's work had entered a distinctly post-modernist phase. A severe Rationalism characterised much of the work of the mid-eighties - for example, the Husum city hall project (1986) and projects for public buildings in Oldenburg and Flensburg. Von Gerkan's office building in the Grindelallee in Hamburg, completed in 1987, is altogether lighter in touch, with a highly developed façade treatment which responds extremely well to the locale - an area of surviving five and six storey 19th century apartment blocks. The themes in this scheme were carried further in other schemes where Meinhard von Gerkan was the design partner - for example, the Lufthansa training centre, Frankfurt, of 1986. This project has a light elegance which harks back to the classic Modern Movement models and the work of Eric Mendelsohn in particular.

During the 1980s, von Gerkan, Marg & Partners' approach to the planning of large commercial buildings developed markedly. The office development at Mainz (1981-1984) is divided by a series of internal "streets". This element came more strongly to the fore in the project for a publishing house for Gruner & Jahr in Hamburg (1985).

Von Gerkan's "Energy saving building" for the IBA in Berlin, built in 1983-1984, presented a staid front to the street. On the garden front, it erupted in a series of metal balconies. Many of the practice's housing schemes adhered closely to the rationalist aesthetic, although a scheme for a residential development in Hamburg's historic Fischmarkt provided the opportunity to design in a more openly historicist fashion.

The completed buildings are amongst the more convincing of the large number of "infill" schemes recently completed in the historic towns of Europe. Von Gerkan, Marg & Partners' historicism is lively and progressive. The restoration and extension of the 1920s Michaelsen house in Hamburg as a museum was carried out with Karl Schneider's designs of 1923 firmly in sight. The Rickling clinic has the reassuring folksiness of German rural building, while steering away from literal traditionalism. Von Gerkan, Marg & Partners are well able to use simple materials, brick and timber and rooftiles, to produce serious architecture. They have never moralised about materials. Their clinic at Bad Meinberg (1987-1989) includes an uncompromising yet sympathetic refurbishment of an existing block - half-timbered and tile-roofed, and the addition of a new block which, initially reassuring in scale and materials, has a distinct toughness of detail typical of its architects. The old Rationalism is still there in the Hillmannhaus at Bremen (completed 1989) and the residential/retail scheme at Buchholz of 1989-1991. There is little in this manner of recent date in Europe which is as good as this - mid-Atlantic Post-Modernism is, by comparison, lacking in substance while the British Romantic Pragmatist tradition is both self-conscious and mannered.

Yet, above all else, von Gerkan, Marg & Partners have enlarged their reputation of late with a striking series of projects which expand the language of uncompromisingly modern design. They had established their place as airport designers some years ago, with the scheme to rebuild Berlin-Tegel. The new Stuttgart Airport ranks high amongst the second generation of airports in Europe. Though it may lack the cool and calm simplicity of Norman Foster's Stansted, it has a presence which is far from the anonymous passenger containers of the past. The terminal does not try to be simple or understated. Its structural system is boldly, even wildly, expressive. The structural "trees" here are trees, almost literally, an introduction for the arriving traveller to the German mystique of the forest. Everything here is dramatic, creating one of the most memorable gateways to any European city.

The new terminal at Hamburg airport also promises to be as exciting. Meanwhile, von Gerkan's multi-storey car park at the same airport is a remarkable achievement: a metallic Guggenheim which must be exhilarating to use. The new shed for jumbo jets at Hamburg is, in effect, a grand bridge structure. Von Gerkan's projects for smaller airports are equally exciting, as direct in form as the best of 19th century railway stations. There is none of the straining for effect here, for the building as giant machine, which characterised high-tech

Bielefeld Town Hall, 1980-1990

Architect's office and house, Hamburg, 1986-1990

Interior of architect's house, 1992

Miro Data Systems, Braunschweig, 1991
Overleaf: Carl Bertelsmann Foundation, Gütersloh, 1989

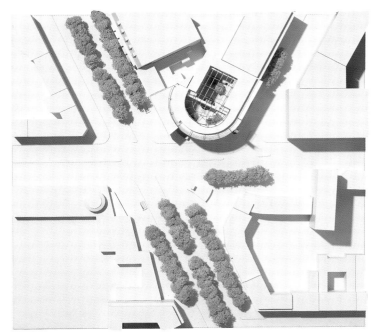

Hotel Ku'damm-Eck, Berlin, 1992

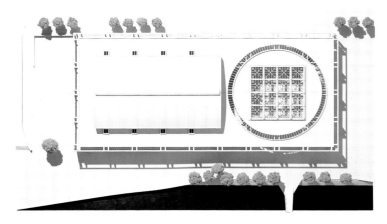

Concert and Conference Hall, Lübeck, 1990-1994

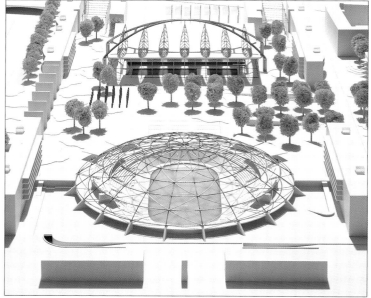

Olympia 2000, Berlin, 1992

buildings of the eighties. Von Gerkan's intentions are more traditionally architectural. But his technology is always leading edge. His partner, Volkwin Marg, was responsible for a dramatic transformation of the Hamburg Historical Museum, where the 17th century quadrangle is now covered in a lightweight glazed roof of swelling, shimmering form. Von Gerkan, Marg & Partners seem able to move rapidly from large-scale, bold gestures to intricate detailing. Their architecture has a totality of approach rarely seen in practitioners whose work is so diverse.

A number of recent projects illustrate this diversity (which remains the keynote of their work). The reshaping of the main railway station in Bielefeld (1989-1991) has both high drama and cool logic. A huge wedge of glass brings daylight down into the subterranean platforms. Emerging from the station, you immediately see another major work, von Gerkan's City Hall. This vast multi-purpose hall has an external simplicity which looks to Richard Meier. Inside it is austerely grand in a way typical of its architect. Von Gerkan's own house is a masterpiece of contemporary domestic design which, in its understated radicalism, looks back to the heroic days of Modernism but is entirely contemporary in its use of materials (The proposed apartment block in Hamburg promises to be a convincing restatement of this approach.) The new town centre at Schenefeld is admirably simple in concept and developed with a clarity and attention to detail typical of the architect. There is a new fluidity and expressiveness in schemes like Ku'Damm Eck, Berlin, the Munich museum project, and the Lubeck conference centre and concert hall - the architecture is growing, expanding its horizons. But it has not lost its roots in rational modernism and the engineering tradition - look at the ordered radicalism of the Berlin Olympia 2000 bid. The Mira Data Systems building at Brunswick is a model for the industrial buildings of the next century - finely made, good to work in, democratic in atmosphere and plan.

The work of this German practice typifies, on one level, the very best in the new public architecture of Europe: its urbanist credentials are never in doubt. Von Gerkan's projects (for Sony and Daimler Benz) on the Potsdamer Platz area of Berlin are confidently modern, assuredly urban. It repairs and complements, is positive rather than dissonant. But it would be wrong to present it as some comfortable middle way between traditionalism and the avant garde. Von Gerkan, Marg & Partners' work has a traditional integrity which is balanced by a willingness to experiment and a commitment to the public realm which are true to the best modernist canons.

THE THEORY OF DIALOGICAL DESIGN
by Meinhard von Gerkan

Architecture is not an autonomous art, like painting, sculpture, music and literature. It involves social application and is dependent on the conditions in which it is to be used, its location, the materials and techniques to be employed, and the capital available. Above all, it is conditioned by human needs.

Hence, all architecture evolves from a dialogue between the existing conditions and the ideals and models of the architects involved.

Architects react to their task in different ways. They may see themselves as receiving orders, as holding a complacent monologue, or as partners in a discussion. The pluralism of architecture today is partly the result of these different attitudes and reactions.

High school sports facilities, Kiel, 1976

The Conformist Pragmatic Position
Here, architecture is seen as a social commodity; such architects are prepared to adapt to the prevailing conditions without taking a clear position of their own. Synthesis is achieved by following the line of least resistance.

The architect taking this position assumes the role of an assistant helping fulfil a project or idea. He is a product designer, giving the required stamp or appearance.

The Complacent Monologue
This tends to be dogmatic; existing conditions are largely ignored and every proposal is given the stamp of ideology. Many contemporary architects tend to indulge in such monologues. They cite theories they have invented and then made into conditions. The conditions are imaginary, and do not represent the real requirements of concrete tasks.

Townhouses, Hamburg, 1978

Changes in social values create new ideologies and new formal doctrines. Periodicals, exhibitions and theoretical discussions are full of such monologistic designs.

Graphic visions, or ideas that can effectively be demonstrated graphically, use architecture as a subject; in doing so they do not provide information about a concrete architectural intention; they produce illusions with alienations, painterly intensifications and associative embellishments, avoiding deliberate confrontation with existing conditions.

Deutsche Shell AG Headquarters, Hamburg, 1975

The Dialogue
As I see our profession, the architect should be a partner in a dialogue. His use to society

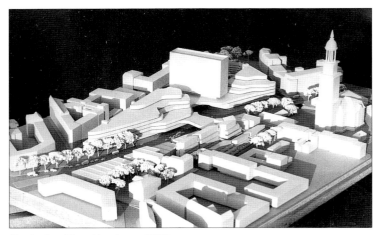

Deutscher Ring, Hamburg, 1976

Lufthansa Training and Computer Centre, Frankfurt am Main, 1986

Pahlavi National Library, Teheran, 1978

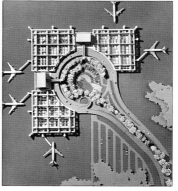

Dar El Beida Airport, Algiers, 1975; alternative proposal, 1975

derives from the fact that as an expert on the design of the environment, he reacts to conditions according to his subjective system of values. In this view, architecture is an art with social applications, and the result emerges from the interplay of inherent and external factors. The dialectic lies between the intellectual position of the architect and the opposition of existing conditions.

Neither the predetermined regimentation of an intellectual or artistic prejudice, that is, the dictate of a formal concept, nor the totally free play of forces, in which the coincidental and the chaotic can gain the upper hand, should dominate. Only the interplay of free forces and natural elements with the structure of an intellectual and artistic concept will result in their synthesis in a "true" image of human society in architectural form. All major cultural achievements are the result of that dialogue.

Design in Dialogue

I cannot put forward here a complete and finished theory; these remarks are analytical reflections on my own work.

I should like to characterise my position in four key sentences:

Simplicity

- Search in your designs for the most obvious and the simplest solution. Try to make the simplest the best.

Variety and Unity

- Create unity in variety and variety in unity.

Structural Order

- Give the designs a structural order. Organise functions into clear architectural forms.

Unmistakeable individuality

- Give the design an identity using the specific features of the situation, location and task.

These are my general aims and form the inherent "design philosophy" I use to respond to conditions during the design process.

The Need for Simplicity

What I mean by simplicity is what is plausible, self-evident, clear and unadorned, in the sense that a sun umbrella is a simple solution. The most elementary simplicity, I am convinced, is also a guarantee of beauty and durability. But it is extremely difficult to achieve. Simplicity is also aiming at modesty, reduction and unity of materials. And, above all, simplicity is a maxim in the organisation of function.

Variety and Unity

The better the balance between variety and unity, the higher the quality of environmental design. The discomfort of our living environment is due either to an excess of uniformity, which we feel is monotonous, or an excess of variety, which we register as chaos.

So I see a balance of unity and variety as a particularly important objective. However, this problem in design arises in every task with different and often totally opposing conditions. While rows of identical houses can lead to monotonous uniformity, there is always a risk, when designing shopping precincts and corridors, of overloading the design.

My own objectives do not result from an idealisation of variety, nor a dogma of strict order; my aim is to enter into a dialogue with the prevailing conditions.

Structural Order

The purpose of structural order is: to create clear architectural forms; to make the architecture visually legible; and to give clear spatial orientation.

Each design must be based on a structural principle, which subdivides the building and organises its functions. The ground plan and elevations must be derived from that structural principle. For me, the structural principle is the grammar of the design process. My organisational principles are generally simple or composite geometries, sometimes overlaid with free forms.

Unmistakeable Individuality

Every design concept is derived from the search for a specific identity in its solution. The concern here is not uniqueness for its own sake or a formal arbitrary act but the endeavour to develop unmistakeable individuality from the specific conditions of the given situation and the task in hand.

Conclusion

How our environment is shaped is not only determined by us as architects. We can respond to the demands of the tasks in hand with designs. Whether our answers are accepted and have a chance of becoming part of our architectural environment depends in part on the extent to which we are prepared to listen during the dialogue.

Finding suitable and acceptable answers and solutions to the problems of designing the environment requires being ready for dialogue and adapting one's standpoint to changing conditions.

The decision as to what will be built and how, affects society with its complex political and economic mechanisms. We architects are obliged to face up to these conditions by entering into a dialogue and to participate in the discussion with inner conviction.

Multi-storey car park, Hamburg, 1980, and Townhouse, Mannheim, 1978

Berlin-Tegel Airport: Passenger Terminal, 1974

Workshops, 1975

Exhibition hall, AMK, Berlin, 1986

ELBCHAUSSEE

NER MÜHLENWEG

MUSEUMSHAFEN
ÖVELGÖNNE

ELBSCHLUCHT
Hamburg (1986-1990)

Preliminary design: 1986
Building commenced: 1987
Building finished: 1990
Design: Meinhard von Gerkan
Assistants: Jakob Kierig,
Peter Sembritzki, Sabine von Gerkan,
Volkmar Sievers
Client: Meinhard von Gerkan

*Ensemble consisting of a public square,
a restaurant, an architects' studio, an art
gallery and private housing.*
The Elbchaussee runs for more than
9km along the top of the Geest slope
parallel to the river Elbe. The buildings
on the river side, known as the "wet
side", give way in places to parks
offering a view of the fascinating scenes
in the harbour and its shipping. The
sites here are of a size that befits the
residences of the wealthy - the shipown-
ers who send their vessels round the
world or, with hanseatic understate-
ment, participate in world trade.

   Although the Elbchaussee has
suffered in the past, it is still one of the
finest streets in the world. I know of no
other place, anywhere on the globe,
where the world of work and transport -
ships, containers, cranes, docks - and
the world of distinction and wealth lie so
close together. The direct experience of
activity twenty-four hours a day is
intensified by its position high on a hill,
and from these sites it is like looking
down from an observation platform at a
permanently busy harbour scene.

   It is a place with a very strong identity,
a "genius loci" par excellence, to use a
term that is somewhat overused in the

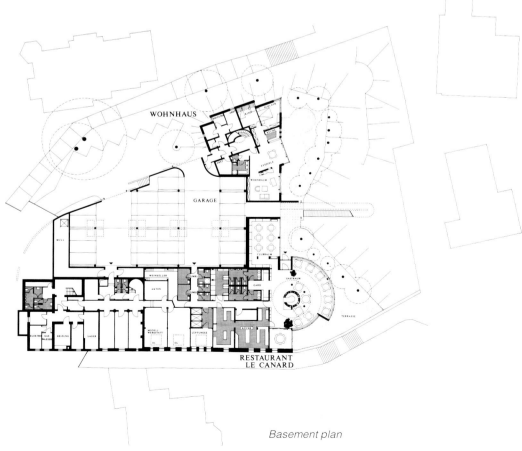

Basement plan

vocabulary of architects today. A view of the sea, a lake or a river always upgrades a site, and the activity of an ocean harbour makes the scene a stage set with an endless drama in progress. If, in the sun-starved north, the view is also to the south, with the noisy road on the northern side, then conditions could not be more superb.

And so there have always been recreation and leisure facilities set among the great villas - inns and restaurants that enticed visitors from Hamburg and Altona even in those days when a trip of some five or ten kilometres was a considerable undertaking.

Around the turn of the century the Elbchaussee was dotted with such establishments - Kröger's "Gasthof zur Erholung", Ritscher's, Groth's, the Elbburg, Louis Jacob, the Parkhotel Teufelsbrück and the Duve'scher Elbpavillon to name but a few.

Best of all was the Elbschlucht, a restaurant and beer garden. In an advertisement in the "Zwischenakt" in 1889, the then owner, Wilhelm H. Ahrens, recommended his services to his clients in the following words:

"The largest establishment on the Elbchaussee. I beg to draw the kind attention of the public to an establishment that is unique of its kind. Now that the extensive programme of building

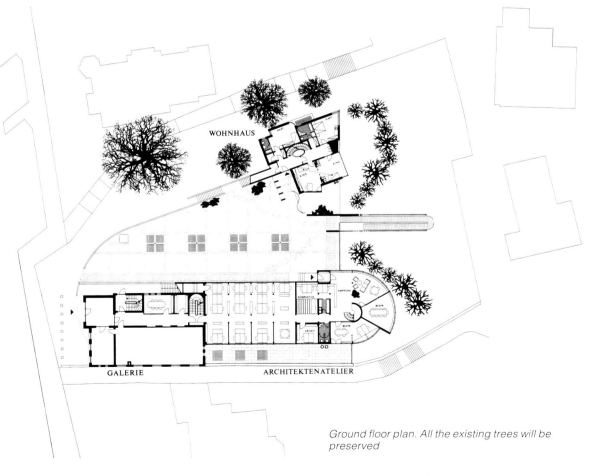

Ground floor plan. All the existing trees will be preserved

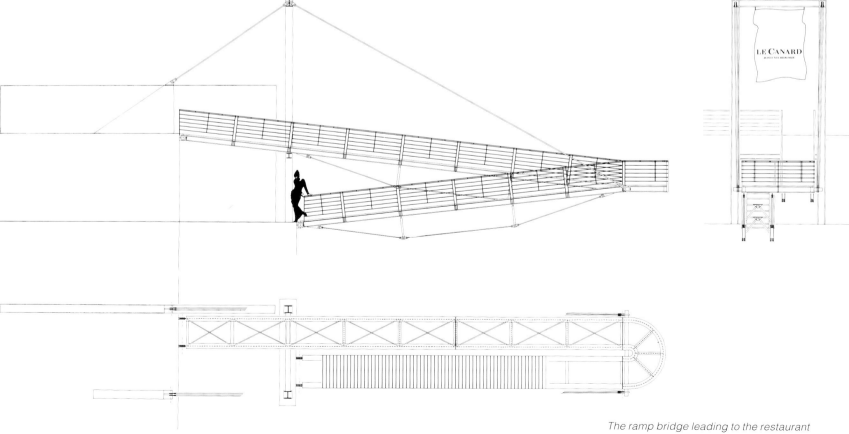

The ramp bridge leading to the restaurant

and conversion is complete, I would like to remind my honoured guests very particularly of the view now afforded from the verandas and the tower, which may well be described as the finest and most magnificent panorama along the whole of the Elbchaussee.

I also recommend my establishment most warmly for wedding parties, social gatherings and reunions of all sizes, for all of which I can offer very fair terms. Larger luncheon parties, dinners and suppers must be booked in advance."

Most of these recreational facilities and inns have fallen victim to changes in habits. Now people go on excursions to Majorca, the Bahamas or at the very least to Sylt. Large family parties are celebrated with barbecues in the garden at home. Antipasti di mare or navarin of lamb in a thyme and vinaigrette dressing are no longer consumed in dance halls or beer gardens.

Although the site at Elbchaussee 139, which is about 4000sq.m in size, has a restaurant licence in the current development plan, it is in a district that otherwise now consists entirely of top-quality residential housing, and the restaurant, which changed hands frequently, had been showing evident signs of going downhill for years. The majestic old ensemble with its pavilion, its neo-classical turret and its glass

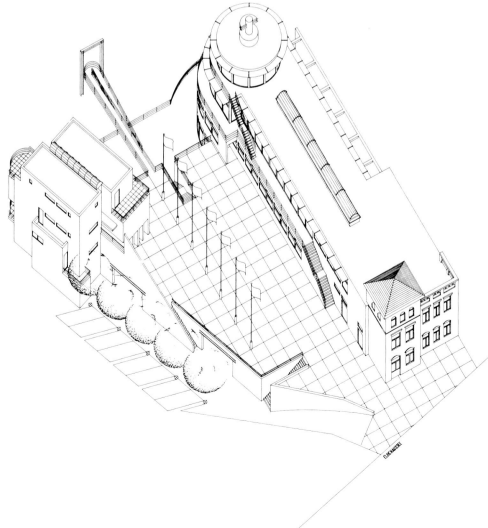

conservatories had long been spoilt by a single-storey cross-wing. It stood like a barracks, dividing the site into an ugly parking area facing the road and a garden terrace facing the river. More extensions, conversions and additions had further marred its appearance. The general impression was desolate, and not even a seasonal gathering or Terramotto's special spaghetti sauce could now breathe new life into it.

For many years I had been driving past the site almost every day. The gradual decay suggested that the property might be for sale, and in my mind I could see the same horrific visions that had already taken shape in other parts of the Elbchaussee - pseudo-patrician housing consisting of conversions or new buildings, packed full of owner-occupier apartments, the prescribed hipped roofs a caricature with incisions, dormer windows and shapeless superstructures. For years the architectural changes in the Elbchaussee have been a depressing sight, demonstrating only the incompatibility of the pompous gesture and petty-minded maximisation of profits.

For years, too, the office of our firm, Gerkan, Marg + Partners, had also been located in a former patrician villa, converted to a use for which it had not originally been designed. We were being urged to find new premises because the local council wanted the area to be purely residential and they thought that architects' offices should be located in the business ghettos.

We were not prepared to accept that we, as architects, should face the challenges of creating a better environment in some anonymous office block. But many unusual ideas for a new home for our company foundered on the rigid norms of urban planning and building regulations. For the planners, architectural work is office work, and office work should only be done in office blocks!

Nevertheless, I ventured to do something which my partner Volkwin Marg urged me not to do: I made a preliminary planning enquiry, and asked whether an architectural project, which would reflect both the spirit of changing times and our own social needs, could be built on the site at Elbchaussee 139, which was gradually falling into a state of ruin and was now indeed up for sale.

What I proposed to the planners was that I design a building that offered an unusual solution with respect to shape

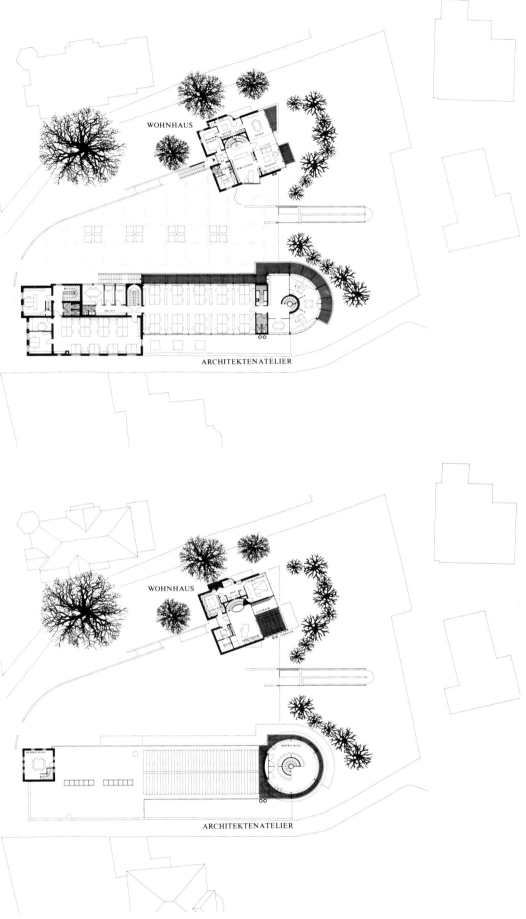

First and second floor plans

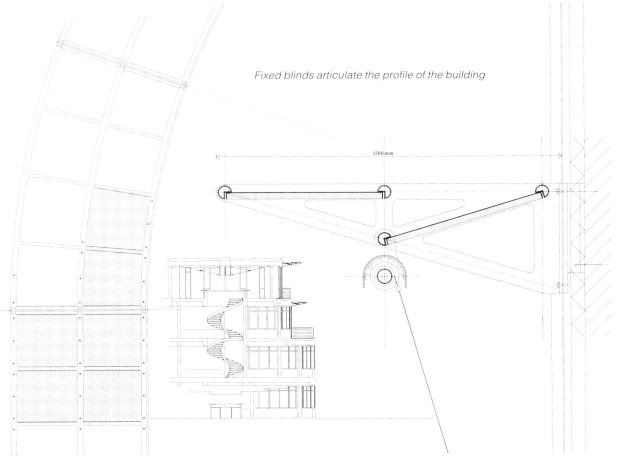

Fixed blinds articulate the profile of the building

1200 mm

and use. The best and most characteristic parts of the old building would be preserved: both the neo-classical turret on the Elbchaussee, which had given the complex its particular identity for so many decades, and the long wall along the Övelgönner Mühlenweg.

The site, which is flanked on both sides by public steps linking the Elbchaussee to the riverbank, has a landmark on the western side which is a wall more than 50m long which rises in height as the path descends. This wall is particularly unpopular today, when people prefer front gardens, lawns and groups of trees. But we could only cite the building regulations which state that the existing state must be maintained.

Every potential investor I approached about the project proposed the obvious solution of a long building parallel to the Elbe that would ensure maximum river views. However, I did not want to do what I so disliked in other new buildings along the river. All the pseudo-villas with the owner-occupier apartments so skilfully fitted in, looked as uptight as their genuine predecessors.

I wanted to experiment with a "private building open to the public". We would utilise the slope and banish the cars below the level of the Elbchaussee; above, we would create an open space with an unobstructed view of the river and the harbour. It would be accessible to passers-by and, most important of all, it would be completely free of cars.

If we could carry out our plan of including an art gallery, it would also provide a space where sculpture could be shown so that the harbour panorama would provide a backdrop for the visual arts. On the other side of the square, the path would lead up to the restaurant.

At the front, the open space is approached through a steel gate, which frames the view of the harbour, and steps lead to a ramp which takes the visitor across the steep slope towards the Elbe and then, halfway along, turns at 180 degrees to lead back to the building and the entrance to the restaurant. The visitors' room is on the floor on the slope, in the semi-circular bow of the steamer. In front of it is an open terrace which is hidden but unmistakeable and offers a rich and varied feast.

On the upper deck is our workplace. Our working habits have not changed and the lights are on until well into the night, proof, if it were needed, that architecture is not normal office work.

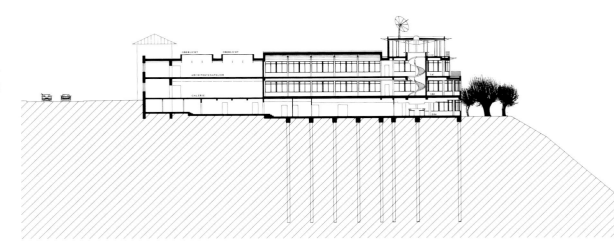

The cylindrical upper storey counterbalances the neo-classical turret, and it soars above the bow like the captain's bridge. The spiral staircase in the middle leads to the large conference room which has a panoramic view.

The main body of the building has a strange appearance: a steamer 50m long, drifting at right angles to the current, along the wall on Övelgönner Mühlenweg and connected with the Elbchaussee by a neo-classical turret.

Opposite, on the other corner of the site, which opens out in a trapezoid to the Elbe, stands a cubic villa. It is the owner's residence and the legal basis for this mixed use, with its combination of residential housing, an architects' studio, a restaurant and an art gallery.

The formal language of the new defies analogy with the other buildings along the Elbchaussee. Where the drawing boards stand, the window axes follow the design of the workplace. The upper storey is a large drawing studio. A vaulted roof with a visible steel construction gives the room its unity and the character of a workshop.

Open access routes resemble the deck of a ship. The fixed blinds outside articulate the profile of the building. Glazed toplights, strong enough to bear the weight of pedestrians, have been set into the surface of the open space, providing daylight for the garage beneath. In the evening, artificial light shines up out of the garage, and with the four "light steles" creates an almost supernatural atmosphere in the square.

The residence has the dimensions of a cube, swung out of axis and set parallel to the eastern edge of the site. It corresponds with the base of the buildings on the open square. The access to the first storey is articulated through a triangular arrangement on the wall to which the staircase is attached. All the rooms in the house have a view of the Elbe. The trees that have survived provide contrasting greenery.

My proposal to use the site in this way met with the approval of the authorities, and we were able to embark on the experiment: of working and living, dining and exhibiting incorporated in an architectural symbiosis, not in an office block and not in an alienated villa, but in a type of building that presumably has no parallel anywhere. In a place that could not be more hanseatic - in front a "first-class address", and behind the breath-taking scenery of the harbour.

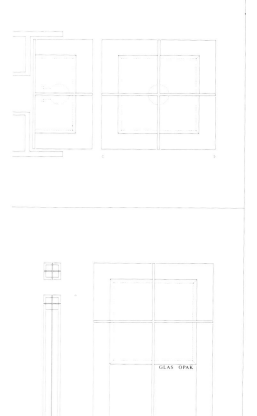

GLAS OPAK

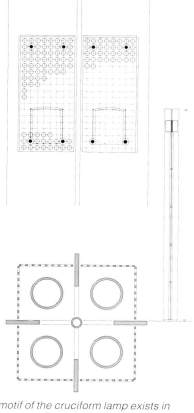

The motif of the cruciform lamp exists in numerous variants throughout the building

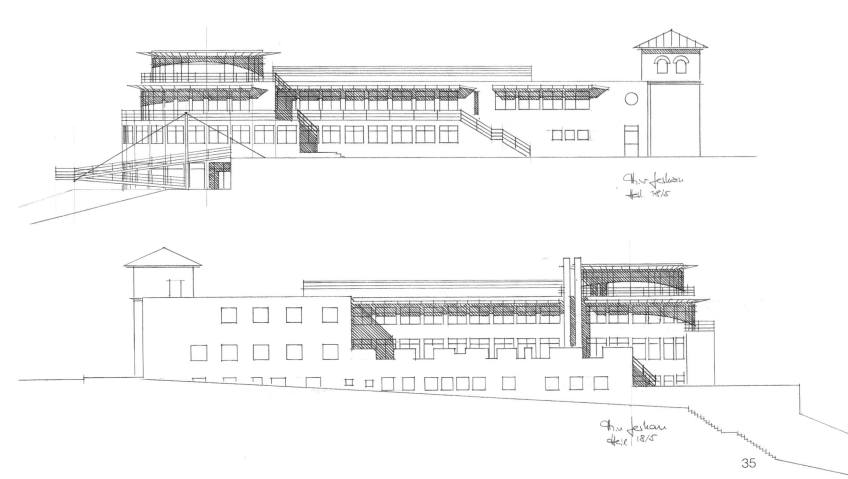

THE MUSEUM OF HAMBURG HISTORY - A ROOF FOR THE COURTYARD
(1989)

Design: Volkwin Marg
Assistant: Klaus Lübbert
Engineers: Schlaich, Bergermann + Partners
Building Supervision: Volker Rudolph

The Museum of Hamburg History, which was designed by Fritz Schumacher, was built between 1914 and 1923 and now has a preservation order on it.

Although the possibility of grouping the buildings around a glazed inner courtyard was discussed when the Museum was built, the plan finally chosen had an open forecourt.

The new glass roof is extremely delicate and is designed to give the lightest possible impression while affording protection from the weather. It is in the form of a fully transparent bowl, which is a structural innovation. The historic buildings have been treated with respect and exhibits which had been exposed to the weather are now under cover. In addition, there are attractive new opportunities for using Hamburg's finest covered courtyard.

The courtyard covers an area of 10,000sq.m with an L-shaped ground plan. It has a system of cross-supports consisting of two vaulted bowls and a covering dome. The geometry, with its fluid transitions between the three main elements, is the result of a process of optimisation. The reduction of the structure to a system of membranes also meant that the necessary diameters of the bowls were minimised.

The supporting structure consists of 60mm x 40mm galvanised flat steel

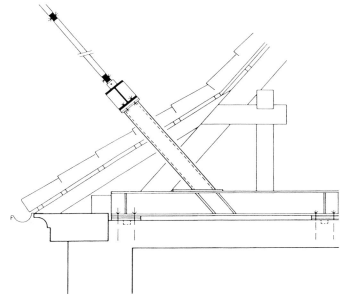

Section and top view of the network of roof supports

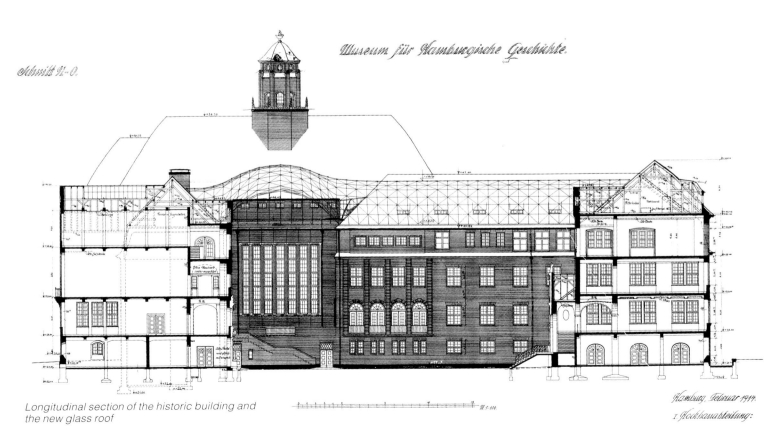

Longitudinal section of the historic building and
the new glass roof

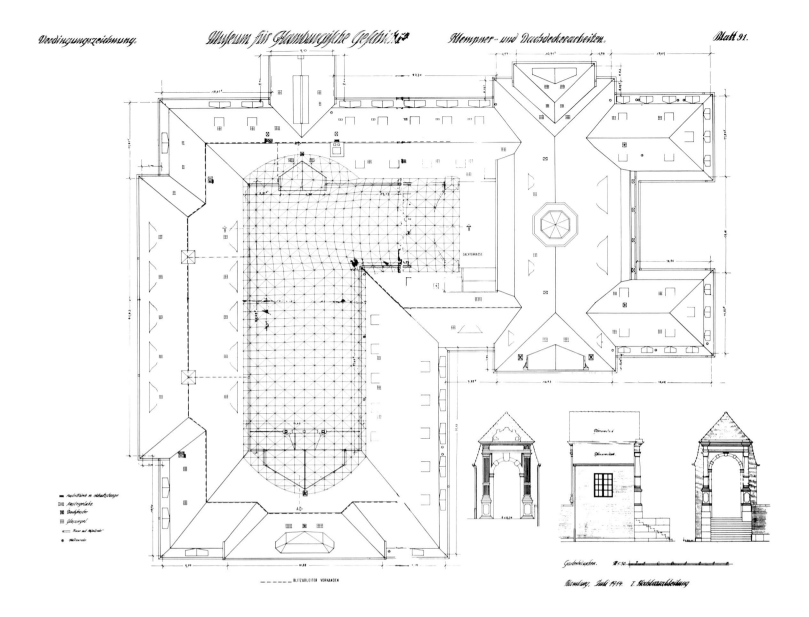

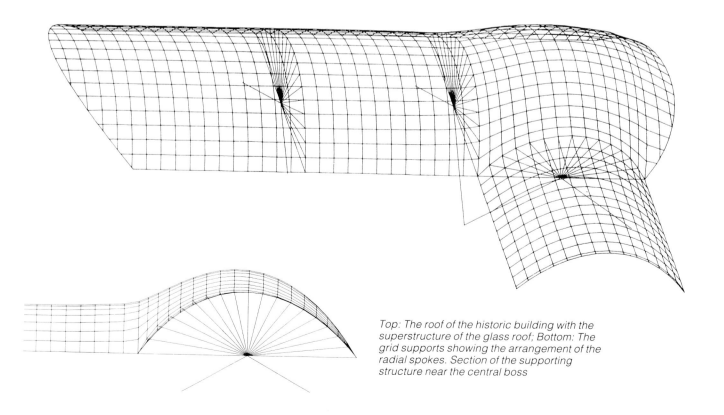

Top: The roof of the historic building with the superstructure of the glass roof; Bottom: The grid supports showing the arrangement of the radial spokes. Section of the supporting structure near the central boss

profiles, painted white. They are only as wide as is necessary to hold the panes of glass. These profiles, which create an orthogonal network of supports with even widths between, are held at the intersections by rotating screws. As the squares between the supports could become rhomboids if the intersections permitted a sliding movement, the diagonals have to be such as to permit the squares to become triangles and still provide a firm support for the bowl. Since the diagonals act as ropes, they are arranged in both directions, so that one of them can always act as a pulley.

The glazing consists of 10mm thick safety glass in single sheets laid directly on the flat steel profiles. It is held at certain points in the intersections with plates. A firm supporting edge has been slid right round the roof, about 70mm to 90mm above the existing roof. At certain points it is fixed to the reinforced concrete ceilings or walls.

To allow for heavy snow falls and any drifting, the vault-shaped bowls have been reinforced with radial spokes .

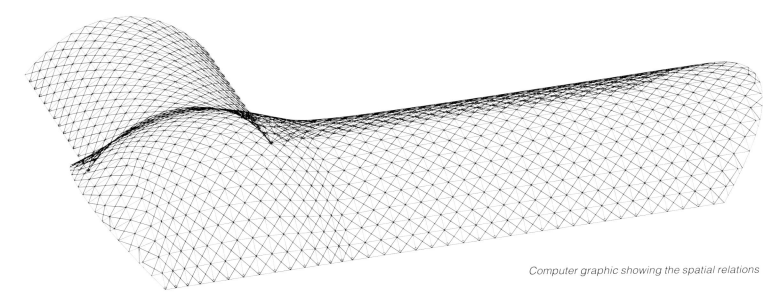

Computer graphic showing the spatial relations

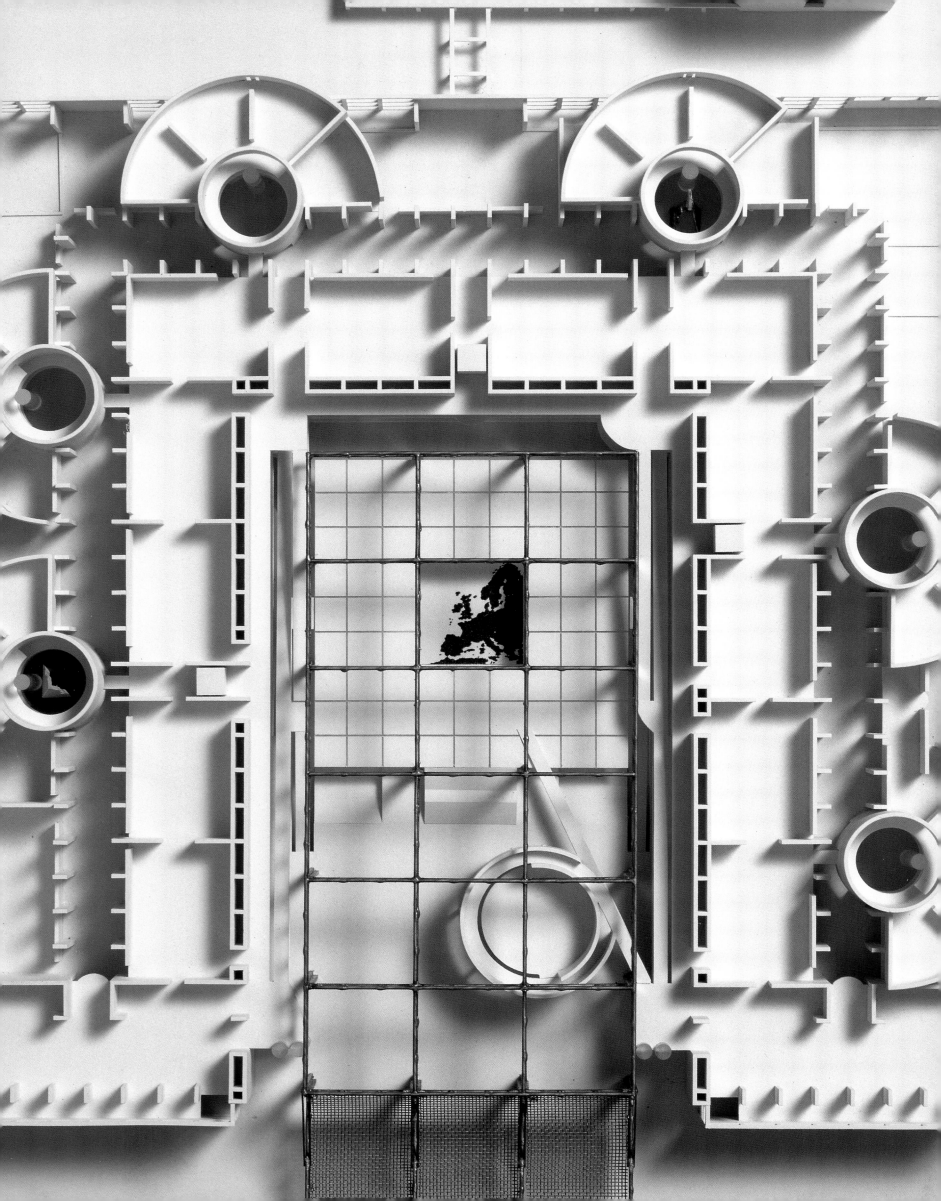

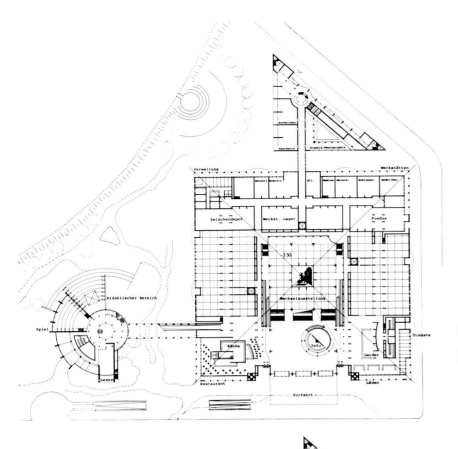

GERMAN HISTORY MUSEUM
Berlin

Competition: 1988
Design: Meinhard von Gerkan
Assistants: Manfred Stanek, Arturo Buchholz-Berger, Gerhard Feldmeyer Thomas Rinne, Jacob Kierig, Marion Ebeling

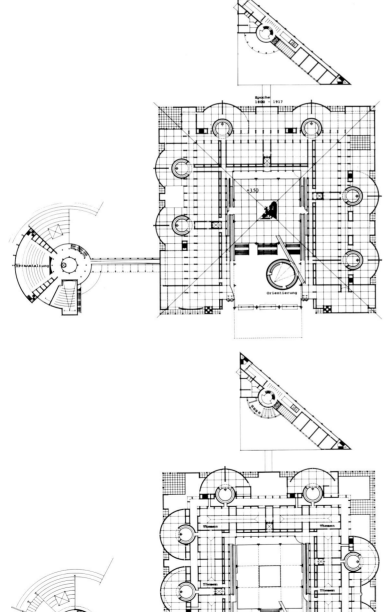

The complex comprises three buildings:
-The museum itself, with a square ground plan 132m x 132m., based on the classical models of the Altes Museum in Berlin and the Glyptothek in Munich. The exhibition spaces are set around a central hall thus permitting visitors to make a tour of the collections.
-The Education Programme Building, a pavilion-type rotunda, which is linked directly to the entrance area.
-The Research Centre and Offices along Moltkestrasse which look out over the Spree countryside to the south-west.

This tripartite division of the complex reflects the different purposes of the buildings and the design ensures that each has its own identity.

The large solitary monuments of the Reichstag and the Kongresshalle dominate the urban context, and the buildings around the Alsenplatz form a block structure. The Museum provides a link between the two. It faces the two monuments and its subsidiary buildings provide the required demarcations to the south, east and north.

The open-plan, well-organized interior offers maximum scope for the design of individual exhibition rooms with as much structural ordering as necessary but as much freedom as possible in the arrangement of rooms. It

From top: Ground floor; First floor; Second floor

43

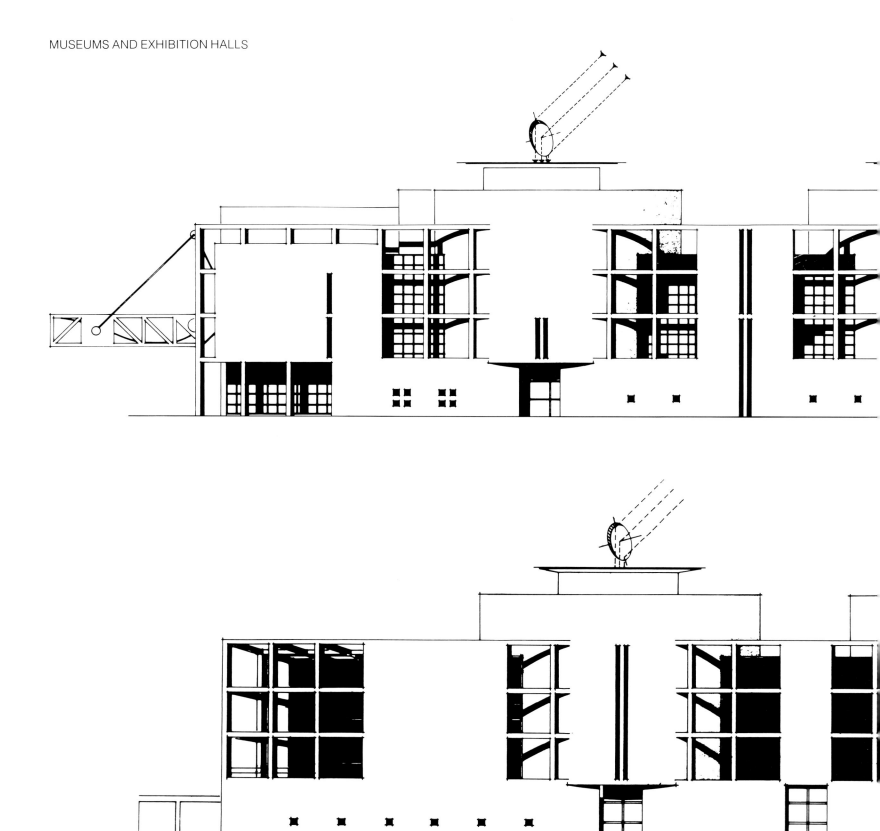

From top: Alsenplatz elevation; The Spree elevation

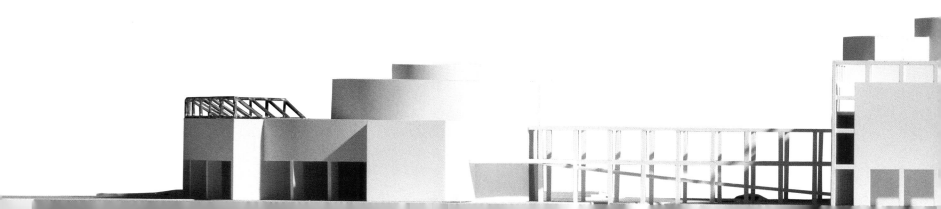

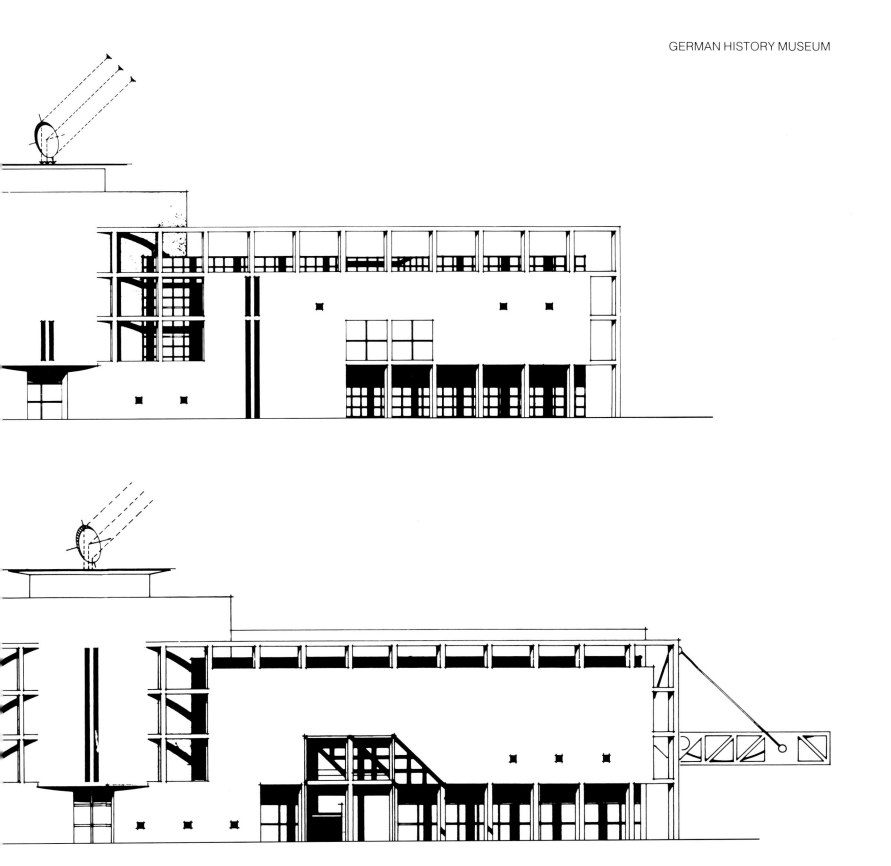

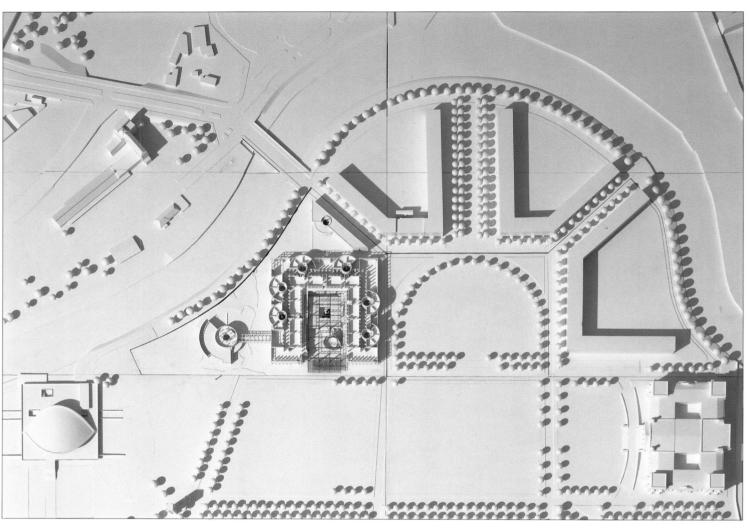

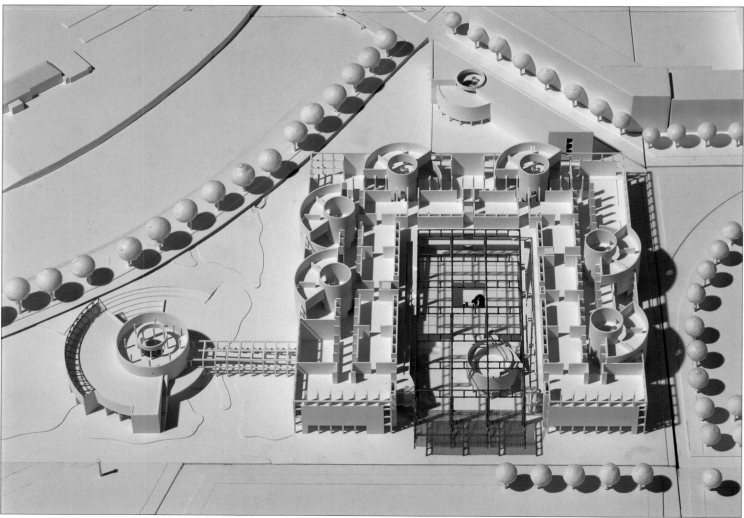

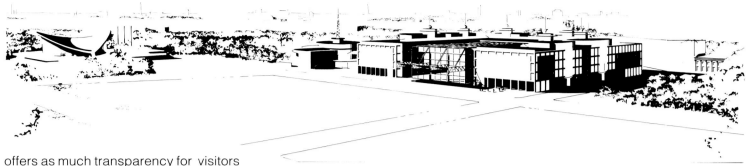

offers as much transparency for visitors as possible even before they enter, with clear orientation and obvious directions for the two self-contained tours. The rooms devoted to the different periods of history and historical themes are each arranged on one floor and can be inspected on a single tour.

The large central hall, which is spatially integrated with the entrance area and flanked on either side by surrounding galleries and ramps, is a multi-purpose area. Its glass roof has a light control system.

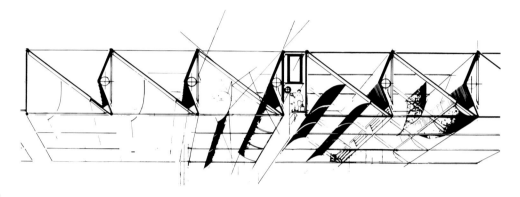

The areas for temporary exhibitions lead directly off this central hall; they are on a lower level in the centre under a glass floor. The variety of architectural experience is maintained in individual exhibition areas, where room heights vary from 4m to 12m.

The central axis of the surrounding exhibition area contains a high gallery with direct top lighting which acts as the "spine" of the orientation, both for each floor and for the cross section of the building. The inner courtyards and terraces form part of the gallery circuit.

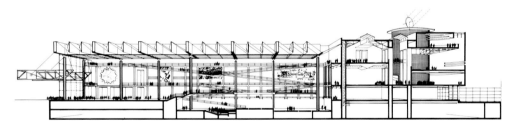

"Recessed rooms", which are places where visitors will linger, are arranged at right angles to the horizontal chronological progression through the ages. They consist of six round towers, 12m in diameter, each containing a spiral ramp and a lift connecting the two upper floors with the floor exhibiting the various periods of history; they provide a cross-link with the rooms devoted to historical themes. The towers are lit by a daylight reflection mechanism on the roof and have enough space for large objects specific to each period.

The façade structure links the main body of the building with the surrounding area; its two layers give it both depth and plasticity. The interplay of open and closed areas creates variety within the unity of the overall structure and affords views into the building and its activities. To the south, where the entrance is located, the building's large projecting roof, which offers protection from the weather, invites the visitor to enter.

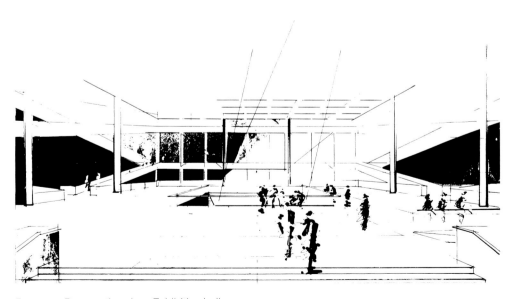

From top: Perspective view; Exhibition hall ceiling with light control system; Longitudinal section; Upper floor of the exhibition hall

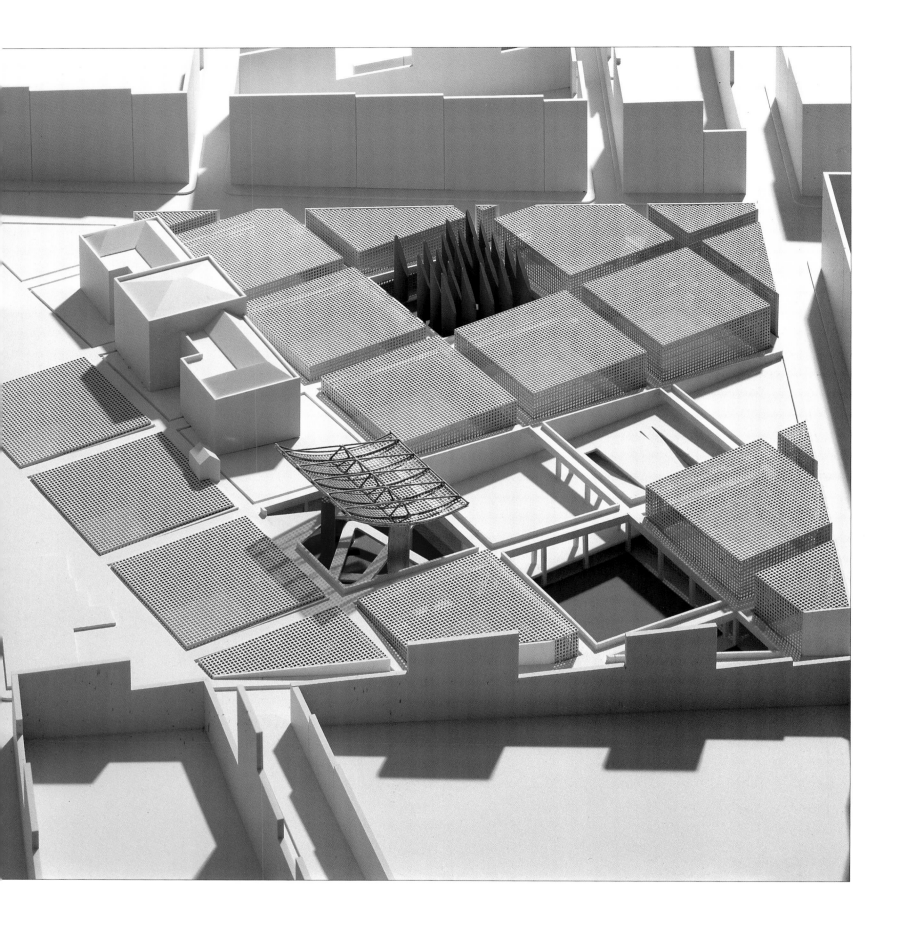

ACROPOLIS MUSEUM
Athens

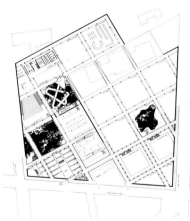

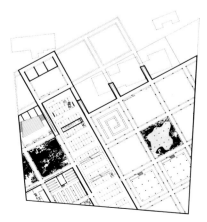

Competition: 1990 - Second Prize
Design: Meinhard von Gerkan
Assistants: Hilke Büttner, Kai Voss

The design concept is based on three main aims:

- As a public building the museum complex must be part of the city's public space. The buildings overlap with the topography to create paths which afford views into the museum, awaken curiosity and create a desire to enter.

- The Museum must have some specific characteristic relating to a symbolic interpretation of its contents - archaeology. The symbol is an archaeological excavation. A system of paths resembling the walkways of a dig covers the whole site and intersects the complex, creating square buildings.

The exhibition area lies below ground. The slope of the site makes the main body of the Museum emerge more from the land to the south, and the paths become narrow lanes cut into the terrain. The interpenetration and overlayering of building and site, and the square structure of an excavation area are reminiscent of Hippodamic city plans.

- The Museum had to be linked to the Acropolis. It is dug into the ground and thus counterbalances the Acropolis, which towers high above the city. The view from the Acropolis clearly reveals this reversal.

The entrance to the Museum is marked by a large sloping roof. Below this roof the visitor enters over a ramp which extends obliquely into the recessed entrance courtyard.

49

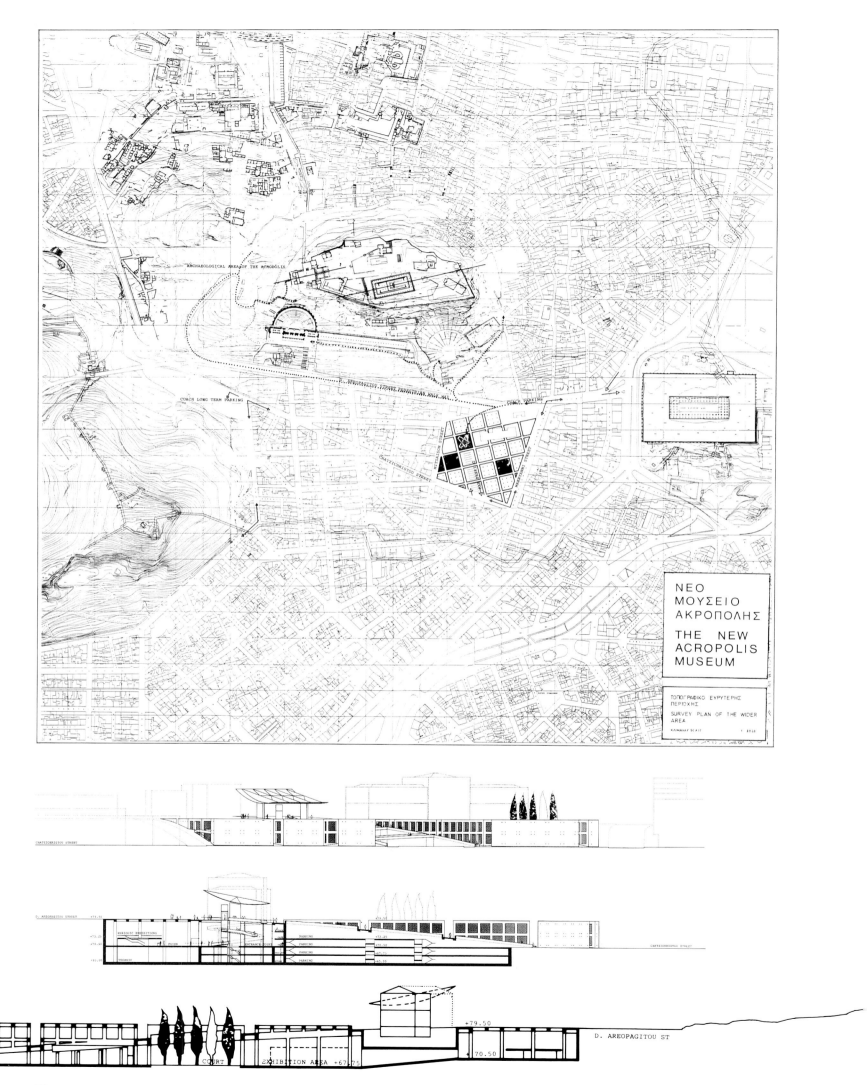

ΝΕΟ
ΜΟΥΣΕΙΟ
ΑΚΡΟΠΟΛΗΣ
THE NEW
ACROPOLIS
MUSEUM

ΤΟΠΟΓΡΑΦΙΚΟ ΕΥΡΥΤΕΡΗΣ
ΠΕΡΙΟΧΗΣ
SURVEY PLAN OF THE WIDER
AREA
ΚΛΙΜΑΚΑΣ SCALE   1 : 2000

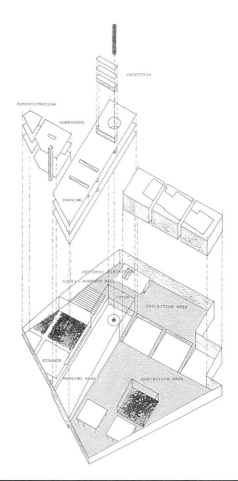

Within the walkway system are large halls, 27m by 27m and 8.5m high, with no supports within the span. They are high enough for the insertion of mezzanine floors so that the design of future exhibitions can be varied. The roofs of the individual exhibition halls and their side walls, which extend out of the site, have a surface structure in which windows and top lights can be inserted to let in daylight and permit a view inside from the lanes above. These surfaces will have a second façade inside, to deflect the heat of the sun.

Three of the squares are structured like inner courtyards thus creating a horizontal external reference on the exhibition floor.

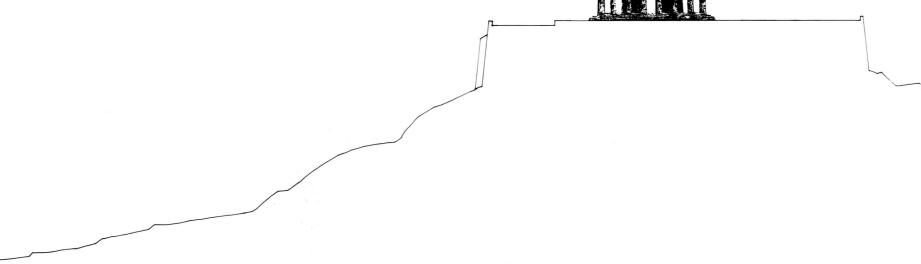

From top: Dissected use diagram; The design concept is based on the structure of an archaeological excavation
Opposite from top: Site plan; South elevation; Longitudinal section; Longitudinal section with the Acropolis

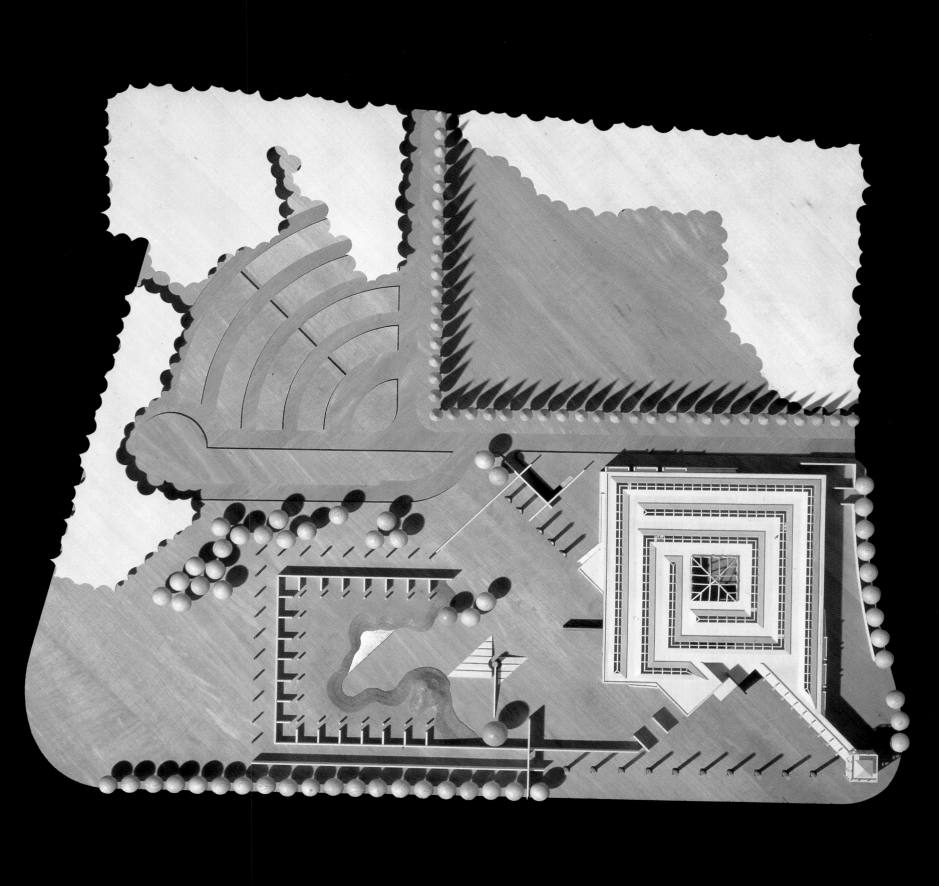

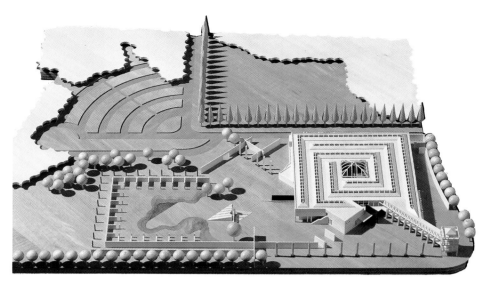

MUNICIPAL ART MUSEUM
Bonn

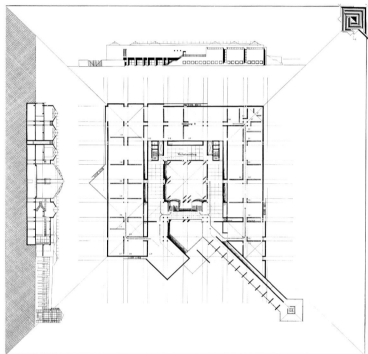

Competition: 1984
Design: Meinhard von Gerkan
Assistants: Thomas Bieling, Arturo Buchholz-Berger, Klaus Petersen, Michael Zimmermann

To create a suitable urban environment for the new arts complex in Bonn, it was necessary to create large open spaces with clear demarcations. Our design incorporates urban leisure zones using walls, arcades and rows of columns to give the location a specific identity.

This will permit the site for the art gallery, which will be built at a later date, to be clearly defined without establishing its architectural design in advance.

The museum interior is arranged in such a way as to guide visitors round the various parts of the collection along an easy-to-follow route.

In the middle is a two-storey hall with a glass roof in the form of a groined vault, which allows direct light to enter and which will give the hall the character of an air-conditioned inner courtyard. The route follows the square shape of the building, beginning and ending at the central staircase.

Two straight ramps provide additional routes from the entrance hall to the upper floor, offering shortcuts to the different parts of the collection.

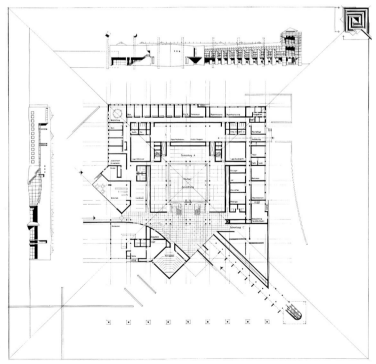

Middle: Upper floor; Bottom: Ground floor

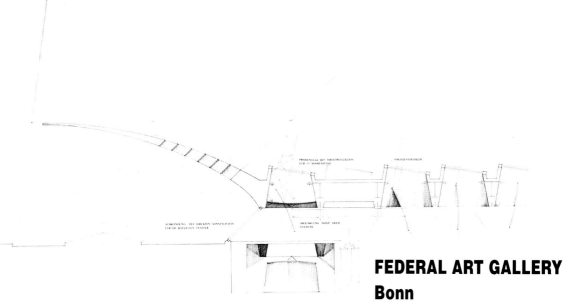

FEDERAL ART GALLERY
Bonn

Competition: 1986
Design: Meinhard von Gerkan
Assistants: Joachim Zais, Karin Müller-Reinecke, Sabine von Gerkan, Uwe Welp, Tuyen Tran-Viet, Jacob Kierig, Arturo Buchholz-Berger

The design concept prescribed for the municipal art museum is followed but with some variations.

The wall opens onto Friedrich-Ebert-Strasse with high arcades which form the entrance to the sculpture garden. Elsewhere the "wall" is a three-storey building surrounding the large hall. The hall itself has its own architectural topography, a landscape of open areas and steps.

It is covered by a large "umbrella", which rests on nine supports placed at intervals of 24m x 24m. The edges are curved, and the roof extends in a great sweep over the surrounding wall, emphasising the independence of the art gallery from the smaller municipal art museum opposite.

Numerous spatial cross-relations and related vistas enhance one another. Between the great central hall and the surrounding exhibition spaces lies an interim zone, 3m deep.

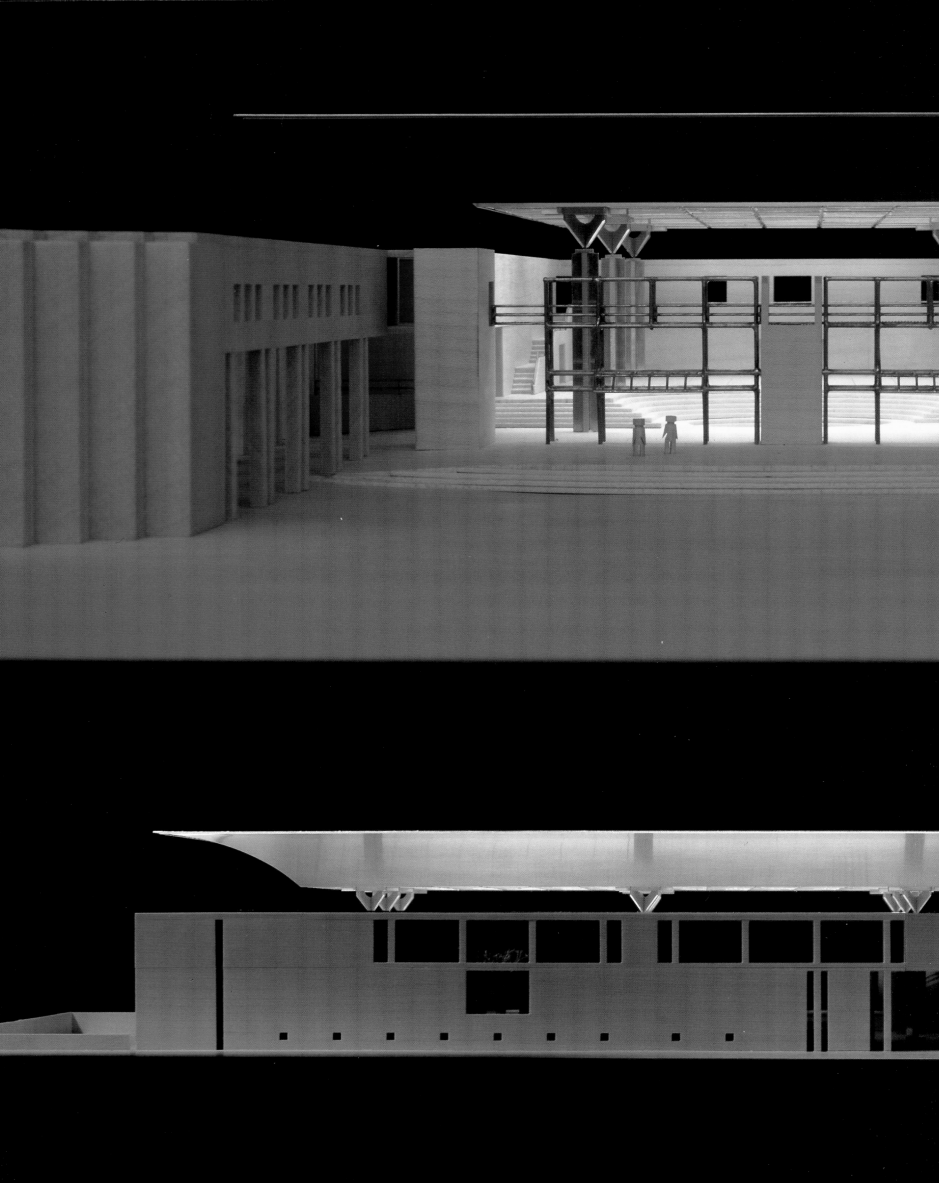

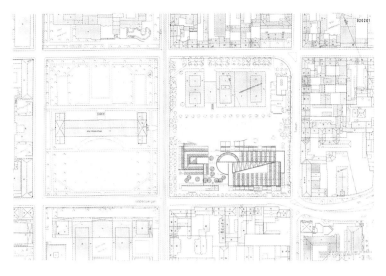

TÜRKENKASERNE MUSEUM
Munich

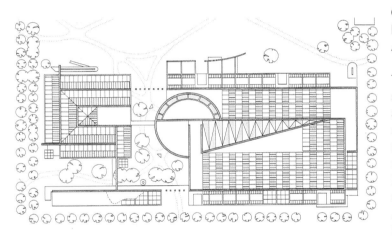

Competition: 1992
Design: Meinhard von Gerkan
Assistant: Clemens Schneider

The urban environment has a block-like structure. The Alte Pinakothek occupies a special position and this should be retained, as should the generous open spaces to north and south. Hence, the new museum is designed to give new block edging along the surrounding streets, while the longitudinal axis of the Alte Pinakothek is extended inside the block in a large continuous green area.

The floor space for the museum incorporated in the design is grouped in an ensemble of three buildings. Multi-storey bridges provide internal passageways, but pedestrian access is also possible at ground level.

The main building comprises all the exhibition space to be constructed during the first phase of building. The cylindrical entrance hall functions as an architectural junction, providing direct access to all other parts of the complex.

In appearance, the complex as a whole should convey an aesthetic of reduction and simplicity, with very precise detailing. The large solid areas of the buildings will be panelled in light grey and white; extensive glazing and delicate profile constructions will add plastic depth and some degree of transparency to the more sober parts of the walls.

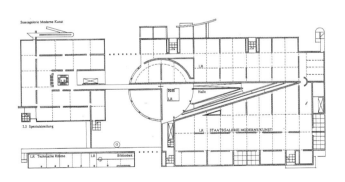

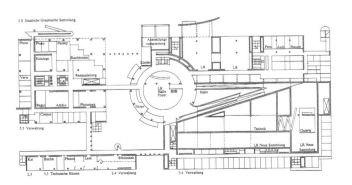

From top: Site; Roof plan; Level +13; Level +5

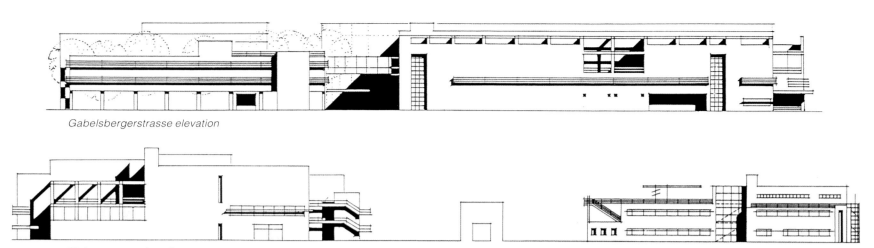

Gabelsbergerstrasse elevation

Türkenstrasse elevation

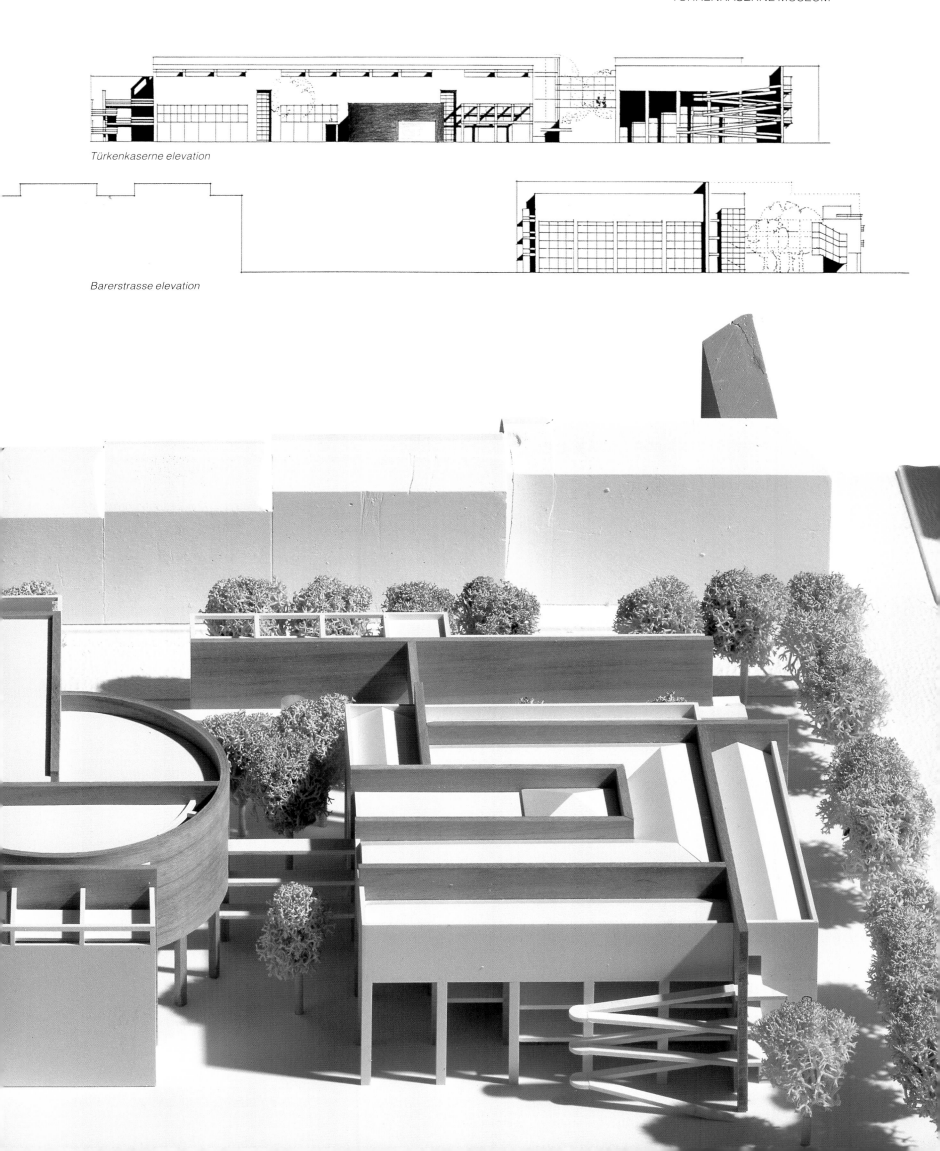

Türkenkaserne elevation

Barerstrasse elevation

Perspective view

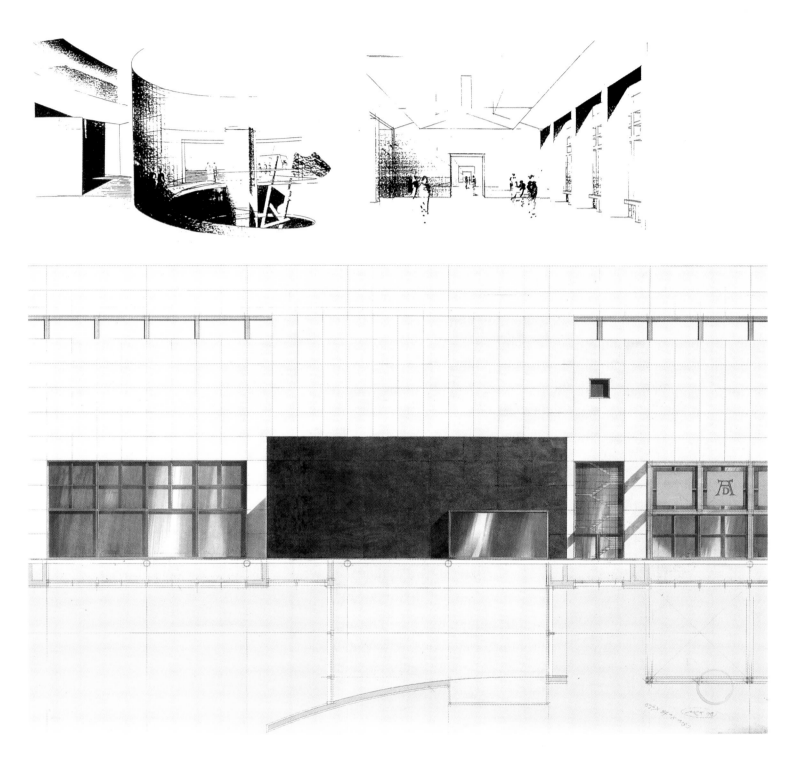

Top and bottom: Perspective views; Middle:
Detail drawing of façade

LEIPZIG TRADE FAIR

Competition: 1992, First Place
Design: Volkwin Marg
Assistants: Hubert Nienhoff, Michael Pohl, Jutta Hartmann-Pohl, Björn Bergfeld, Christian Hoffmann
Landscape design: Wehberg, Lange, Eppinger, Schmidtke
Assistant: P Köster

The reinterpretation of the traditional "MM" sign as "menschliche Messe" (user-friendly trade fair) is the leitmotif of the revised design.

A user-friendly trade fair has to offer physical well-being in addition to intellectual stimulation and our design allows for a compact arrangement with short access routes.

The centre is a linear park evolving from the surrounding urban landscape. In part, it consists of a large glazed conservatory, that will encourage visitors to linger at all seasons.

We have taken up the nineteenth-century idea of the great glasshouse, the crystal palaces of London, Paris and Munich, and we have linked this to the shape of the hall in the main railway station and the pool of water in front of the monument commemorating the Battle of the Nations at Leipzig.

The central glass halls of the new trade fair grounds and their pools will offer the visitor a visual experience, in which references to the past are enticingly combined with a belief in a promising future. The design language used by the architects derives from garden architecture, from the function of the trade fair itself and the hall construction.

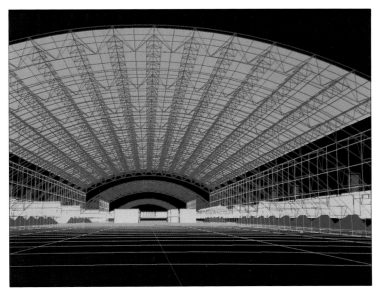

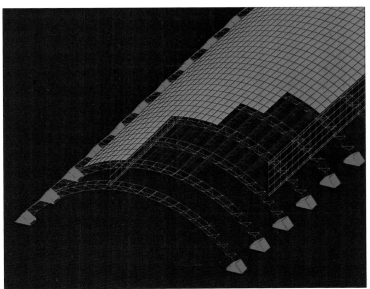

The animated scene under the glass roof; View along the main axis towards the main entrance; Site plan

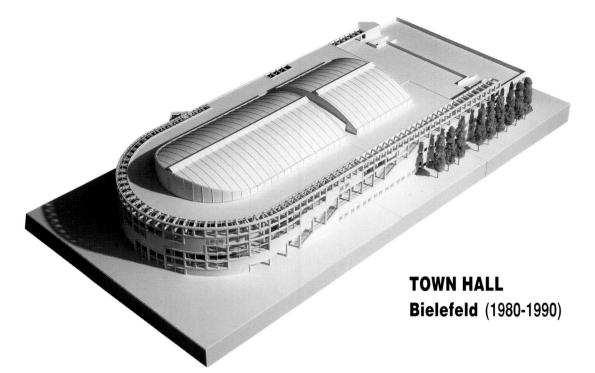

TOWN HALL
Bielefeld (1980-1990)

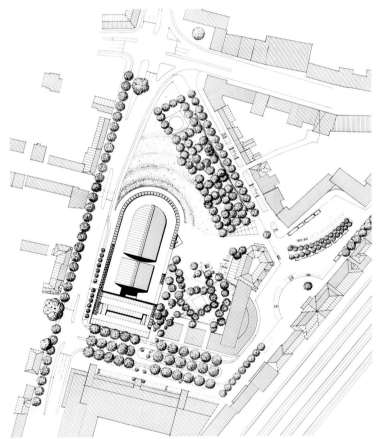

Site plan

Competition: 1980 - First Prize
Design: Meinhard von Gerkan
Assistants: Michael Zimmermann, Marion Ebeling, Frauke Hachmann, Jochen Hohorst, Martina Klostermann, Peter Kropp, Hanns Peter, Detlef Papendick, Stefan Rimpf, Thomas Rinne, Peter Sembritzki, Dieter Tholotowsky, Hans Schröder

Our idea was to make this large, isolated town hall appear like a great steamer floating in the proposed new Railway Station Park right in the centre of the town of Bielefeld.

The building lies in axial symmetry with its semi-circular bow pointing to the inner city, pushing a few earth waves before it. The façade enclosing the building has two layers. Between the two, the open access stairway ascends from the cloakroom hall on the ground floor to the conference hall on the first floor and the balcony level above. The fire escape staircases, which are enclosed, are also located in this intermediate zone and stand out as solid areas on the façade.

Simplicity

The interior of the building is simple. In the centre are the two halls, arranged asymmetrically. The stage area can be opened up, making them into one large hall; they are surrounded by a foyer. The position of the halls on the first floor offers a simple organisational concept both for access by visitors and the work

Herforder Strasse elevation

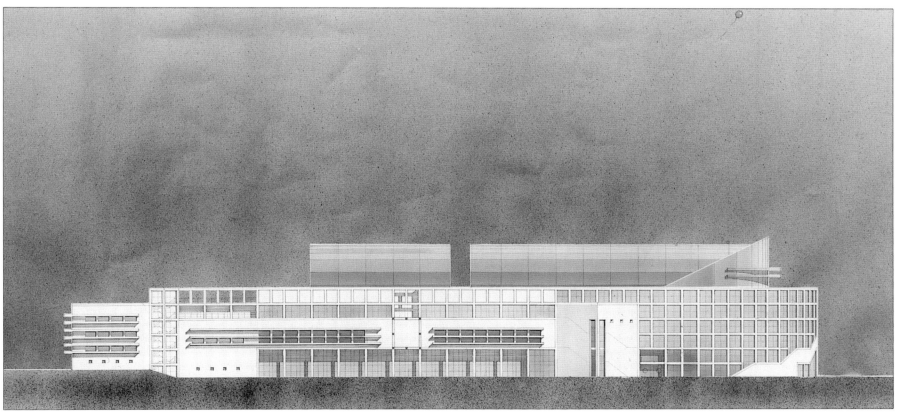

Elevation as seen from the station

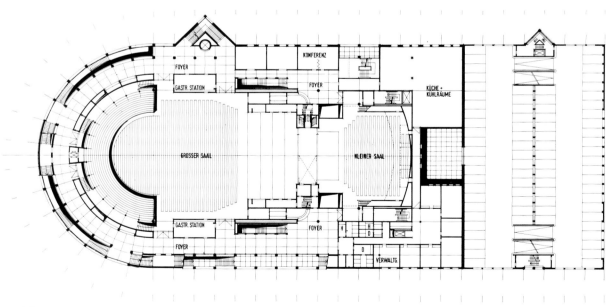

Second tier

of the stage staff. The multi-storey car park, its parking bays easily visible, adjoins the rear of the building. The principle of clarity and simplicity dictated the design of the halls themselves and the arrangement of the seating.

Unity in Variety

The façades of the building are based on a modular scheme; the visible integration of the functional elements of the access stairs gives the building dynamism and life. Although each detail is designed to be functional, it is still subject to the overall design concept. Apart from the grey sheet-metal roof and the glass panes, the only "colour" on the exterior is white.

Structural Order

The great geometric form of the building, which is shaped like an elongated steamer with a round bow and a curving roof, reflects the divisional structure of each part of the building. In the entrance foyer and the cloakroom hall the circular geometry is evident in the position of the columns and the gradation of the mirrored ceiling. On the upper storey the shape of the hall is very clearly defined, both by the surrounding foyer and by the interior.

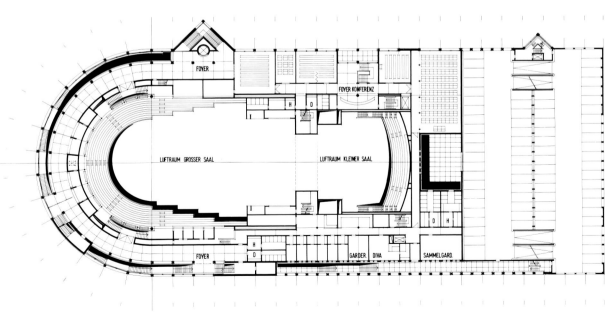

Stalls + 1

*The straight stairway within the double façade
also leads to the parking facilities at the rear*

Cross section of the large hall

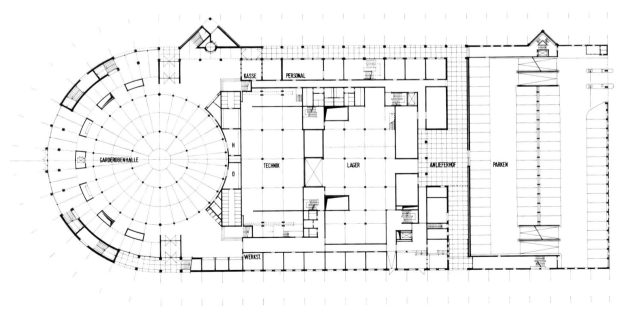

*Top: View from below up into the space between
the two façades. The roof is glazed;
Bottom: Ground floor*

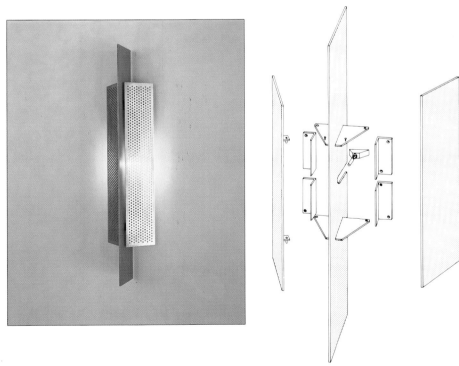

The long axis of the vaulted roof and the rear of the hall, which is semi-circular, sustain this clarity of form.

Identity

The building had to be easily recognisable and reflect its specific use. Hence, the declared aim of the architects was to ensure that the building has both an unmistakeable and highly individual architectural identity, through its special features and size, its design and colouring, lighting and materials.

Function

The large hall has a seating capacity of 2,300 and the smaller 700. They are placed head to head on the central symmetrical axis of the building, so that when the two rear stage walls are opened the entire length can be used.

The stairs set in the two-layer façade are in a transition area between the interior and the exterior. Large panes of glass and toplights provide weather protection from the outside. The stairs to the foyers and lobbies are open, offering good visual orientation to the halls and the town. Visitor flows are a characteristic element of this public building. The action is not concealed inside the building; it becomes a part of the urban scene and visitors have a permanent link with the city.

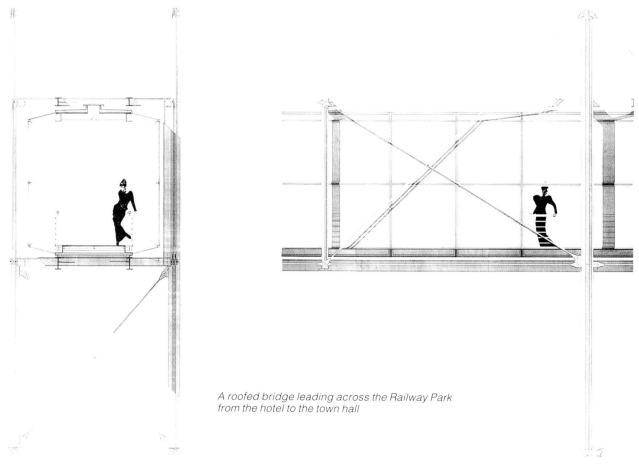

A roofed bridge leading across the Railway Park from the hotel to the town hall

The ceiling of the big hall has an open grid structure which is perceptible, but can be faded out by means of appropriate lighting. Technicians and stage-hands can walk all over the ceiling, and the possibilities for variations ensure that the hall can be altered and re-equipped at short notice for a wide variety of uses and events.

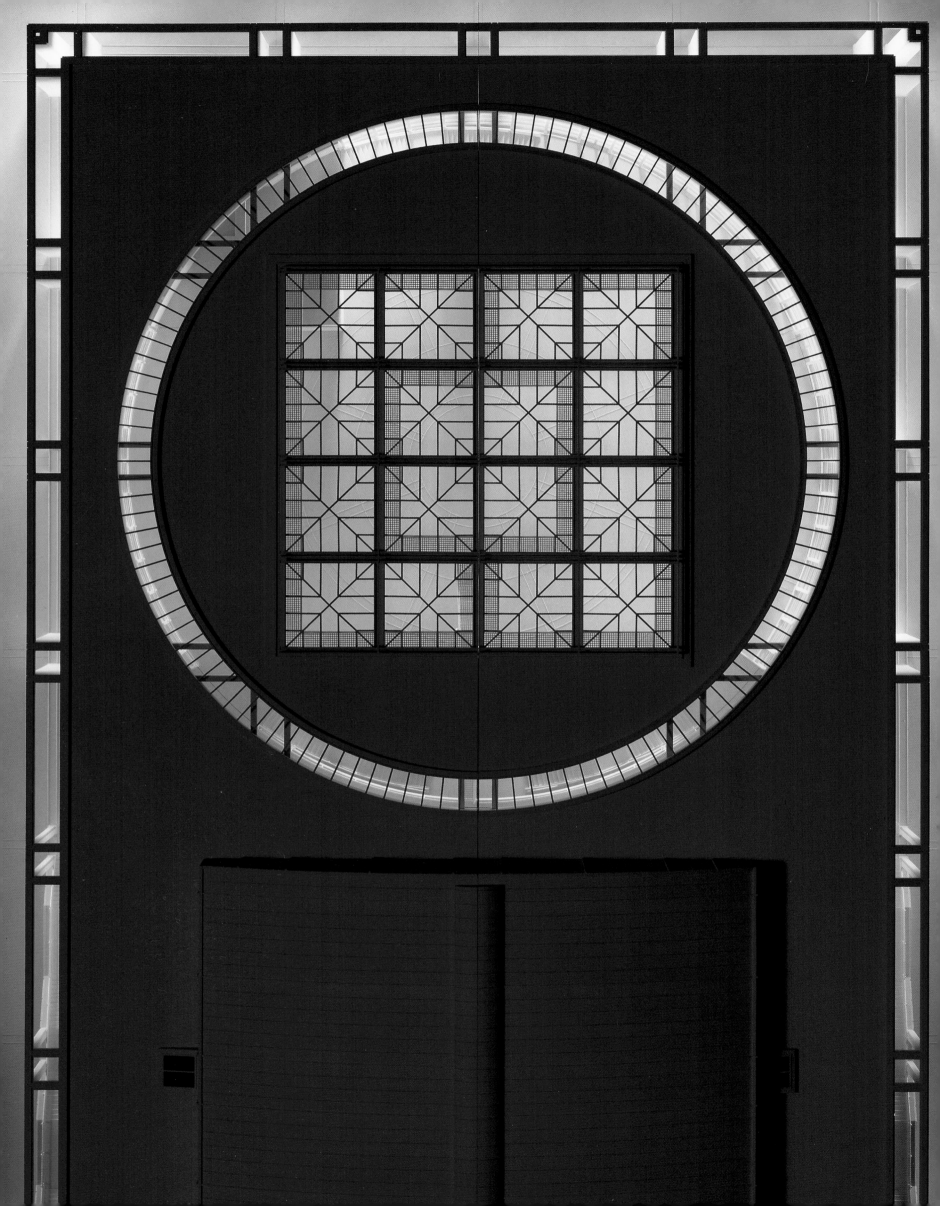

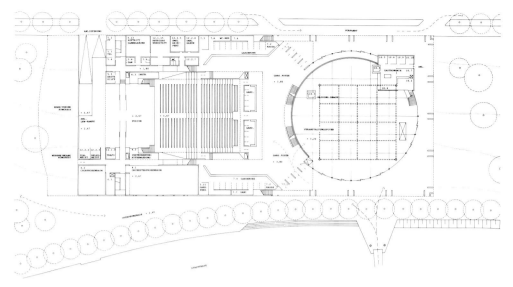

CONCERT AND CONFERENCE HALL
Lübeck (1990-1994)

Competition: 1990 - First Prize
Design: Meinhard von Gerkan
Project Manager: Thomas Rinne
Assistants: Christian Weinmann, Volkmar Sievers, Daniela Kruth, Arne Starke, Martina Klostermann, Peter Kropp, Dirk Sehnkar, Henning Wulf

The aim of the design is to turn the Wallhalbinsel into a park with the Concert and Conference Hall as its dominant feature. The building is rectangular, its long side parallel to the water. The northern tip, with its multi-purpose foyer like a recessed cylinder, forms a large arcade jutting out into the pedestrian passage that intersects it.

Instead of an open space in front lined with buildings, the proposal is that the building itself with its arcades, its open staircases, and the walks around it, should form a public building with a multi-purpose foyer open to the public.

The entrances to the building on both the east and west façades are recessed into the building. The entrance foyer lies between the concert hall and the multi-purpose foyer, offering equally good access to both parts of the interior.

The building is austere in shape, the concert hall a simple rectangle with access all round. The multi-purpose foyer consists of simple geometric elements (squares and circles). One side is glazed with a view of the old city.

The artistes' dressing rooms are located on one side of the concert hall and the conference area is on the other side. The capacity of the auditorium can be varied from 1200 to 2000.

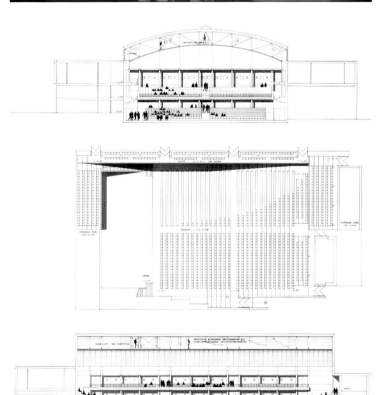

From top: Ground floor plan; Cross section of the auditorium; Auditorium plan; Longitudinal section of the auditorium

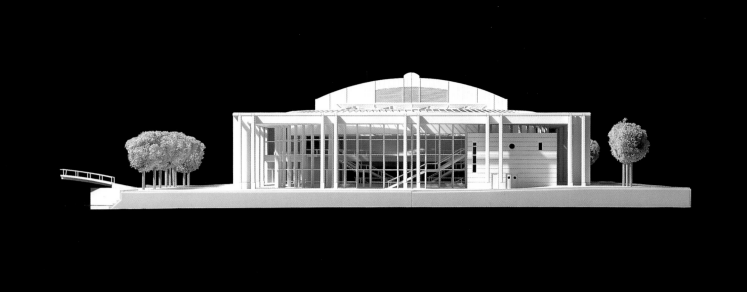

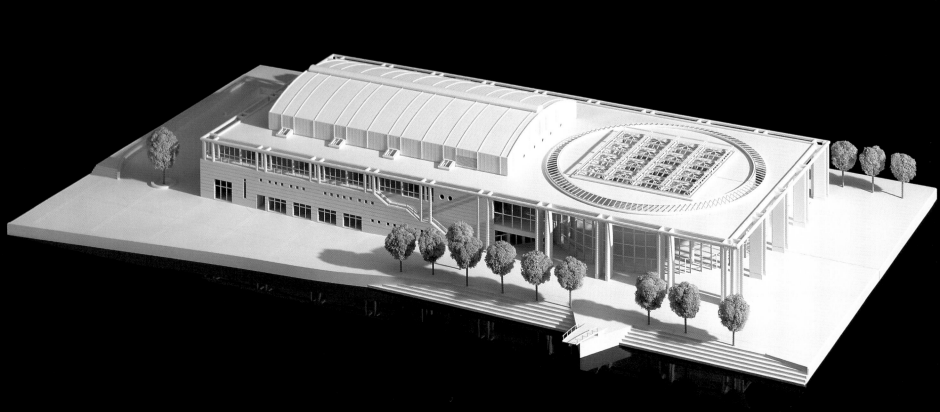

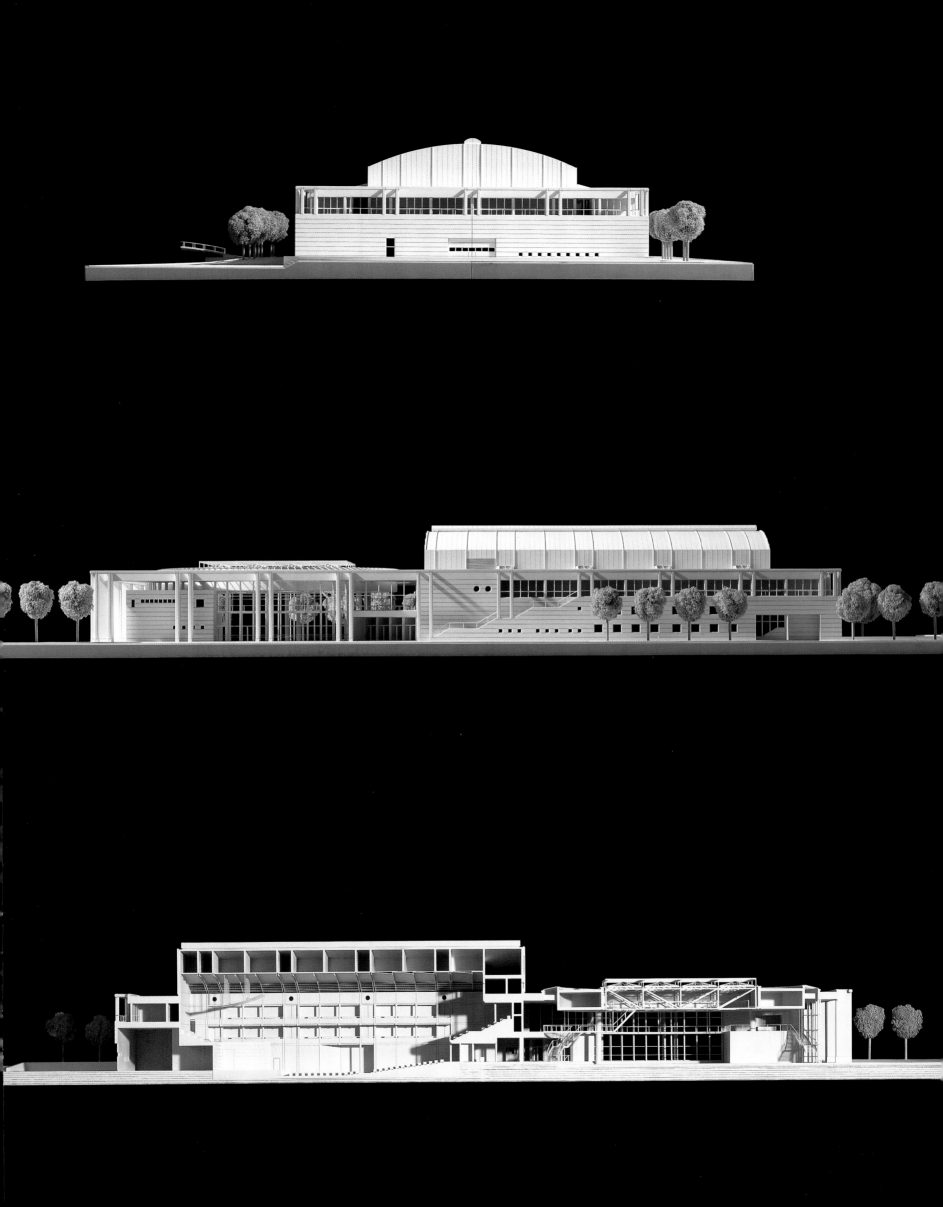

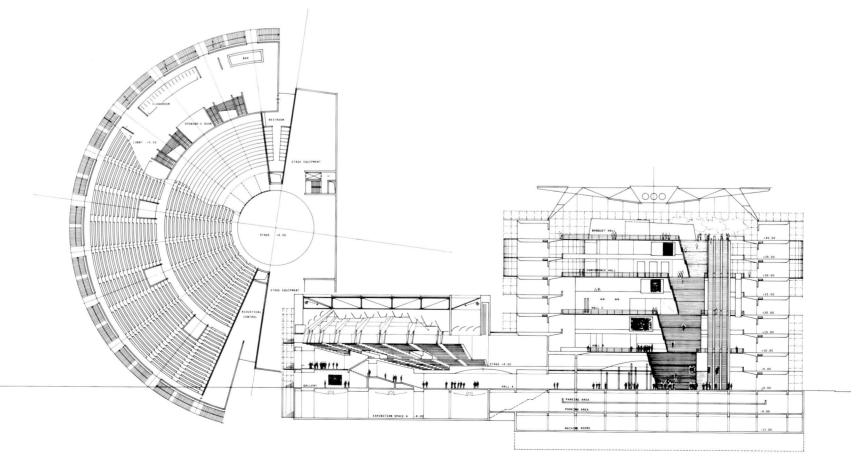

TOKYO INTERNATIONAL FORUM

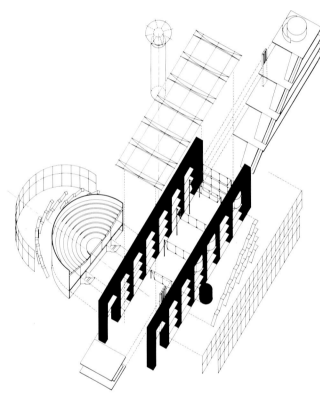

From top: Perspective view; Design concept
Opposite: Plan and section of Hall A

Competition: 1989
Design: Meinhard von Gerkan
Assistants: Christian Weinmann, Volkmar Sievers, Hilke Büttner, Arturo Buchholz-Berger

The main principle of the design is to create a public indoor square adapted to city life. The square rises in terraces, like steps, to the top. All the Forum facilities have direct links with it.

The different levels are organized like a bookcase. The columns contain staircases, service shafts and lifts. Small and medium-size rooms fit into the 5m and 10m high shelf compartments. Balconies make them accessible and open onto the indoor square.

A second façade forms a transparent grid 3.6m to the outside of the main building. The space between the two contains emergency exits, projecting volumes such as conference rooms, shading systems, lighting, technical equipment,cleaning units, advertising.

Large rooms are located on terraces accessible by a wide flight of stairs narrowing at the top. Even the terraces have interchangeable functions. The proposed design does not provide an exact plan of the rooms on each floor but creates only a structural three-dimensional principle of order.

"Hall A", because of its size, forms a separate volume in the form of a half-cylinder located outside the main structure. The cylinder-like tower contains air-conditioning plant and additional fire escapes. A helicopter pad could be located on the roof.

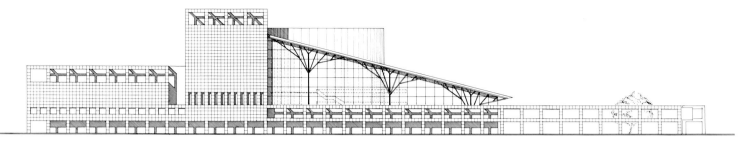

Shibuya Ward Street elevation

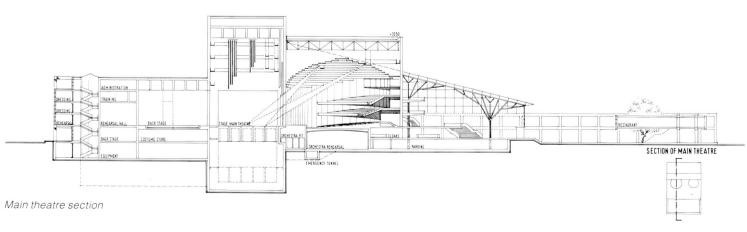

Main theatre section

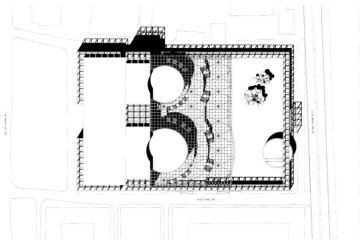

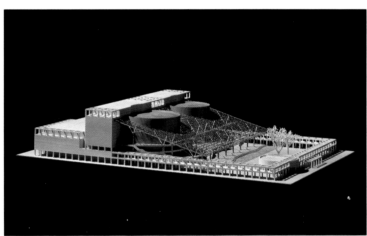

NATIONAL THEATRE
Tokyo

International Competition: 1986 - In top thirty
Design: Meinhard von Gerkan
Assistants: Manfred Stanek, Tuyen Tran-Viet, Jacob Kierig

The theatre is an event which reflects life as seen by artists. It is also a place where the audience leaves the world of reality to enter into the world of the imagination. It is a building for social encounters and intellectual currents. It is a focus of living culture.

Our design embodies these functions by representing them in clearly definable architectural elements. Each element symbolises one component.

The design combines the elements in a simple, logical way. The entire area of the site is utilised but the building masses are compressed to leave space all round for a forecourt. This is delimited from the adjacent noisy streets with arcades. The provision of a forecourt is in the tradition of Japanese temples.

The roof of the great hall is supported by a steel tree-like structure and consists of two glass layers, one above the other. The tree supports are in tubular steel of varying diameters, whereas the junctions are moulded.

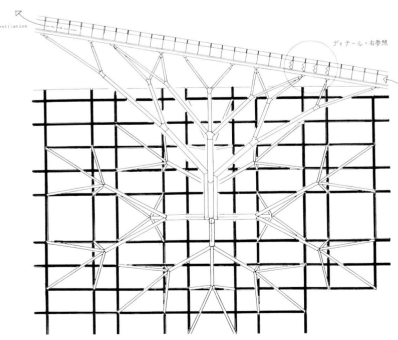

The steel tree-like structure of the roof supports

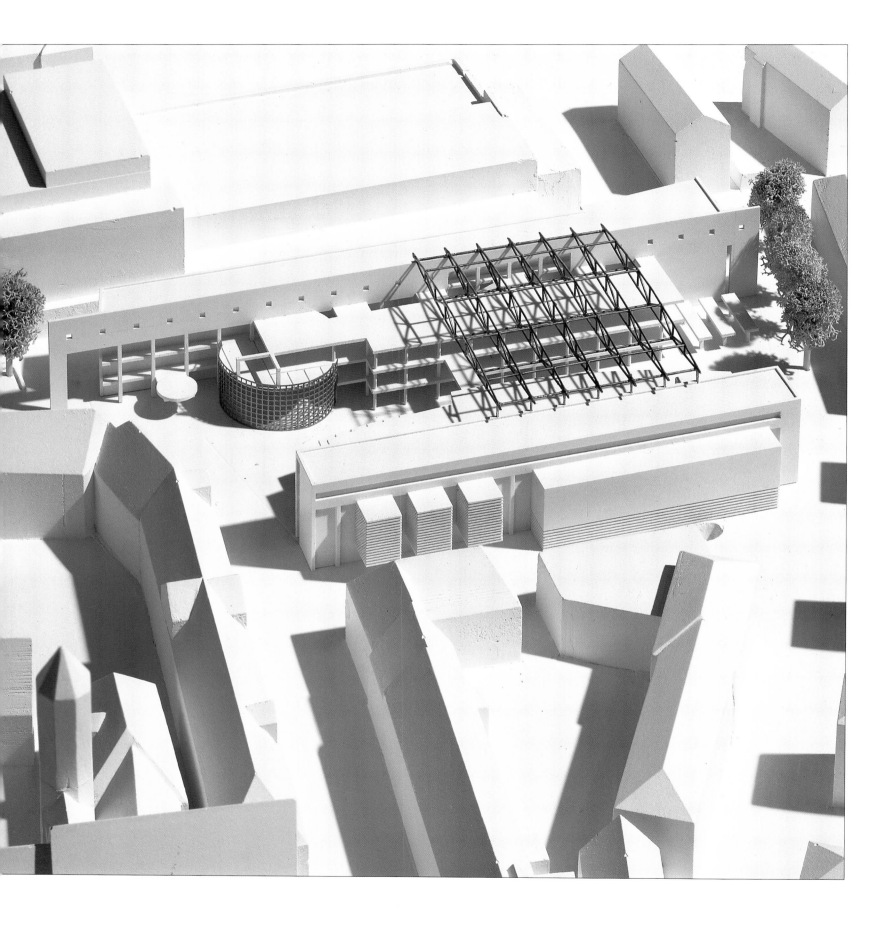

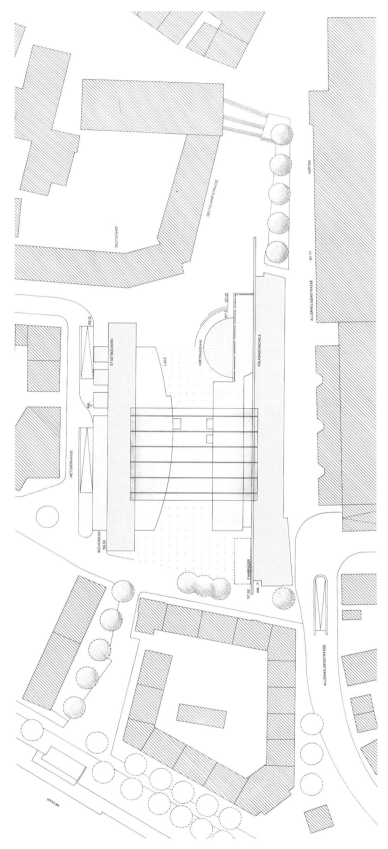

Site plan

ADULT EDUCATION INSTITUTE AND MUNICIPAL LIBRARY
Heilbronn (1990-1994)

Competition: 1990 - First Prize
Design: Meinhard von Gerkan
Assistants: Hilke Büttner, Volkmar Sievers, Hito Ueda, Clemens Schneider

The design is conceived as an open "house", with all the various buildings along the street forming a harmonious complex in the urban space.

The overlayering and interpenetration of the public urban space with the facilities of the adult education institute and library are the main feature of the design. The facilities are conceived as independent units, but have a joint roof.

The longitudinal section of the two buildings creates clearly-defined street spaces: to the north Metzgergasse and to the south Allerheiligenstrasse. In the middle, the public street and square cut through the building complex creating a visual and pedestrian link between the Deutschhof and the steps to the Neckar.

The connecting glazed roof provides a public space protected from the weather and, as the dominant architectural feature, it underlines the importance of the public buildings without competing with the historic buildings.

The interior façades of the buildings are mostly glazed, but the exterior ones are clearly differentiated, in keeping with the surrounding streetscene.

VOLKSHOCHSCHULE

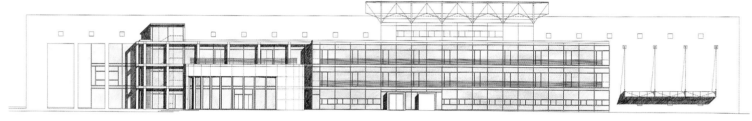

VOLKSHOCHSCHULE

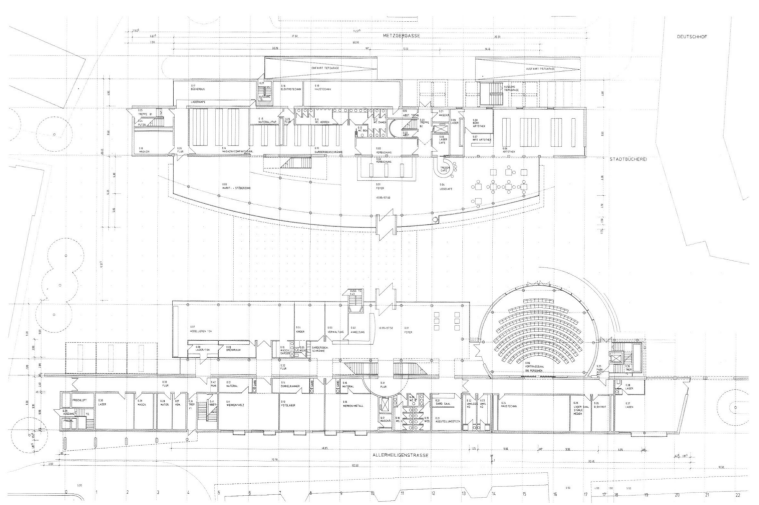

From, top: South and North elevation of Southern building; Ground floor plans

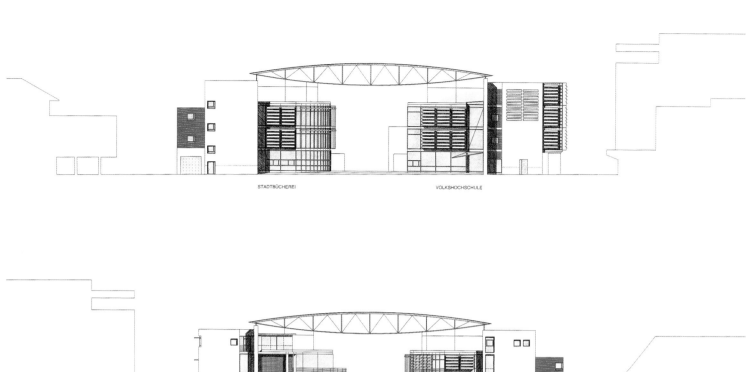

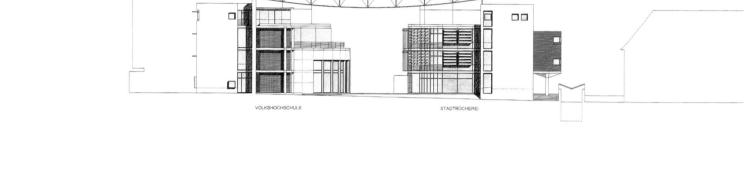

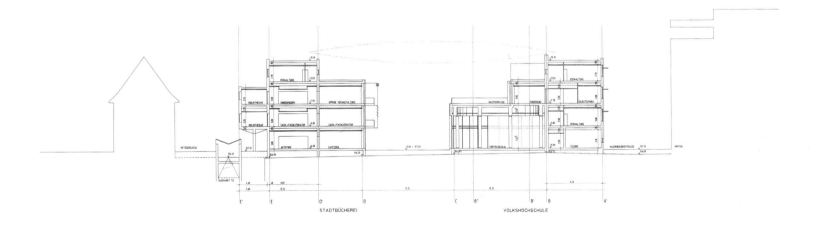

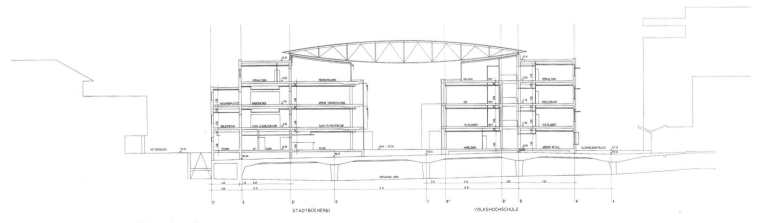

*From top: West elevation; East elevation;
Cross section*

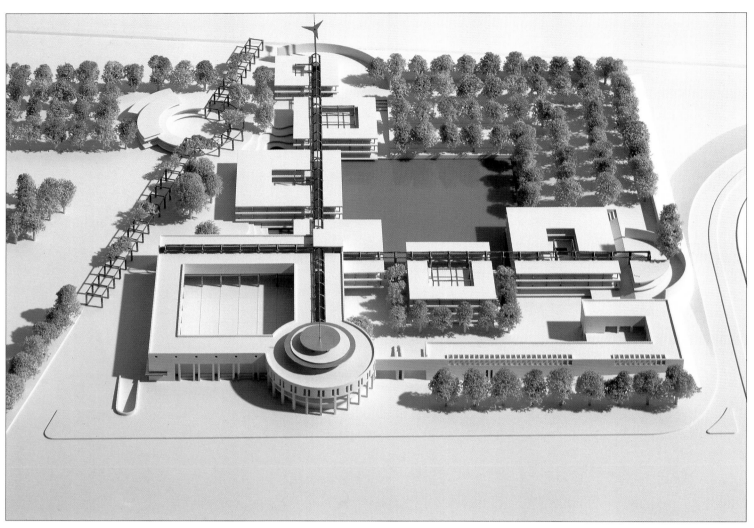

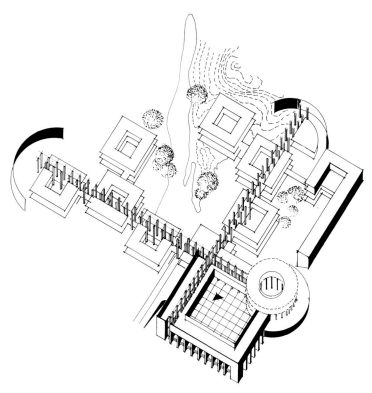

MINISTRY OF THE ENVIRONMENT
Bonn

Competition: 1988 - First Prize
Design: Meinhard von Gerkan
Assistants: Gerhard G. Feldmeyer, Michael Zimmermann, Daniela Hillmer, Andreas Perlick, Sybille Scharbau, Jörg Schulte, Clemens Zeis

The planning aim here was to retain the character of the artificial Rheinaue Park lying on both sides of the Rhine and extending into the grounds of the various ministries. Hence, most of the buildings have only two or three storeys, depending on the contours of the terrain, which acts as a noise barrier.

While the office pavilions have an openwork structure and are well integrated into the landscape, the square structure in front of them is both solid and monolithic. The area in front of it is designedin the form of a city square.

Two intersecting interior "access routes" form an austere grid system, in front of which the office pavilions are set freely, although they also follow a geometric principle. Despite the clear systematic structure, this principle affords a high degree of freedom for the design of individual areas and for adapting building units to requirements.

The interior could include an inner courtyard or a two-storey hall. The main interior thoroughfares have the symbolic significance of "nature" and "technology". The main entrance lies at the intersection of the two. The axes lead to semi-circular niches in the walls intended for works of art on the subject of the conflict between nature and technology and their mutual dependence.

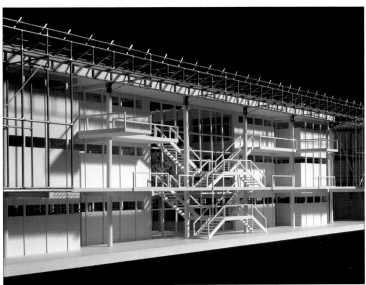

Top: Concept sketch

North elevation

East elevation

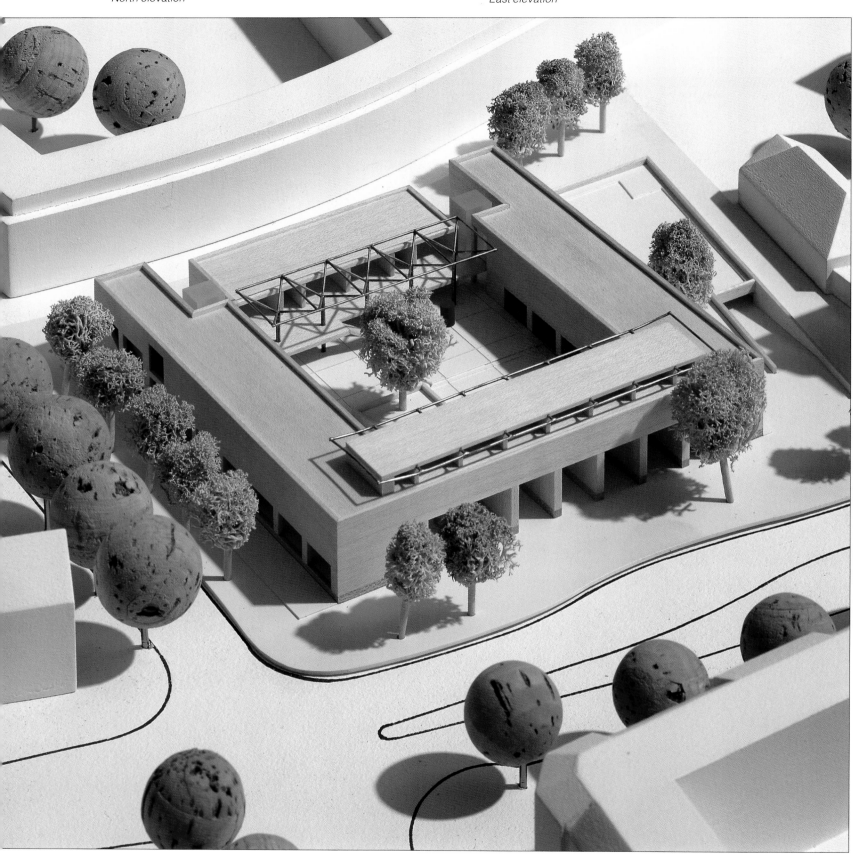

West elevation

South elevation

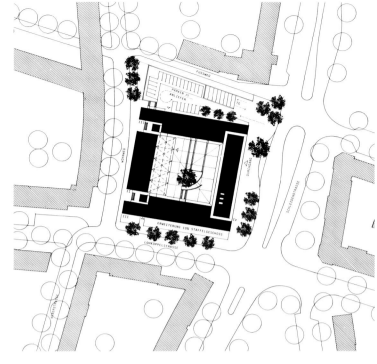

DISTRICT COURT
Hamburg-Nord

Competition: 1992 - First Prize
Design: Meinhard von Gerkan,
Joachim Zais

The design consists of a simple, cubic building with a block structure enclosing an inner court. Along Schleidenstrasse the court terminates in a two-storey arcade opening onto the street. This provides a covered public place and is also the forecourt of the entrance. We have thus used a traditional type of building in Hamburg, like those of Fritz Schumacher and others.

The structure emphasises the fact that this is a public complex. It also allowed us to set the entrance back from the street and locate it with the courtrooms in the main part of the building. Access and orientation should be obvious to both staff and visitors.

The three-storey building rests on a base and is adapted to the scale of the surrounding area; the recessed top storey adjoins the cornice level of the Industrial Court on the street façade.

Our intention was to create a clear, unambiguous formal language for the building, making the facilities easily legible. The three sides of the block where the offices are located have a brick façade, again in keeping with Hamburg tradition. The fourth wall, at the back where the entrance hall and courtrooms are located, is in deliberate contrast, being a light, transparent steel and glass construction. This transparency helps lessen the threshold fear of the court as an institution. The inner court will be a pleasant seating area.

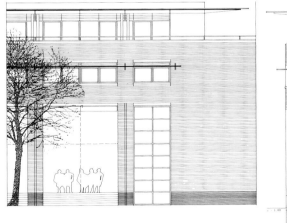

From top: Site plan; Groundfloor; Façade details

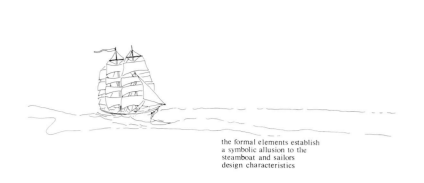

the formal elements establish
a symbolic allusion to the
steamboat and sailors
design characteristics

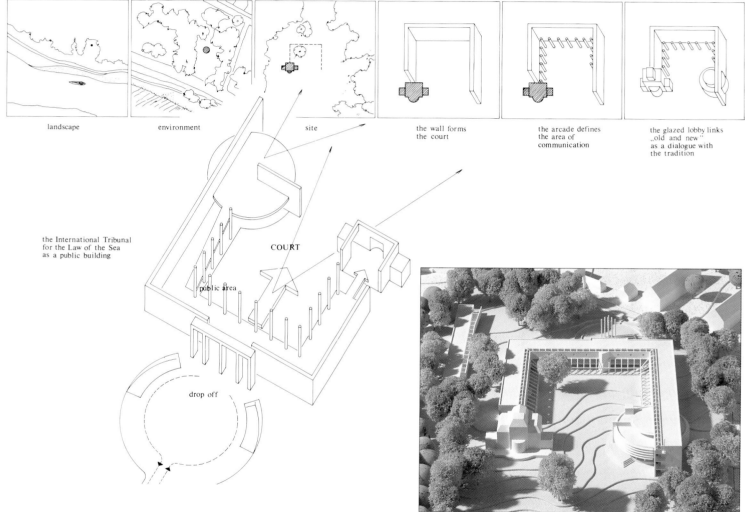

landscape

environment

site

the wall forms
the court

the arcade defines
the area of
communication

the glazed lobby links
„old and new"
as a dialogue with
the tradition

the International Tribunal
for the Law of the Sea
as a public building

COURT

public area

drop off

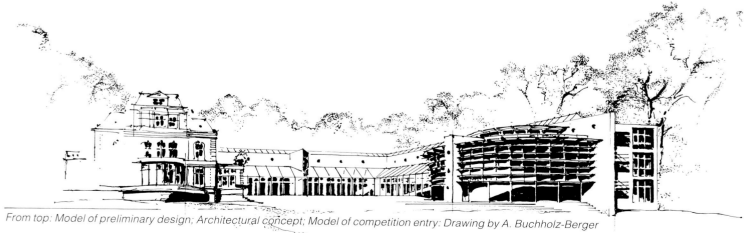

From top: Model of preliminary design; Architectural concept; Model of competition entry: Drawing by A. Buchholz-Berger

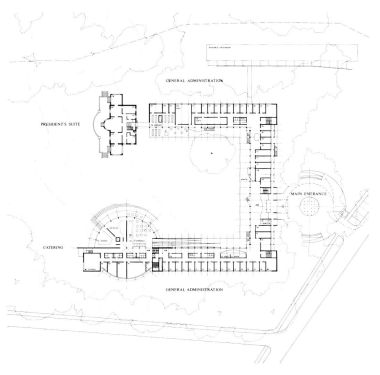

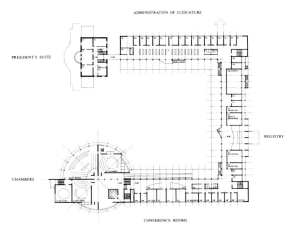

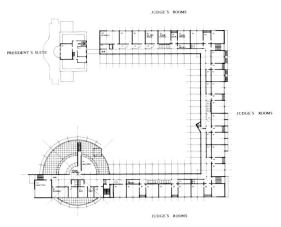

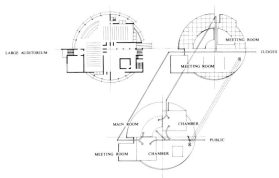

From top: Ground floor; First floor; Second floor; Schematic drawing

INTERNATIONAL COURT FOR THE LAW OF THE SEA
Hamburg

Competition: 1989 - Third Prize
Design: Meinhard von Gerkan
Assistants: Christian Weinmann, Volkmar Sievers, Hilke Büttner, Clemens Zeis, Arturo Buchholz-Berger

The site had such characteristic features as many fine old trees and a neo-classical villa and which our design took into account. Our intention was to preserve the villa, which stands asymmetrically on the site, and to use it for official occasions. To counterbalance the historic building, we planned a circular building for the courtrooms.

The two corner buildings stand as signs representing the dialogue between "old" and "new". They are linked by a U-shaped section around a south-facing court in an arrangement offering an architectural interpretation of the concept of a "law-court". The spine of this section is a wall with open arcades in the lower storeys; this is spatially integrated with the glazed front hall and provides general foyer areas.

On entering, the visitor has a largely uninterrupted view of the Elbe and a visual orientation over the whole complex. The glazed foyer opens onto the court, which is built on three sides and opens onto the river on the fourth. It serves as a public lobby and as an access foyer. The courtrooms in the main corner building are cylindrical. Each courtroom has interpreters' cabins, toilets and a visitors' gallery.

The three-storey, neo-classical villa dates from 1871, and will be the residence of the President of the Court.

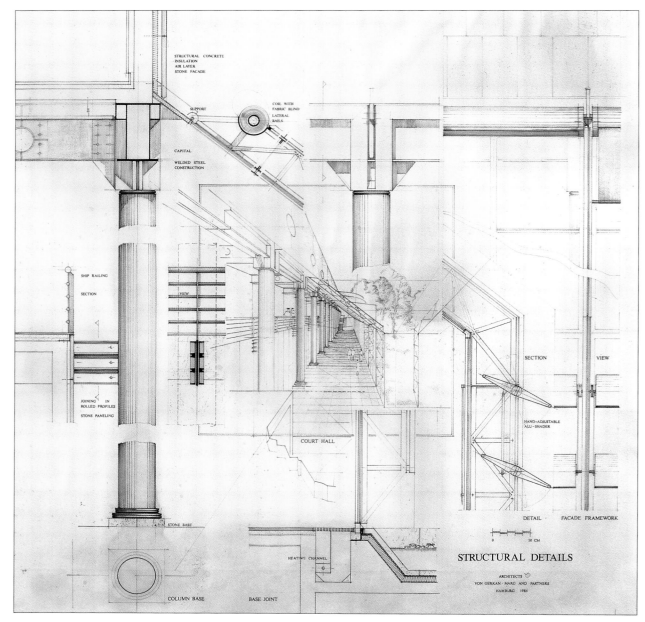

STRUCTURAL CONCRETE
INSULATION
AIR LAYER
STONE FACADE

SUPPORT

COIL WITH
FABRIC BLIND
LATERAL
RAILS

CAPITAL

WELDED STEEL
CONSTRUCTION

SHIP RAILING

SECTION

VIEW

SECTION   VIEW

JOINING IN
ROLLED PROFILES

STONE PANELING

HAND-ADJUSTABLE
ALU-SHADER

COURT HALL

STONE BASE

DETAIL · FACADE FRAMEWORK

0   50 CM

STRUCTURAL DETAILS

HEATING CHANNEL

ARCHITECTS
VON GERKAN · MARG AND PARTNERS
HAMBURG 1984

COLUMN BASE   BASE JOINT

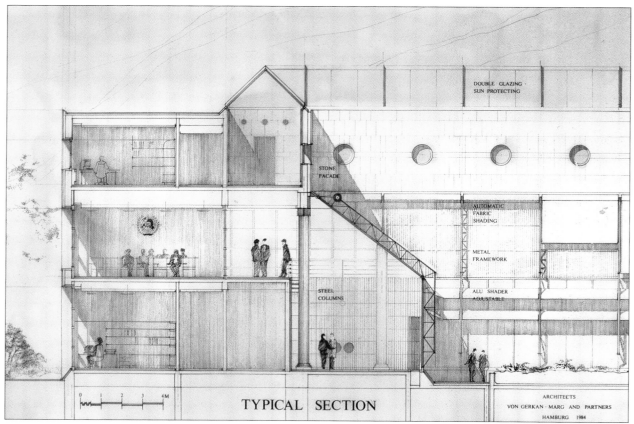

DOUBLE GLAZING ·
SUN PROTECTING

STONE
FACADE

AUTOMATIC
FABRIC
SHADING

METAL
FRAMEWORK

STEEL
COLUMNS

ALU SHADER
ADJUSTABLE

0 1 2 3 4M

TYPICAL SECTION

ARCHITECTS
VON GERKAN · MARG AND PARTNERS
HAMBURG 1984

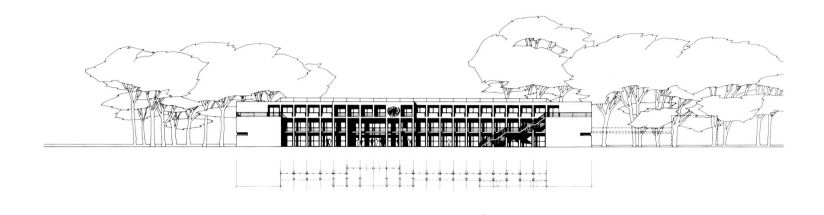

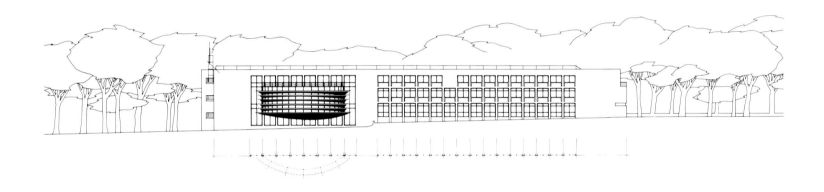

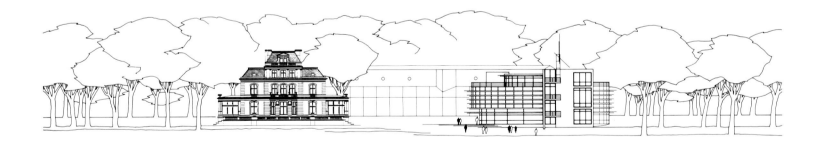

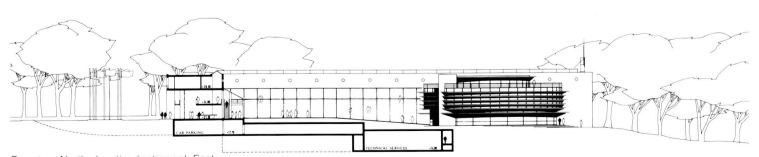

From top: North elevation (entrance); East elevation; South elevation; Elevation from courtyard

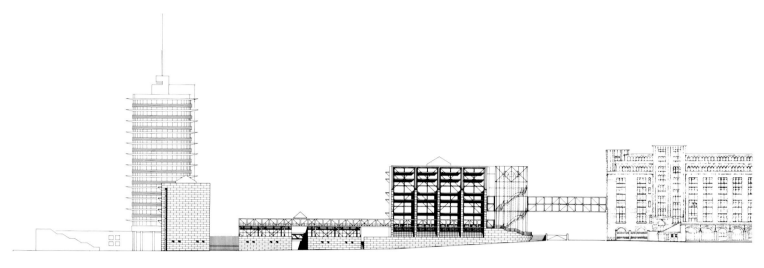

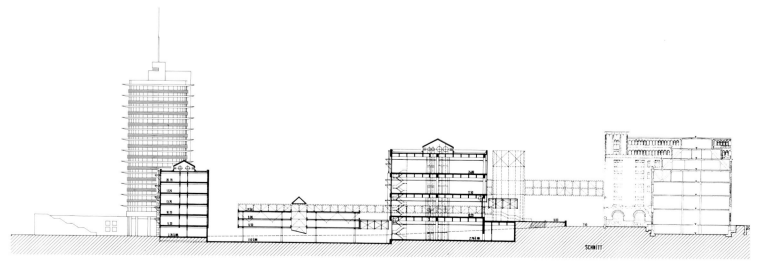

POST OFFICES 1 AND 3
Hamburg

Competition: 1985 - Second Prize
Design: Meinhard von Gerkan
Assistants: Manfred Stanek, Thomas Bieling, Gerhard Feldmeyer, Marion Meews, Marion Ebeling

The design envisages all the new buildings as a uniform complex that will be totally independent of the existing post-office buildings.

The stone bases which interlink the individual buildings support columns which criss-cross the openwork structure of the steel façade and the blinds. The walls are largely glazed in order to let as much daylight as possible into the offices and ensure optimal efficiency for the work within the building. Thus the "inner functions are reflected outwards".

The cylindrical office tower will be a contrasting element and an unmistakeable marker on Amsinckstrasse.

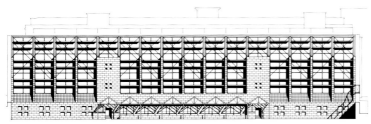

From top: Site plan; Detail; South elevation; Opposite top: East elevation; Opposite bottom: Section

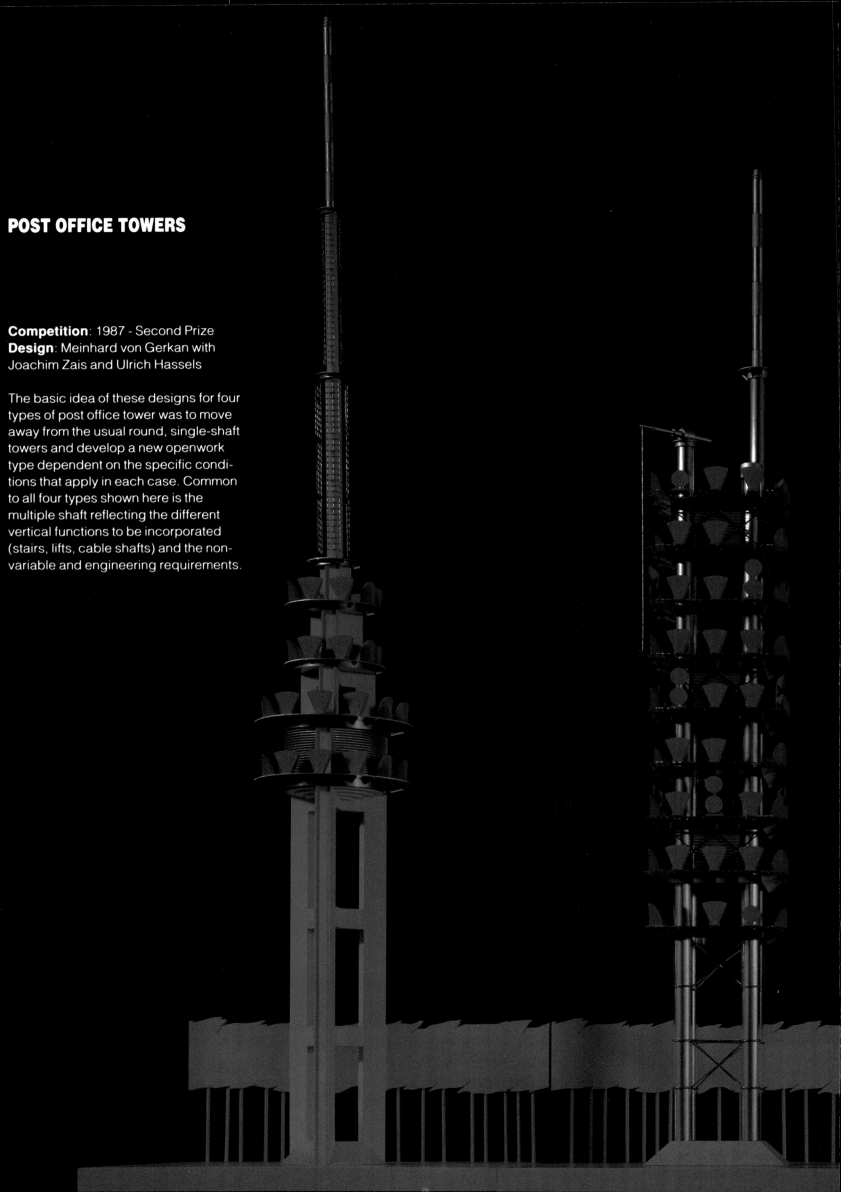

POST OFFICE TOWERS

Competition: 1987 - Second Prize
Design: Meinhard von Gerkan with
Joachim Zais and Ulrich Hassels

The basic idea of these designs for four
types of post office tower was to move
away from the usual round, single-shaft
towers and develop a new openwork
type dependent on the specific conditions that apply in each case. Common
to all four types shown here is the
multiple shaft reflecting the different
vertical functions to be incorporated
(stairs, lifts, cable shafts) and the non-
variable and engineering requirements.

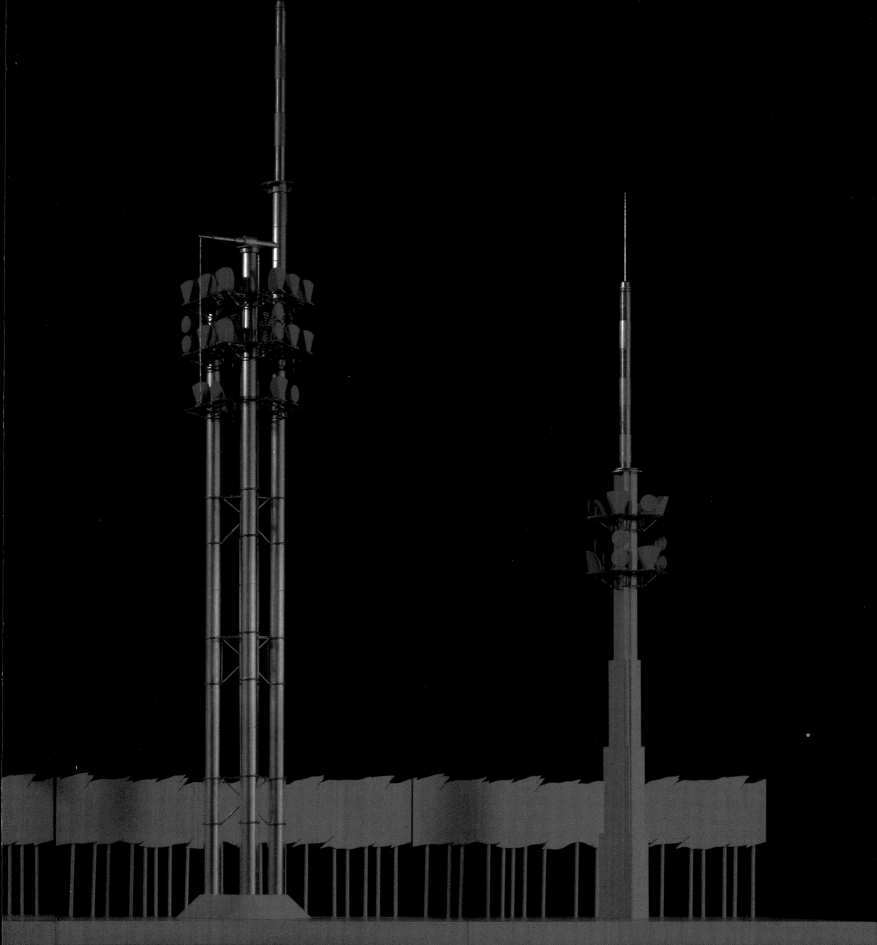

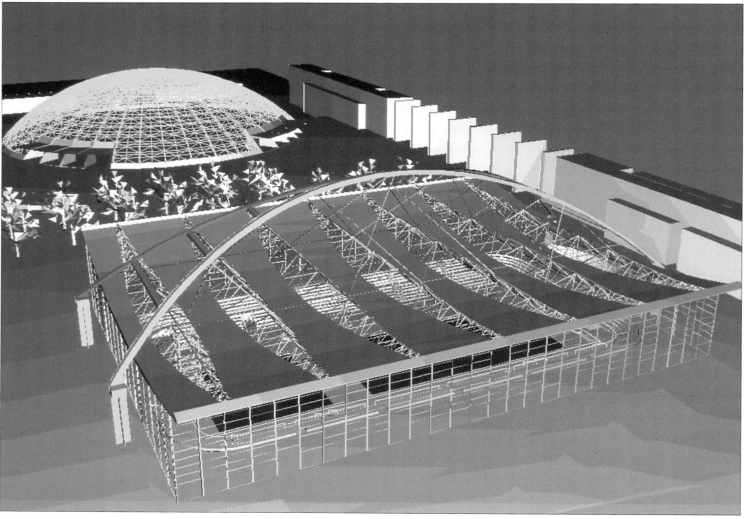

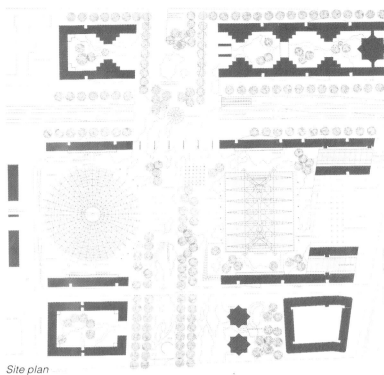

Site plan

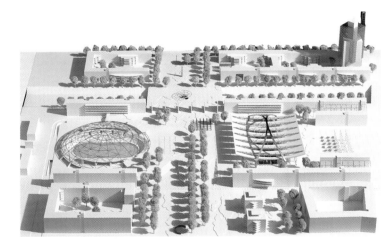

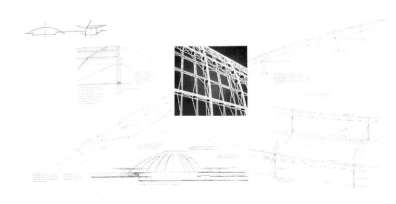

Cycling arena: construction details

*Opposite from top: CAD drawing of the interior view of the cycling arena;
CAD drawing of the aerial view of the swimming pool and cycling arena*

OLYMPIA 2000
Berlin

Competition: 1992 - Second Prize
Design: Meinhard von Gerkan
Assistants: Clemens Schneider,
Manfred Stanek

The Olympic Games are a spectacular event and it is tempting to design spectacular architecture for them but our proposal deliberately avoids the dramatic gesture. The shape and structure of the buildings reflect their function, and, since their requirements are different, they are diametrically opposed in ground plan and elevation.

The circular ground plan for the cycling arena is introverted and closed, as is the bowl-like structure of the building. The stands follow the oval of the track.

The rectangular swimming pool hall has a suspended tent roof. During the Olympic Games it will cover the temporary rows of seats along the long sides, and afterwards act as a projecting roof to shade the façade. The supporting double arch has a geometric relation to the bowl, but the two shapes retain their elementary antagonistic duality.

The terrain round the halls is raised by about 4m. To allow the geometric shapes of the halls to be fully evident, and to ensure that they appear both clear and transparent, all services are banished below access level.

A large green belt intersects the Olympic site and the service centre, which is arranged in parallel sections north and south of the railway ring. The special facilities are incorporated in the zones between so that the two halls are clearly delimited architecturally.

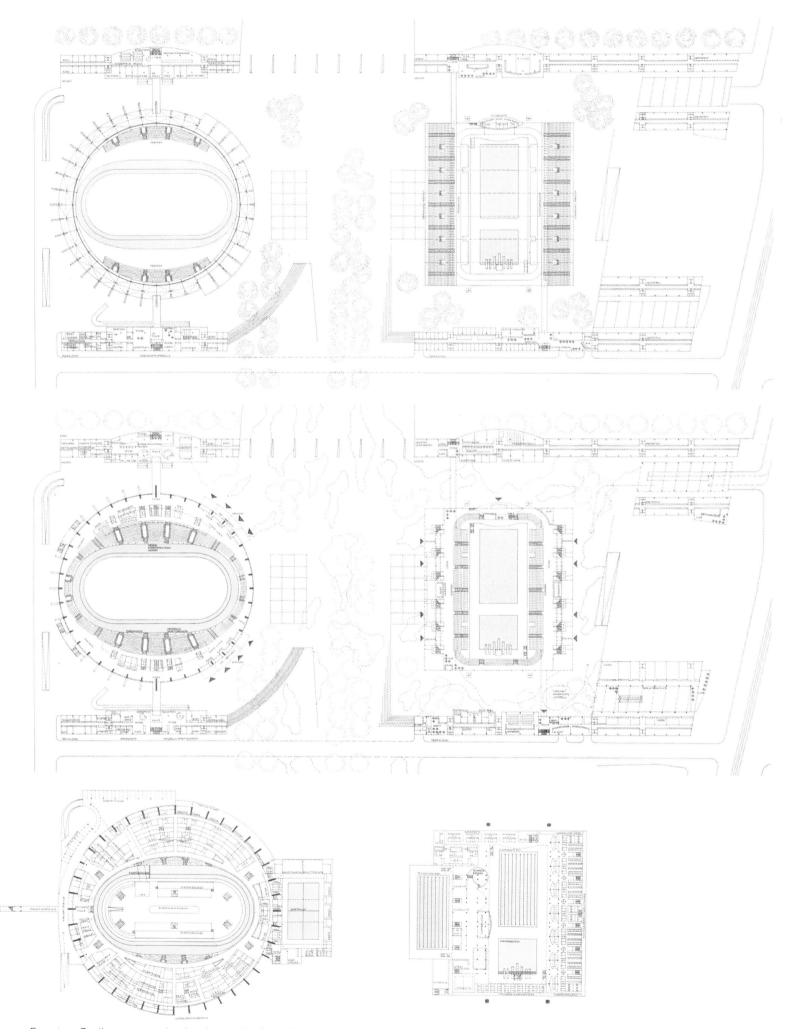

From top: Cycling arena and swimming pool hall at +7m level; at +4m level; at -4m level

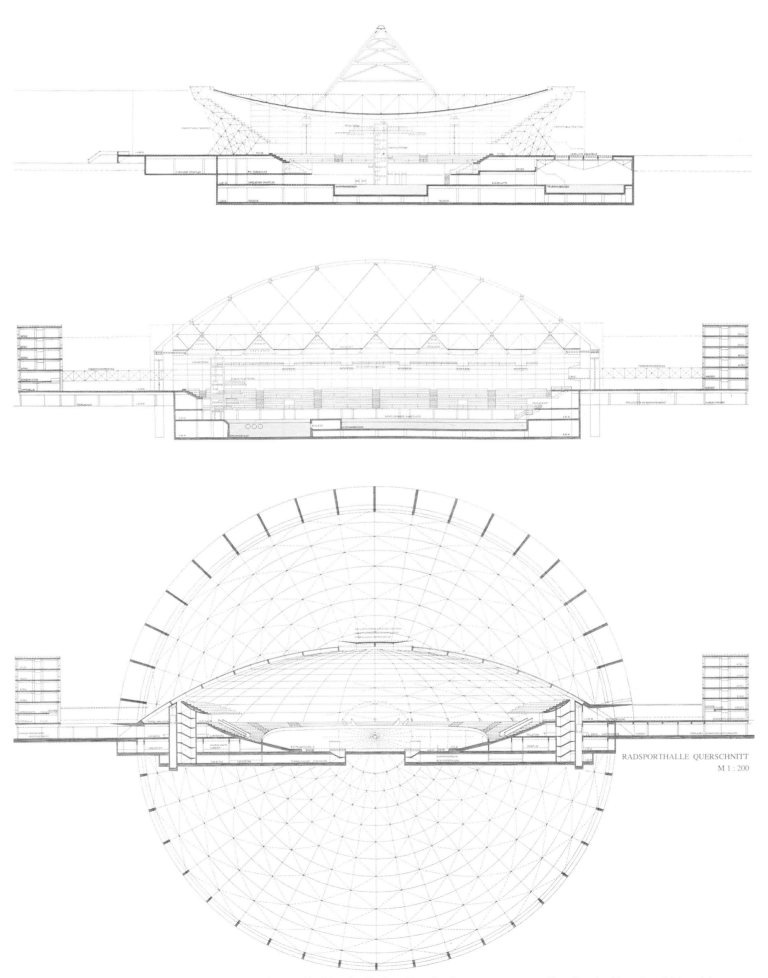

RADSPORTHALLE QUERSCHNITT
M 1 : 200

From top: Swimming pool hall cross section; Swimming pool hall longitudinal section; Cycling arena cross section; Overleaf from top: Alt Landsberger Chaussee elevation; Fritz-Riedel Strasse elevation; Storkower Strasse elevation

111

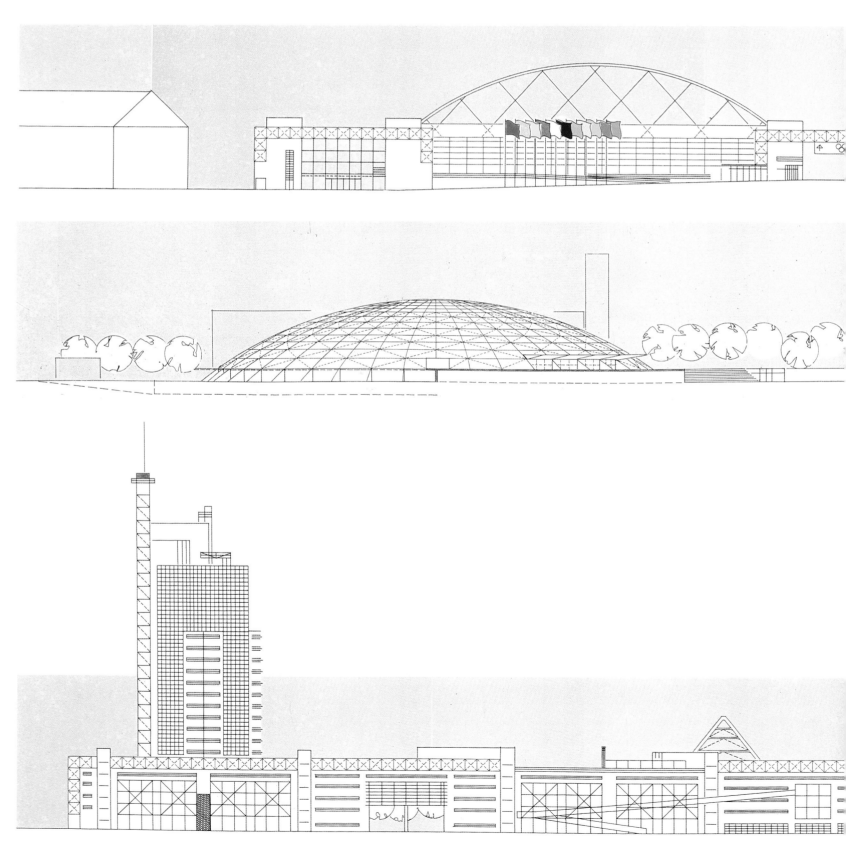

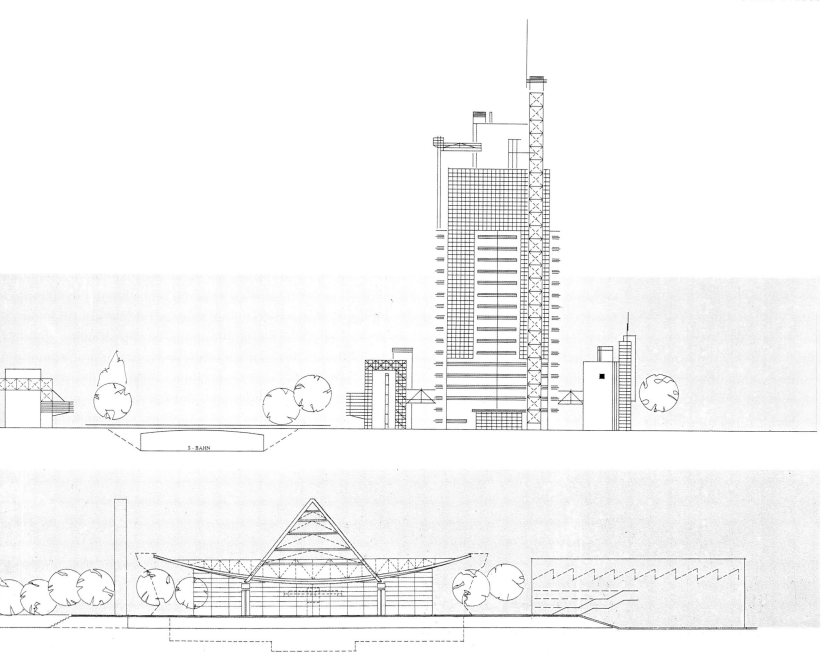

S · BAHN

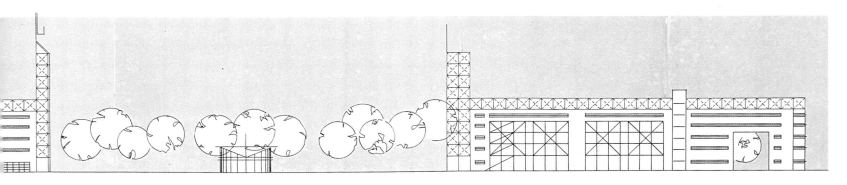

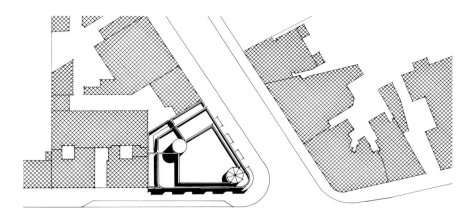

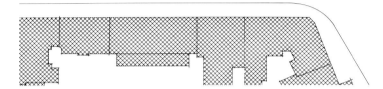

GRINDELALLEE 100
Hamburg (1984-1987)

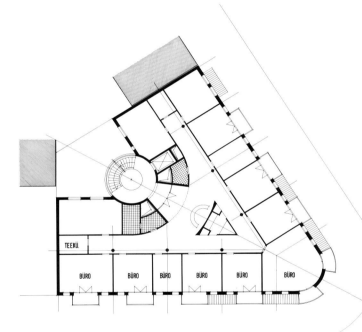

Design: Meinhard von Gerkan with Klaus Staratzke
Assistants: Barbara Fleckenstein, Peter Sembritzki, Harald Sylvester
Size: Shop space 410sq.m; office space 940sq.m; living space 1,070sq.m; and parking for 17 cars

The site is tiny and angular with very little light at the rear. The two façades are on extremely noisy, traffic-bearing streets. Nevertheless, the proximity of the university and many good shops makes this a good area.

The rotunda with its projecting roof accentuates its corner position and ensures that the new building enters into a dialogue with the buildings opposite, which date from the "Gründerzeit", the prosperous years of the late nineteenth century.

The façade is a variegated steel and glass construction forming a second shell in front of the solid, monolithic walls with their deep-set fenestration.

The conservatories provide additional sound insulation as well as extending the living space and shop floors outwards. The windows have single glazing and thermally sealed steel profiles to achieve optimal transparency and openwork. The complementary effect of block-like solidity and openwork transparency is the main objective of the two layers of the façade .

The ground plan is almost exactly symmetrical with the diagonal bisecting the angular corner site. The route from the corner entrance to the rear circular stairway also follows this diagonal.

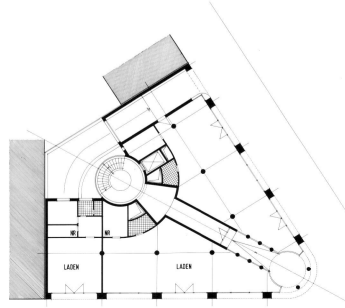

From top: Site plan; First and second floors; Ground floor

The glass brick wall makes the stairway very light and bright, despite its position in the rear court. The inside walls are painted white, while the floors and stairs are terrazzo with dark grey inlays in light grey areas.

The ground floor and parts of the basement can be used as shop floor space. The space on the first and second floors can be subdivided as required for commercial use, such as offices, surgeries or a dental laboratory.

The three top floors contain small apartments since this site is not suitable for large families with children.

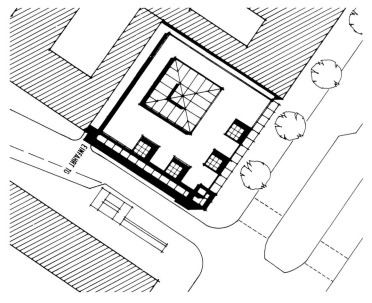

SALAMANDER BUILDING
Berlin (1990-1992)

Design: Volkwin Marg
Assistants: Joachim Rind, Martin Bleckmann, Annette Brücker, Bettina Lautz, Vera Mostert, Christina Tibi, Peter Römer, Sybille Zittlau-Kroos, Beate Lucas, Ute Kretschmer, Karl Baumgarten, Ivanka Perkovic, Benedict Dardin

The main objective of the design is advertising through architecture.

Instead of the usual office block façade, the Salamander Building's main feature is its brilliantly lit winter garden.

The street corner is accentuated by an advertising tower which displays the illuminated Salamander logo.

The transparent two-storey shop fronts with recessed galleries located on the first floor are designed as broad arcades with weather-protection.

The building has a combination of shops, offices and apartments, providing mixed use for inner city needs.

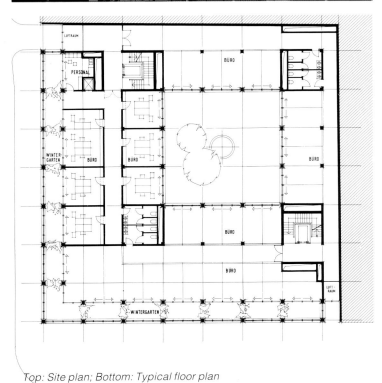

Top: Site plan; Bottom: Typical floor plan

MAIN POST OFFICE BUILDING
Braunschweig (1982-1990)

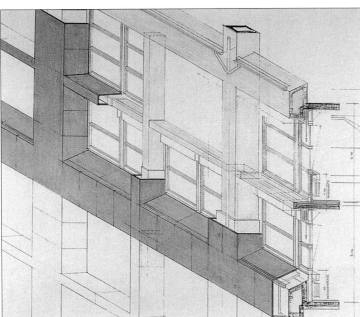

Design: Meinhard von Gerkan
Assistants: Bernhard Albers, Knut Maass, Uwe Schümann, Antje Lucks, Marion Ebeling, Klaus Lübbert, Marion Mews, Sabrina Pieper, Manfred Stanek, Gerhard Tjarks, Jürgen Friedemann, Erich Hartmann, Kurt Kowalzik, Hermann Timpe
German Architects' Federation Prize, Lower Saxony, 1991
Natural Stone Prize 1991
Commended

The organization of the massing evolved from the location in the urban environment and the shape of the site.

The flat four-storey building respects existing squares and streets. At the corner where the two sections meet at an obtuse angle, a tower block rising high above the intersection provides a focal point for the whole complex.

A special feature of the building is the façade. Typologically, it uses the principle of the windowed façade clad in natural stone, with strongly articulated fenestration to give added depth.

The usual repetitive uniformity of small window openings is overcome by a structural arrangement that conceals the location of the floors and, by grouping the windows into sets of four - two side-by-side and two one above the other - creates a basic structure with cross-shaped elements between. The basic element predominates and is woven into the surface structure with smaller window openings and horizontal and vertical accents which give the building unmistakeable plasticity.

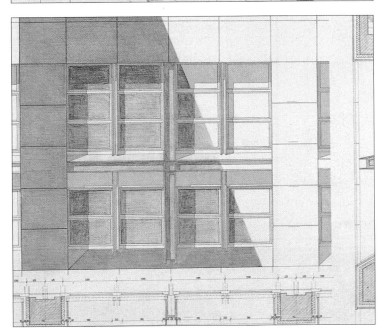

Details of façade

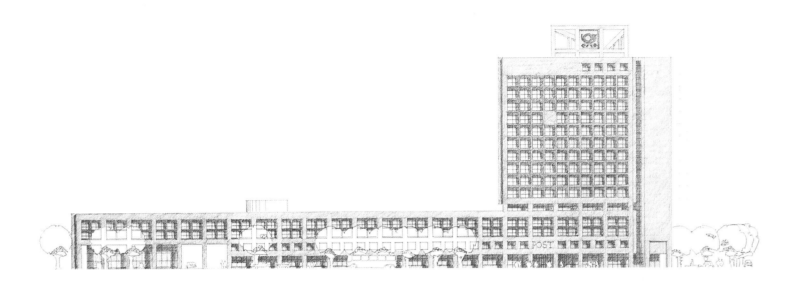

*Top: Drawing of the façade from the Berliner
Ring by M. von Gerkan*

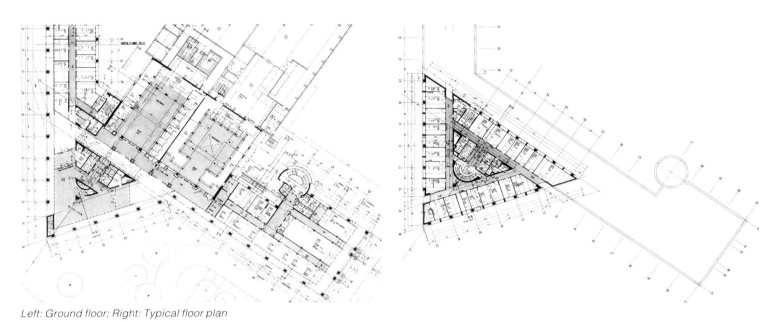

Left: Ground floor; Right: Typical floor plan

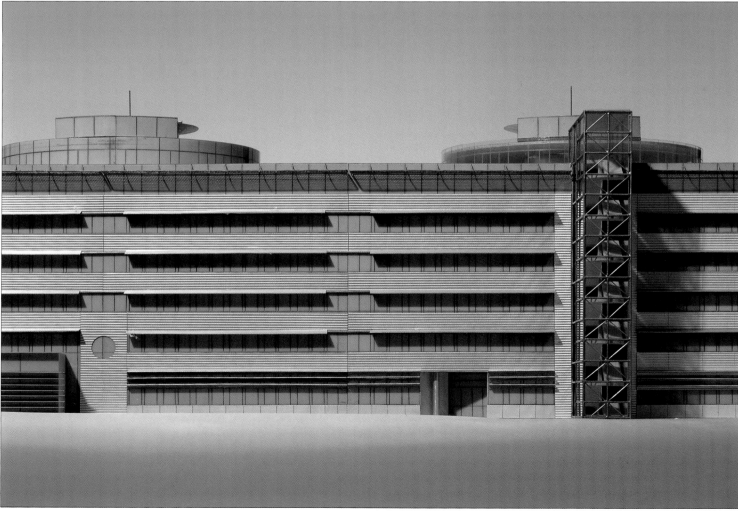

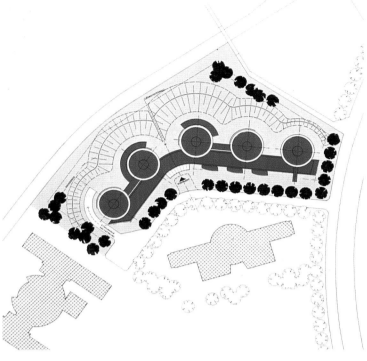

DEUTSCHE REVISION AG
Frankfurt am Main (1990-1994)

Competition: 1990 - First Prize
Design: Meinhard von Gerkan
Project partner: Klaus Staratzke
Assistants: Manfred Stanek, Kerstin Krause, Robert Beyer, Jörn Warnebier, Arturo Buchholz-Berger, Gabriele Hagemeister, Jutta Kaumold, Knut Maass, Birgit Meier

The site has an unusual polygonal shape with a curve. The aim was to design a tense, dynamic building in the same shape as the site.

The curve of the building along the access road forms a spine to which five cylindrical towers are attached. This highly differentiated architectural layout reflects the interior function.

The office block is divided into small manageable units each with a communicating stairway lit by a glass toplight.

The ground plan is such that building work can proceed in self-contained sections, which can be rented out on a temporary basis. It also provides a clear framework for access, avoiding long, boring corridors, and is animated by its spatial accentuations and divisions.

There are 770 underground parking spaces. An earth wall acts as a noise barrier for the two lower floors and its gardens conceal the main road and neighbouring site. For additional noise protection, it is proposed that the office towers have a second skin. If the proposed by-pass is built, this could be glazed to provide sound insulation. Behind the insulation, metal grids on each floor allow the air to circulate ensuring natural ventilation for the offices.

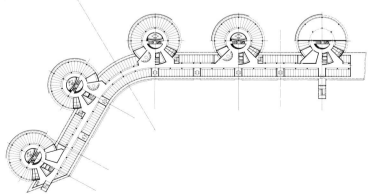

Top: Site plan; Bottom: Typical floor plan

131

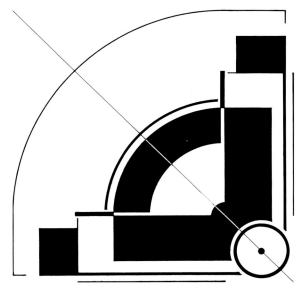

MOORBEK RONDEEL
Norderstedt (1987-1990)

Design: Meinhard von Gerkan with Joachim Mais and Uwe Hassels

The four-storey building presents itself on the city side as an austerely-structured walled façade with a protruding ground floor. The side overlooking Moorbek park to the north-west has a light, transparent glass and steel façade curving like the segment of a cylinder.

The main body of the building is designed in such a way as to offer units of differing sizes and therefore a high degree of flexibility in use.

The side facing the city has a red brick façade with a projecting glass structure enclosing the conservatories.

The park side of the building, which is curved, is an openwork glass and steel structure with sunblinds.

The top of the building consists of fixed metal shades with sharp-edged contours that highlight the geometry of the structure.

South elevation

North elevation

133

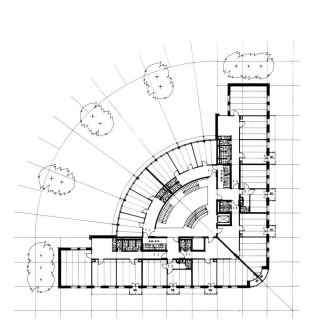

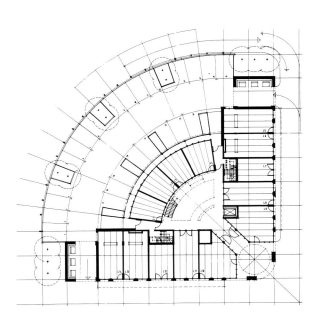

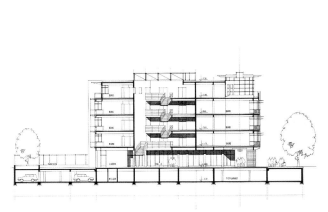

From top: Typical floor plan; Ground floor; Cross section

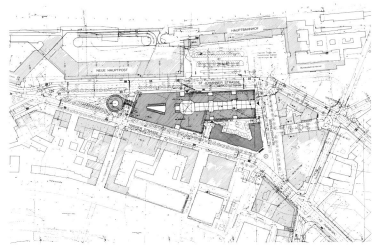

Site plan

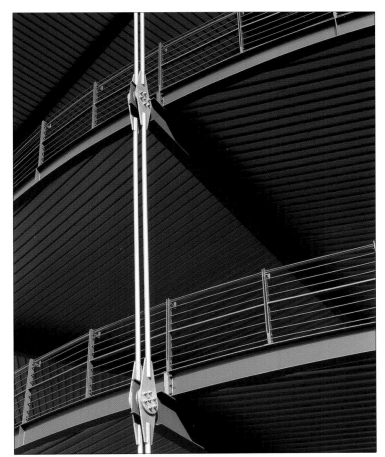

West elevation

East elevation

SAAR-GALERIE
Saarbrücken (1988-1991)

Design: Volkwin Marg
Assistants: Hakki Akyol,
Christian Hoffmann, Hubert Nienhoff,
Joachim Rind
GMP Aachen: Martin Bleckmann, Björn
Bergfeld, Klaus Brand, Annette Brücker,
Roland Dorn, Jutta Hartmann-Pohl,
Christian Hoffmann, Franz Lensing,
Christa Rath

The Saar-Galerie fills one of the last
gaps left in the city by the Second World
War. Its height respects the Saarberg
administration building, and, where they
join, the façades are set back to give
prominence to the historic building.

The steep slope of more than 4m in
the main axis of the gallery has been
utilised to provide an entrance directly
onto the upper floor from the street.

The design is based on a pedestrian
passageway like a nineteenth century
glazed arcade, and develops it to suit
the needs of modern shops and traffic.

It is more than 100m long and 12m
wide with six storeys and ends in an
octagon 38m high, which is a key
feature of the Saarbrücken skyline.

The outside walls of the multi-storey
car park above the arcade are clad in
openwork prefabricated concrete
sections which allow the light to enter.
They are shaped in graduated square
modules set between the main supporting axes. The prefabricated parts are
almost white, in clear contrast to the
black of the steel construction.

A ramp for cars, which is designed as
a spiral steel construction suspended
on ropes, terminates the ensemble.

137

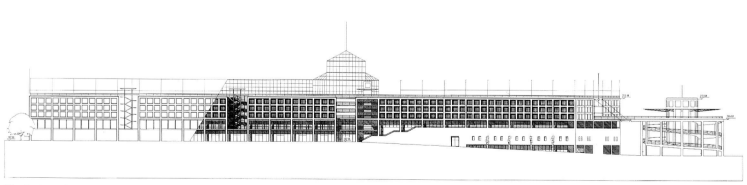

North elevation

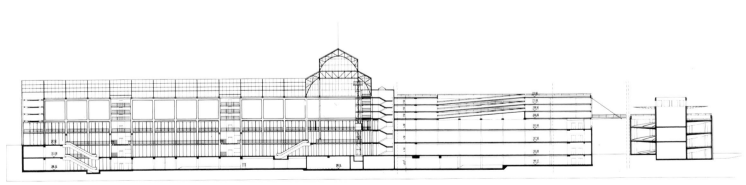

Section D-D

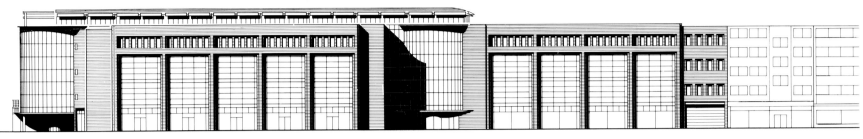

GALERIA
Duisburg (1989-1993)

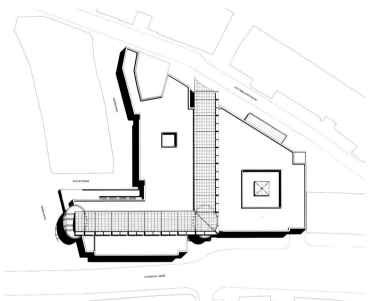

Design: Meinhard von Gerkan, Klaus Staratzke, Otto Dorn
Assistants:Manfred Stanek, Kerstin Krause, Clemens Zeis, Sibylle Scharbau, Thomas Grotzeck, Jürgen Brandenburg, Christine Mönnich

The site is a "slice" of the inner city of Duisburg that has not been utilised to date and will now be brought into use with a new urban concept.

The design offers a broad, attractive glass arcade accentuated by two elliptical glass structures. The project-ing "towers" will be visible from afar and constitute city landmarks. They will mark the entrance. The height of the buildings is on the same scale as the adjacent streets. Retail shops and facilities for the main tenants are located at ground level; the only access is via the arcade.

The upper storeys are reached via open steel staircases, glazed stairways and lifts. On the upper floors are more retail shops and large offices, some combined with facilities on the ground floor. Steel galleries have been pro-vided for restaurants, some of which will be accessible from the ground floor.

The third floor will be mainly offices. The "tower" on Kuhstrasse has a restau-rant with a commanding view; access is by glass lift or staircase.

The flat parts of the roof will be planted with luxuriant vegetation.

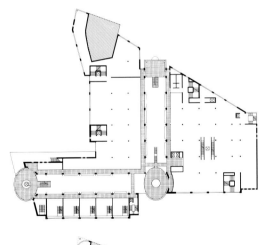

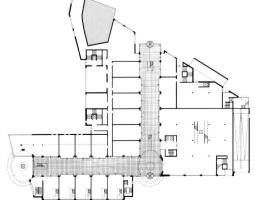

From top: Front elevation; Site plan; Levels +1, +2, +3; Level 0

CITY CENTRE
Schenefeld (1991)

Design: Volkwin Marg, Klaus Staratzke
Project manager: Bernhard Gronemeyer
Assistants: Karl-Heinz Behrendt, Sabine Bohl, Gerd Feldmeyer, Uwe Gänsicke, Thomas Grotzeck, Lene Jensen, Christa Hahn, Andreas Leuschner, Detlef Papendick, Carsten Plog, Karin Rohrmann, Elke Sethmann, Annette Wendling-Willeke

The Schenefeld City Centre project will recreate the middle of Schenefeld as a meeting place for people from the north-western suburbs of Hamburg. It links the districts of Alt-Schenefeld and Schenefeld-Siedlung with the school and sports centre, which had no links.

The city centre is in the tradition of the great market halls and arcades of the nineteenth century, providing for the bustling commercial life of the city as well as its social and cultural activities.

The architecture is both rigorous and simple. These qualities are evident firstly in the clear arrangement of the spaces and the easy orientation, and, secondly, in the handling of details such as the visible steel construction of the roofs, stairs, railings and windows.

The ambience of Schenefeld City Centre is a landscape of space, transparency and light. The planting in the car parking areas, will underline the impression of a natural landscape.

The handling of colour is deliberately restrained with white columns, grey-white walls and silver steel openwork. Only the wooden handrails are in the natural colour of the wood.

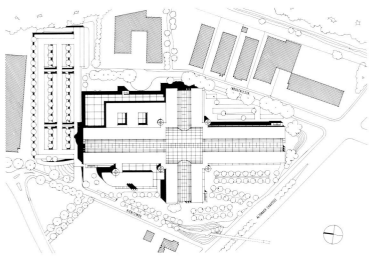

Site plan

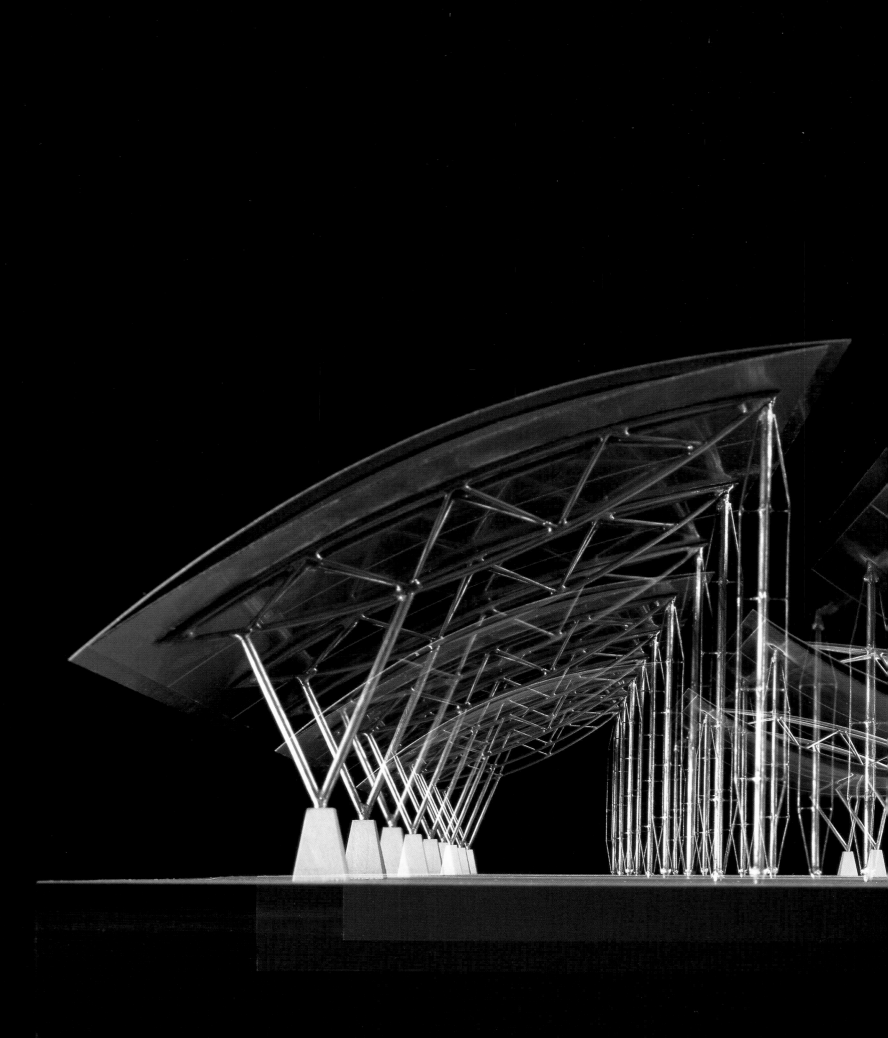

BMW SERVICE CENTRE
Munich (1987)

Design: Meinhard von Gerkan
Assistants: Gerhard Feldmeyer,
Christian Weinmann, Tuyen Tran-Viet

The service centre itself is not conceived as a building but as an architectural landscape arranged on several
levels with tent roofs arching above it.

The roofs also cover open spaces,
access routes and drives.

The division between inside and
outside is created by a transparent
glass skin.

The characteristics of the design
derive from the engineering requirements of the roof. The arching of the
sails has associations with coach-
building. The bowl shape of the roof
facing Petuelring could be enclosed in a
glazed grid construction, so that it can
be lit from inside at night and seen from
the city as a huge illuminated sail.

KAUFMÄNNISCHE KRANKENKASSE
Hanover

Competition: 1991
Design: Meinhard von Gerkan
Assistant: Manfred Stanek

The cylindrical buildings are arranged in pairs, with a common core where they touch. At the rear they are six storeys high, with an attic on top. All four pairs of cylindrical buildings are linked by a glass spine, which in turn is reached through a central core.

   The circular ground plan gives all the offices an almost equally unobstructed view of the surroundings.

DEUTSCHE LUFTHANSA TRAINING AND COMPUTER CENTRE
Frankfurt am Main

Design: Meinhard von Gerkan
Assistants: Joachim Zais, Hartmut Potthoff

The aim of the architectural layout is to enter into a tense dialogue with the surrounding landscape.

Much of the mass is deliberately subordinated to the landscape; this is the case with the technical areas of the computer centre, which are located underground and remain invisible, and the parking floors, which are set like terraces into the steep slopes of the hill.

The visible part of the building aims to emphasise the rural character of the scene with its large-scale design.

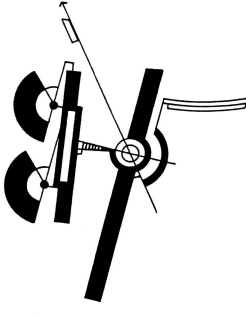

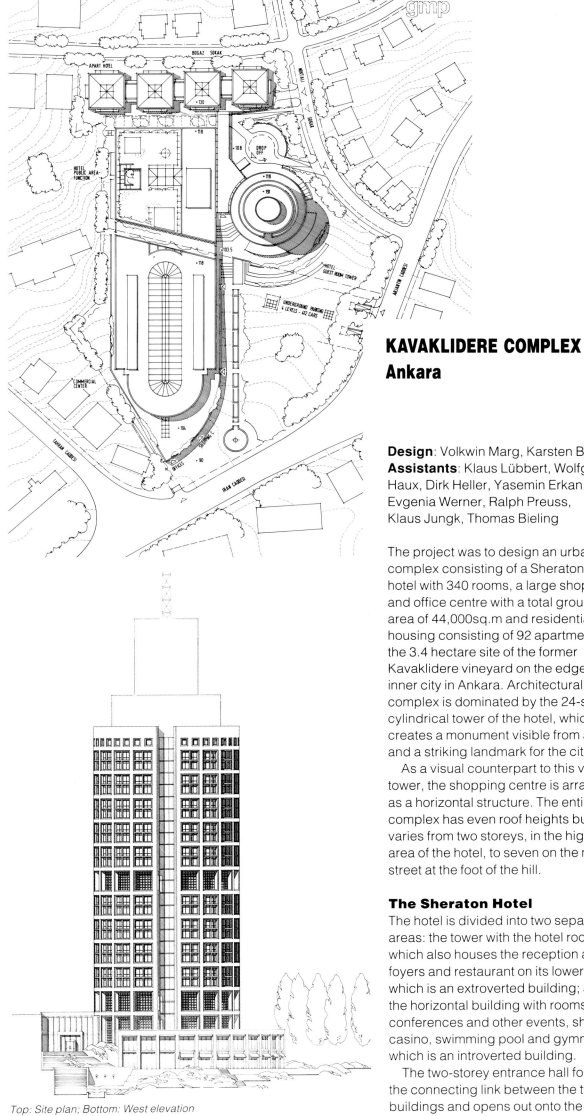

Top: Site plan; Bottom: West elevation

KAVAKLIDERE COMPLEX
Ankara

Design: Volkwin Marg, Karsten Brauer
Assistants: Klaus Lübbert, Wolfgang Haux, Dirk Heller, Yasemin Erkan, Evgenia Werner, Ralph Preuss, Klaus Jungk, Thomas Bieling

The project was to design an urban complex consisting of a Sheraton luxury hotel with 340 rooms, a large shopping and office centre with a total ground area of 44,000sq.m and residential housing consisting of 92 apartments, on the 3.4 hectare site of the former Kavaklidere vineyard on the edge of the inner city in Ankara. Architecturally, the complex is dominated by the 24-storey, cylindrical tower of the hotel, which creates a monument visible from afar and a striking landmark for the city.

As a visual counterpart to this vertical tower, the shopping centre is arranged as a horizontal structure. The entire complex has even roof heights but varies from two storeys, in the higher area of the hotel, to seven on the main street at the foot of the hill.

The Sheraton Hotel
The hotel is divided into two separate areas: the tower with the hotel rooms, which also houses the reception area, foyers and restaurant on its lower floors, which is an extroverted building; and the horizontal building with rooms for conferences and other events, shops, casino, swimming pool and gymnasium, which is an introverted building.

The two-storey entrance hall forms the connecting link between the two buildings and opens out onto the hotel

151

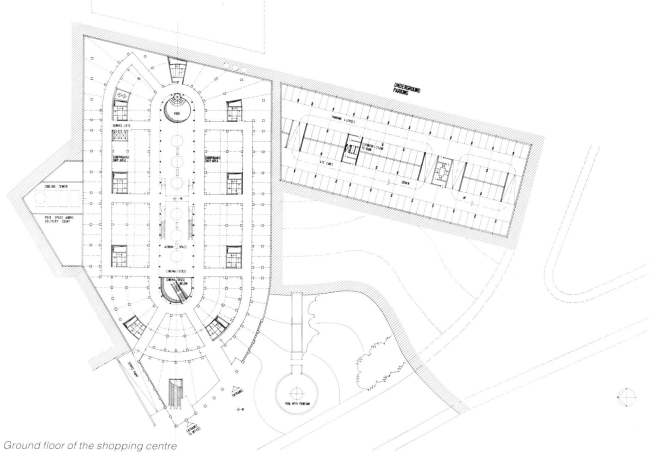

Ground floor of the shopping centre

drive towards the east, and onto the park as well.

The roof garden is divided into a swimming pool area and a patio for barbecues, dances, etc. It is surrounded on three sides by a wall with pergolas. It is thus transparent but at the same time screened from the surrounding buildings making it both exclusive and private.

The Shopping and Office Centre

The design consists of a compact block around a large atrium with a glass cupola. The atrium is seven storeys in height and forms a public space. Simply by its size, 85m long and 20m wide, it offers a completely new kind of shopping gallery in Turkey.

The atrium should be regarded as a large, attractive, animated courtyard, the only difference being that the glass dome protects it from the weather.

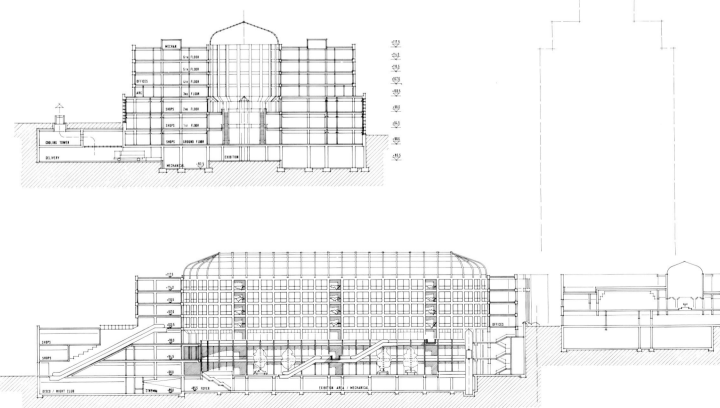

Cross section and longitudinal section of the shopping centre

ARCHITECT'S HOUSE
Hamburg (1992)

Design: Meinhard von Gerkan
Assistants: Jacob Kierig, Volkmar Sievers, Sabine von Gerkan
Project manager: Klaus Tiede

This house is part of the ensemble at Elbschlucht 139 (see page 18)

It is a cube 12m in length measured along its axes, and 12m high. It stands parallel to the eastern edge of the site at an angle of 21° to the other buildings, on the same level as the square, which is directly adjacent to it.

An elliptical stairway in the centre links all four storeys, with a self-contained flat in the basement and a guest apartment on the ground floor.

The main entrance is to the first floor, and is reached by a long single flight of steps leading from the garage over the level of the square to the house. The second entrance is cut into the building on the level of the square. The flat in the basement, the guest apartment and the children's rooms can also be reached separately from here.

A large terrace has been cut into the building on the upper floor.

Seen from the road and the city, the house is like a compact "box", its simplicity enhanced by the white glazed pinewood boarding. The south wall, with the view of the Elbe, is almost fully glazed capturing the unique atmosphere of the harbour.

The materials are simple: beechwood floors; rough finish walls; doors, partition walls and fittings in Swiss pear.

The fittings and furniture were specially designed for the house.

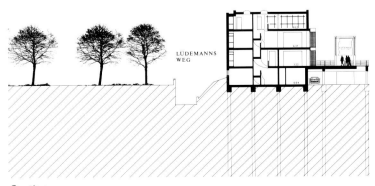

Section

LÜDEMANNS WEG

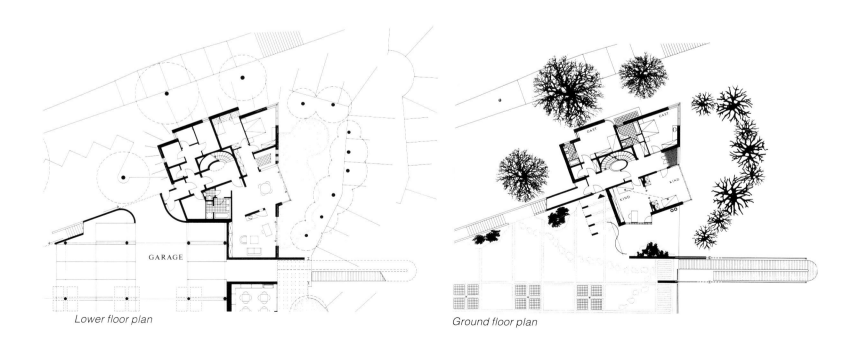

Lower floor plan

Ground floor plan

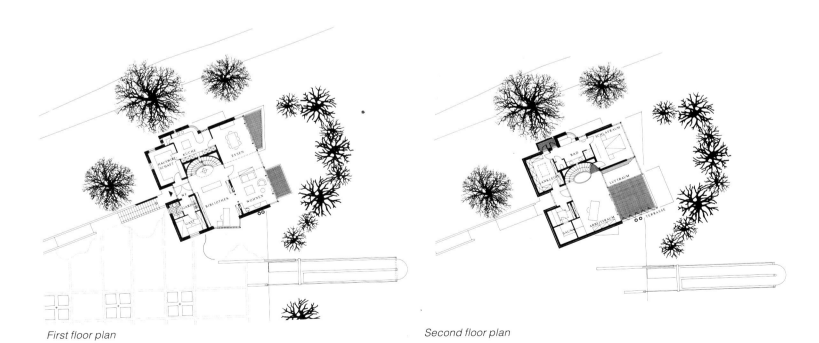

First floor plan   Second floor plan

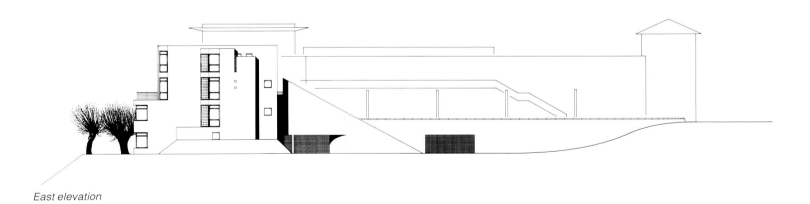

East elevation

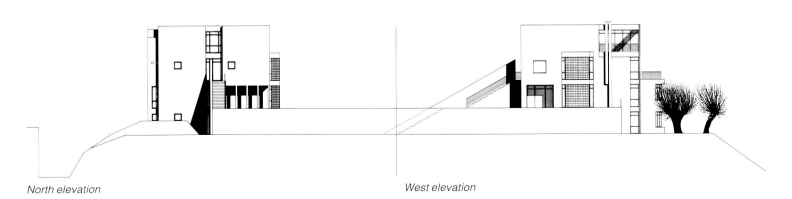

North elevation

West elevation

Site plan

"SCHÖNE AUSSICHT"
APARTMENT BLOCK
Hamburg

Competition: 1992 - First Prize
Design: Meinhard von Gerkan
Assistant: Klaus Lenz

This unique site called for highly individual, unorthodox architecture in keeping with the quality of the location.

Instead of the usual type of apartment block, we proposed a great geometric sculpture in which interior and exterior, architecture and landscaped gardens, are all part of an integrated whole.

The building has none of the traditional demarcations between the interior and the exterior. Walls dissolve into "frames" which define spaces. The exterior penetrates into the differentiated volumes of the building in the form of loggias and terraces.

The interpenetration of interior and exterior, the interplay of mass and space are the main thematic preoccupations of this design.

Each of the eleven apartments has a different ground plan.

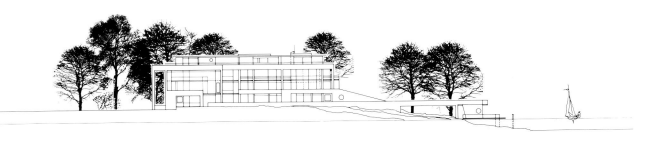

West elevation

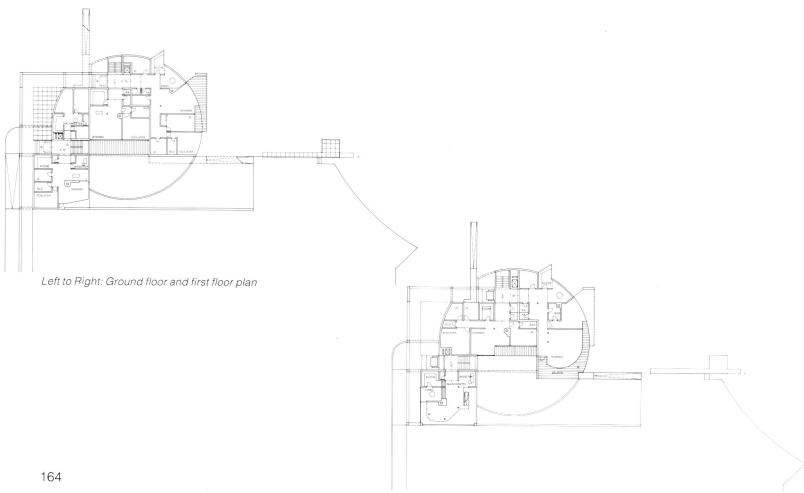

Left to Right: Ground floor and first floor plan

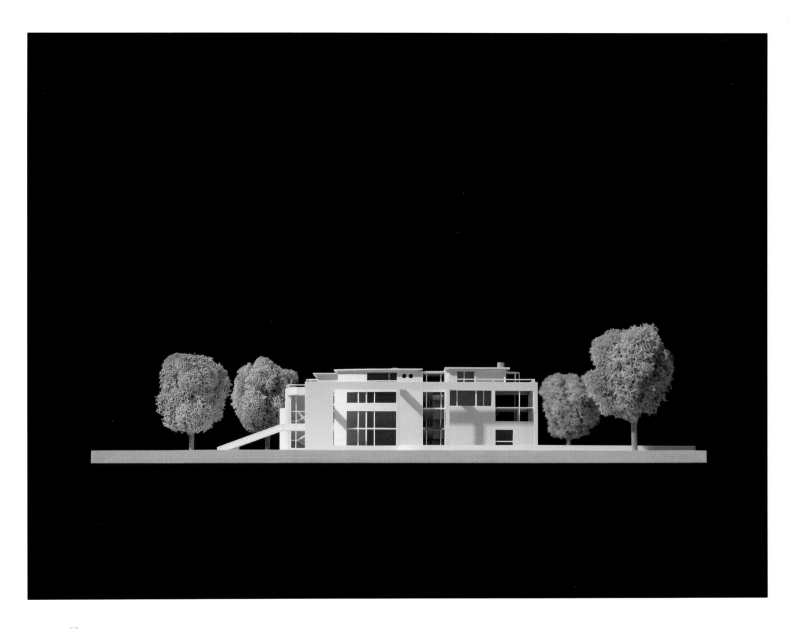

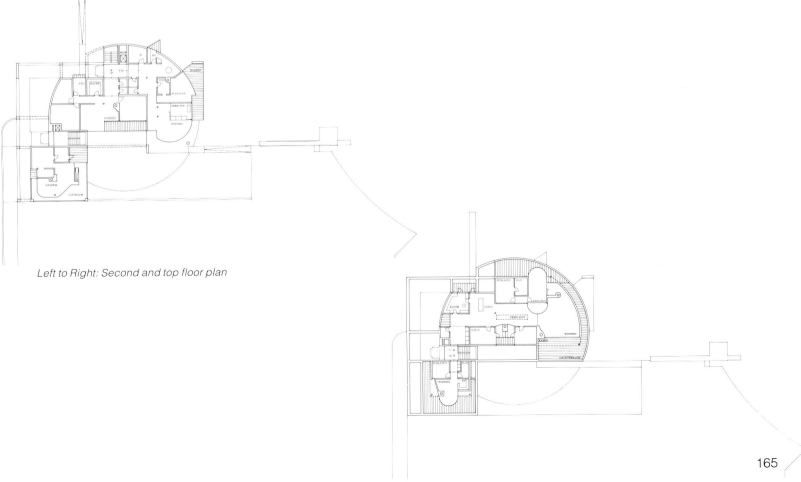

Left to Right: Second and top floor plan

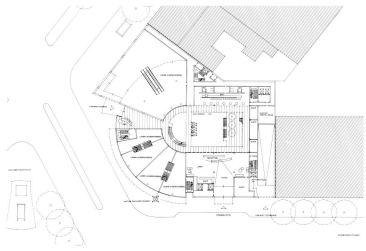

HOTEL KU'DAMM-ECK
Berlin

Preliminary design: 1992
Design: Meinhard von Gerkan,
Klaus Staratzke, Nikolaus Götze

The design for the Ku'damm-Eck hotel is a combination of two building types integrated at a street junction so that they form a corner complex.

The building adapts well to the differing heights of its neighbours, creating a harmonious ensemble.

Its transparent structure rises like the bow of a ship, framed by two natural stone façades on either side. Fronting on the Kurfürstendamm like a well-set diamond, the hotel will be a new jewel on this famous street.

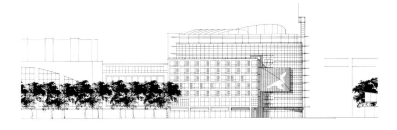

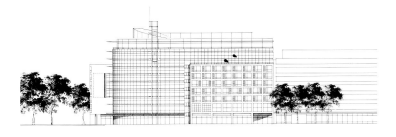

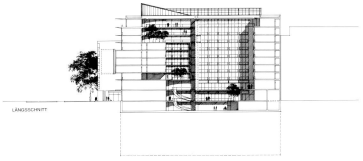

From top: Ground floor; Kurfürstendamm elevation; Augsburger Strasse elevation; Longitudinal section

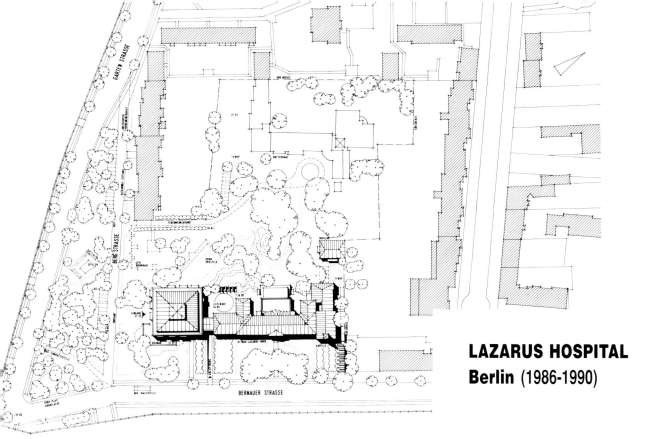

LAZARUS HOSPITAL
Berlin (1986-1990)

Top: Site plan

Design: Meinhard von Gerkan
Assistants:Peter Römer,Joachim Zais, Hildegard Müller,Frank Bräutigam,Karl Baumgarten, Uwe Grahl, Christian Walther, Rolf Kühl, Otto Herzog, Klaus Schimke, Jürgen Kant

The site is in one of the more isolated parts of West Berlin, with the Berlin wall opposite to the south and east; it was the site of many dramatic escapes. A year before the hospital opened, the wall came down but this section is to remain as a museum piece.

The new hospital building is a five-storey structure containing the wards and physiotherapy unit. It is separate from the old building, which is still used, but linked to it by a glazed bridge.

The southern corner of the street block is accentuated by a glass lantern in the attic storey. This provides light for the large hall beneath, which is a meeting place for the residents. In addition to the stairs leading to the upper storeys, there is a glass lift.

The hall cuts through the whole building and at each corner on each floor are alcoves with seats where people can sit and talk .On the ground floor is the public area with the cafeteria and, on a mezzanine, the physiotherapy unit. In the plan the single rooms were of standard size, but it was possible to include a small oriel window with seats giving the rooms a more pleasant atmosphere. The glazed oriels also act as features on the front of the building. The other windows are set flush with the façade, which is clad in natural stone.

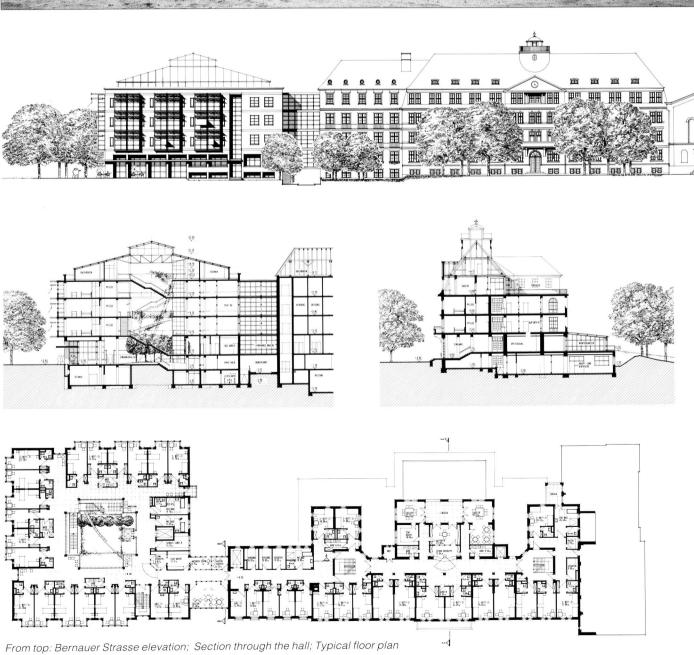

From top: Bernauer Strasse elevation; Section through the hall; Typical floor plan

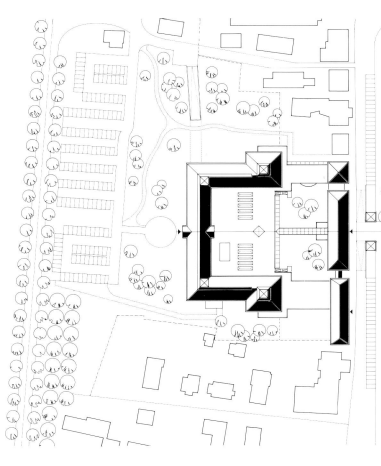

ROSE COMPLEX
RHEUMATISM CLINIC
Bad Meinberg (1981-1989)

Competition: 1981 - First Prize
Design: Meinhard von Gerkan
Project manager: Kirsten Brauer
Assistants: Hans-Rüdiger Franke,
Helmut Ritzki, Barbara Dziewonska,
Regina Sander, Peter Römer

The design evolved from the baroque axis in the urban plan, in which Kurhaus Stern is connected to Haus Rose across the centre of the park.

The park axis is picked up and continued in the system of interior corridors in the clinic, thus determining the symmetrical U-shaped arrangement of the new building which is located behind Haus Rose.

The new building consists of a three-storey structure containing the wards and a lower level below this with the therapy facilities. This one-storey base is next to the old buildings at ground level, but as the terrain rises by about 5m to the south it is entirely under-ground under the ward section.

Thus the new building looks like a three-storey structure to the south, west and east; but the northern end of the U-shaped ward section appears to be a three-and-a-half storey structure at its outer edge. The base joins the bath-house on one side and on the other side, to the west, the front of Haus Rose.

In front of Haus Rose lies an inner courtyard, cut by a corridor connecting it to the new building; it is in the form of a "glazed arcade". The inner courtyard continues into the first storey on the roof terrace of the therapy wing, where it is spatially enclosed by the ward section.

Top: Site plan

173

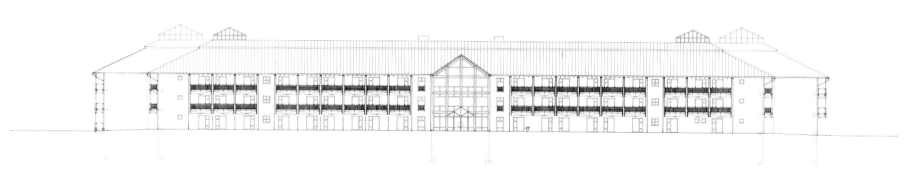

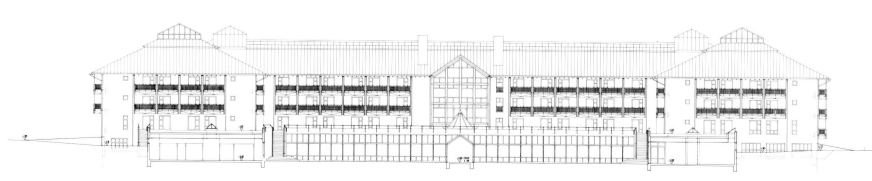

Middle: South elevation; Bottom: Section S1

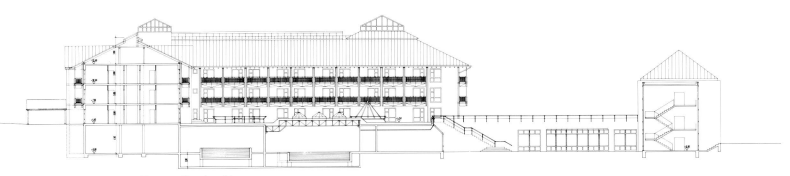

Middle: East elevation; Bottom: Section S4

In keeping with the design of Haus Rose and the type of architecture typical of Bad Meinberg, the ward section has a pitched roof.

The façades are enlivened by balconies, which pick up the design of the half-timbered structure of Haus Rose and extend it by other means.

The clinic has 248 rooms for patients with a total of 266 beds, divided into nine wards. All the rooms for patients have their own bath. With an axial width of 3.35m the standard single room has a ground surface of 11.7sq.m, including the sanitary facilities and the entrance. All the standard rooms in the new part also have an outside balcony.

The therapy facilities are on the lower floor of the clinic, where they are easily accessible both from the wards and from the existing bath-house.

The gymnastics room and therapy pool are located next to the corridors crossing the middle of the lower level. The two halls get daylight from toplights in the roof and these, together with a glazed pyramid above the corridor intersection, create a plastic structure on the roof terrace above. The corridor which crosses them has a glass wall along the pool and the gymnastics hall, so that it is visually a part of these areas and shares their daylight.

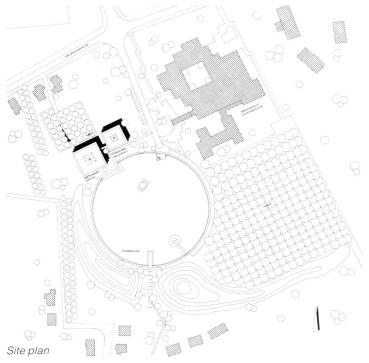

Site plan

CARL BERTELSMANN
FOUNDATION
Gütersloh

Competition: 1989 - First Prize
Design:Volkwin Marg
Project Managers: Hans Schröder, Michael Zimmermann
Assistants:Hakki Akyol, Stephanie Jöbsch, Reiner Schröder, Jörg Schulte
Landscape Design: Wehberg, Lange, Eppinger, Schmidkte

In an earlier competition for a general concept for additional buildings for this growing concern, our design won the first prize because the idea of a central lake in an office park best suited the corporate identity of Bertelsmann AG.

This lake lies in a hollow; it is artificial, which is obvious from its stone basin and circular shape. Smaller-scale pavilions will be built around it, with the same strict orthogonal rationality.

The main building facing the park is sober, light and very transparent. The glazed stairways, halls and corridors provide easy communication. Next to the entrance foyer with its terrace over-looking the lake, is an assembly room that can have a number of uses. It is slightly lowered, and sitting in it is like being in a green hollow. To give even greater transparency and light, the dividing walls are glazed at the top, and the façades dissolve into glazing on the side that overlooks the lake, thus afford-ing a welcome extension of the view.

The building is extremely economical, both technically and architecturally, with no air-conditioning and no sus-pended ceilings. Brevity, clarity and transparency were the objective, both in content and aesthetically.

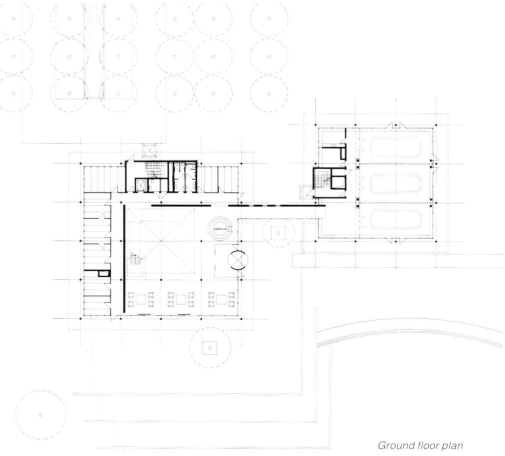

Ground floor plan

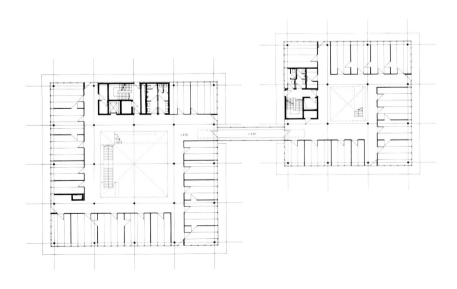

Upper floor plan

Structural order developed from the genius loci

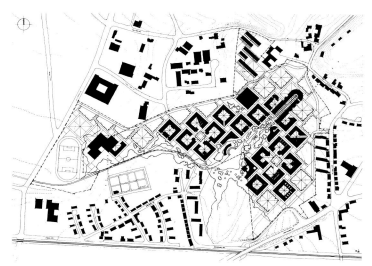

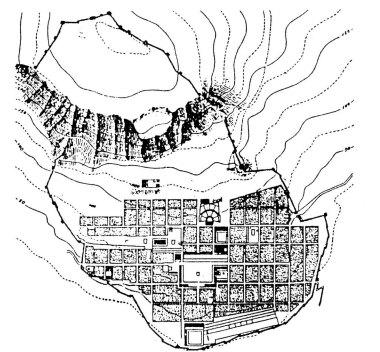

From top: Site with basic structure; Massing plan; Priene's city plan

THE UNIVERSITY
Witten/Herdecke (1986)

Design: Meinhard von Gerkan,
Joachim Zais

The concept is based on ten proposals.
Structural order which determines the
relation between each element and the
whole to ensure architectural clarity,
visual legibility, and spatial orientation.
Genius loci which includes the distinc-
tive topographical features of the site,
its shape, water courses and questions
of general access and environment.
An unmistakeable identity appropriate
to the function of the building and the
local situation.
A network structure consisting of a
clearly differentiated system of paths
and roads. The inside system connects
with the parking spaces on the periph-
ery, and in the central area with a
generous park-like leisure zone.
Trees to be planted as soon as the
general plan is finalised.
*A balance between control and free-
dom,* control coming from the structural
order of the design and urban planning
regulations; but with freedom in the
design of individual buildings so that the
university can develop in future with the
greatest possible degree of openness.
A mix of uses to ensure that no part of
the site is devoid of life at certain times.
Simplicity in the sense of plausibility
and uncluttered legibility.
A balance between unity and variety
to ensure unity of the whole over the
long period of design and development
without monotony.
Living with the car by providing access
driveways and 2m hedges for car parks.

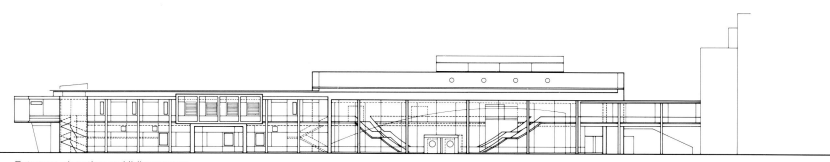

Entrance elevation on Uhlhornsweg

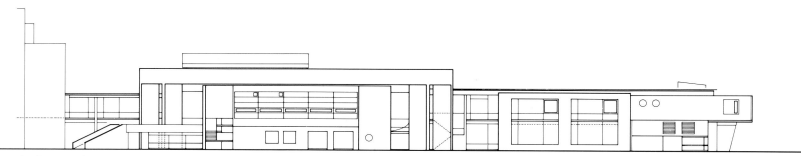

Audimax platform elevation

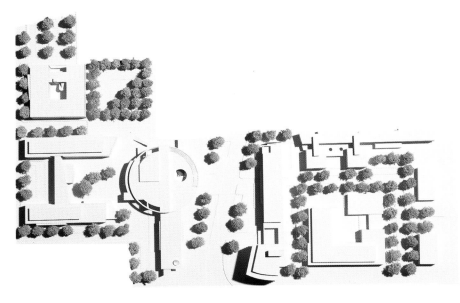

LECTURE CENTRE
OLDENBURG UNIVERSITY

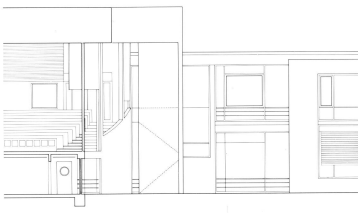

Façade section and elevation

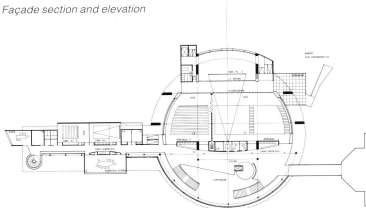

Façade section and elevation

Upper floor, +5 level

Competition: 1992 - First Prize
Design: Meinhard von Gerkan
Assistant: Klaus Lenz

The urban environment of the new buildings contains highly divergent architectural vocabularies; this strident diversity is the dominant feature of the complex, and the existing buildings are incompatible with each other.

None of the architectural languages present was appropriate for the new buildings. We therefore developed a new architectural concept that would not compete with the existing buildings nor add more loud or dominant markers.

First, an overall structural scaffold was developed, which could then be incorporated into the existing location in a linear axial cross, constituting architectural lines of force and providing an intellectual model.

The buildings for individual facilities were deliberately differentiated to achieve integration and incorporation of the individual buildings and spaces into the existing stock creating a complex variety. To absorb the existing buildings into the differentiated subdivision of the individual parts and, where possible, to interrelate them, it was decided not to use clear, simple stereometric shapes.

The circular shape of the main building forms the integrative centre. It creates a strongly differentiated overall complex with overlayerings and additions in keeping with the general objective of the design as explained above.

JUMBO SHED AND WORKSHOPS FOR LUFTHANSA
Hamburg-Fuhlsbüttel (1989-1992)

Design: Meinhard von Gerkan, Karsten Brauer, Klaus Staratzke
Workshops: In co-operation with Pysall, Stahrenberg & Partner Krämer
Project manager: Huhnholz
Assistants:Manfred Stanek, Reinhold Niehoff,Michael Engel, Claudius Schönherr, Dagmar Winter, Elke Sethmann, Alexandra Czerner, Clemens Zeis, Sybille Scharbau, Gregor Smakowski, Winfried Gust, Sabine Oehme, Günter Maass, Peter Klein

An arch spanning 170m and consisting of two individual arches leaning towards each other, each with a cross-section of 2m by 1.7m forms the main load-bearing structure. The weight of this arch rests on two supporting blocks at the sides of the shed and the entire roof of the shed, which is an open grid structure, rests on it. It is like a great suspension bridge, an attractive landmark, its shape visible from afar.

The workshop and offices are adjacent to the shed to the south. This building has striking round glass towers for stairs and lifts, and an industrial façade in steel profiles with large glass or metal panels. The offices are subdivided by patios with gardens, providing good quality working conditions for an industrial building.

The doors to the shed are a particular feature of the design. They are 150m long and 22m high. They are "garage doors", steel constructions subdivided into sections 4m x 4m that are fully glazed. This outsize glass façade faces north, giving the shed ample daylight

north, giving the shed ample daylight and enabling passengers in the aircraft taxiing past to look into a "Lufthansa display case"; this is particularly effective in the evening when the shed is lit.

The decision to carry out the assembly work in the field in front of the building while the concrete foundations were being laid saved about three months' building time.

The roof, which had to be transported, is 170m wide, 60m long and 30m high; it weighs 2800 tons. A 100m glide track was set up under the ends of the arches to shift it horizontally. The steel structure then slid on a construction of refined steel on top and Teflon underneath, made especially for this building. To make the roof slide more easily, lubricant was pressed between the two surfaces which are in themselves very smooth. Hydraulic presses forced the building forwards millimetre by millimetre; the entire sliding time was twenty-eight hours. The roof was also lifted with hydraulic presses. They stood on supports 2m x 2m and 26m high, and lifted the roof up a height of about 26m in twelve hours.

Study for the design of the north façade

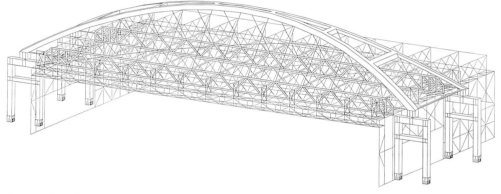

Perspective of structure

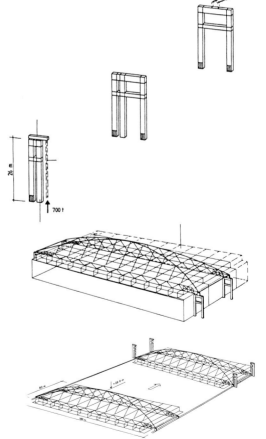

Construction phases

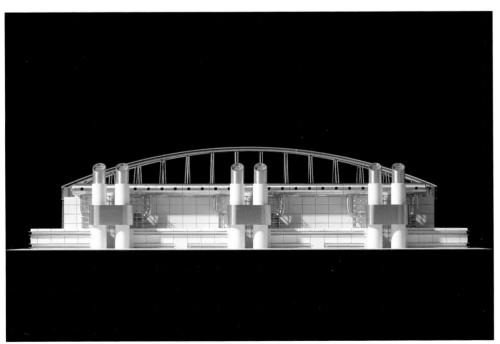

Back view of the original model with the ventilation system visible

191

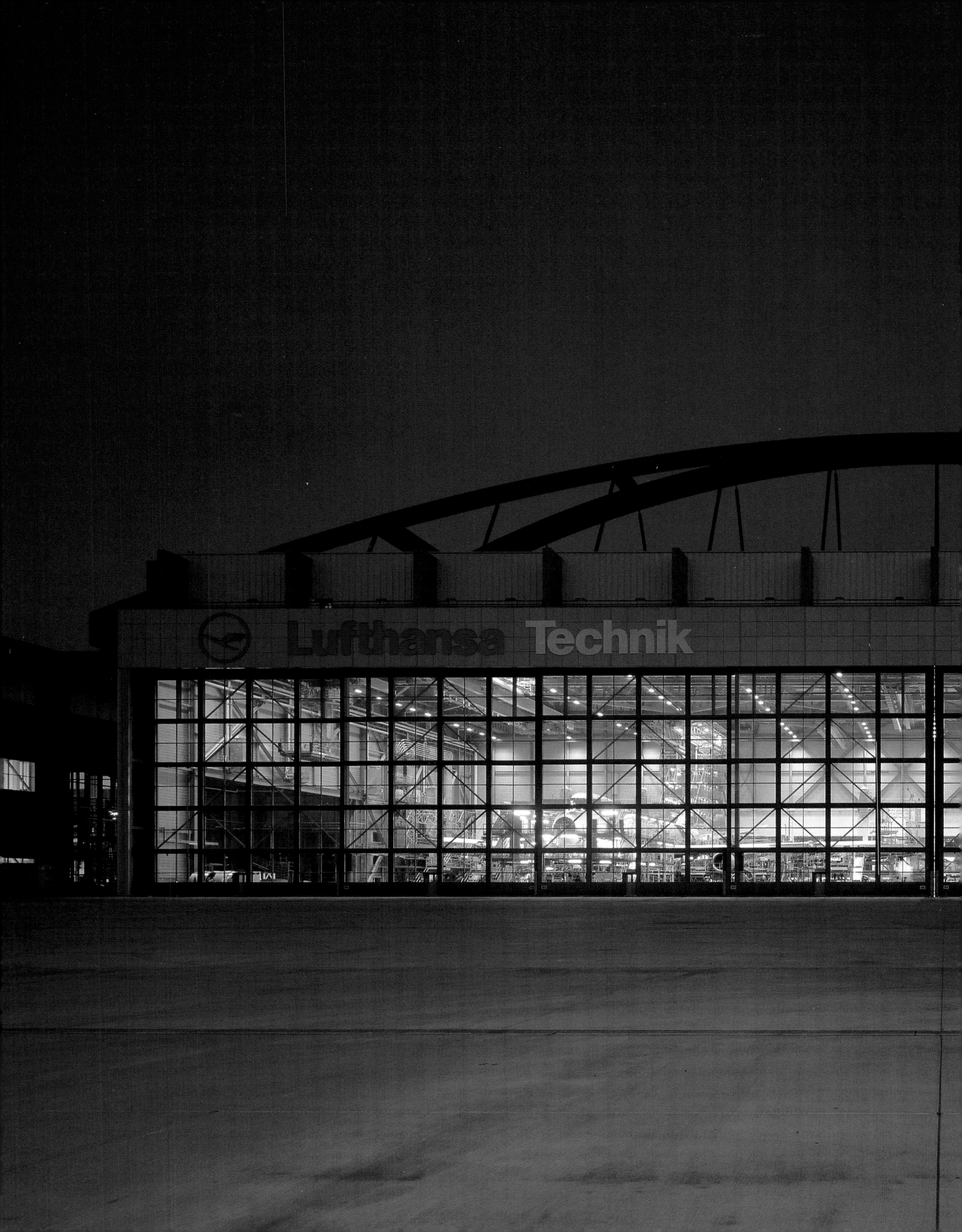
Lufthansa Technik

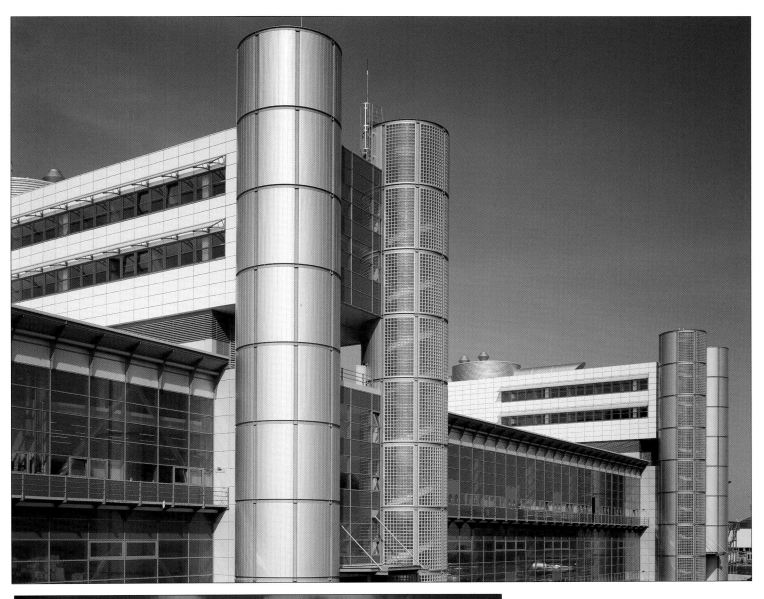

MIRO DATA SYSTEMS
Braunschweig (1991)

Design: Meinhard von Gerkan
Assistants: Ulrich Hassels, Joachim Zais, Walter Gebhardt, Uwe Kittel, Hermann Timpe

Around a central hall, which also serves as a reception, exhibition and training area and can be used for functions, are the think-tanks where new computer elements are developed, products marketed and the commercial side of the business is handled. All the rooms face the communal central area, separated from it only by glass walls, in keeping with the working habits of the staff who are mostly young.

The design concept combines production site and services under one roof. A two-storey factory shed with a direct loading ramp for incoming and outgoing deliveries is at the rear.

The building is like a three-aisled basilica; the central aisle has a vaulted roof which projects out over the reception area in a welcoming gesture .

The materials used are exposed concrete, corrugated metal and raw steel, which emphasise the technical nature of the business.

Our clients, the two founders, asked for one special feature. We translated their self-confident business style into two offices that float like a cylindrical pulpit above the main entrance with a total overview, both inside and out.

The building stands directly on the Braunschweig-Nord motorway exit; it is 96m long, 32.5m wide and 21m high. Floor space per storey is 10,920sq.m, the volume about 43,000cu.m.

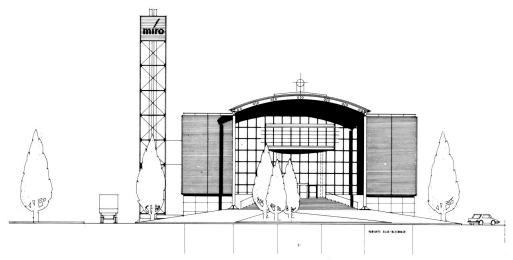

West elevation

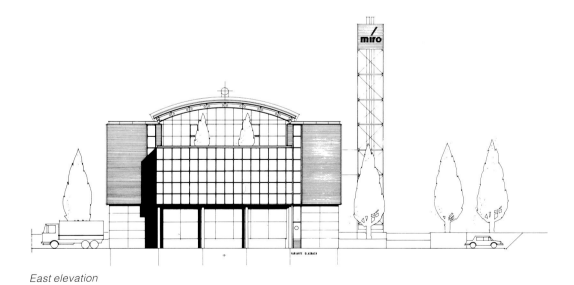

East elevation

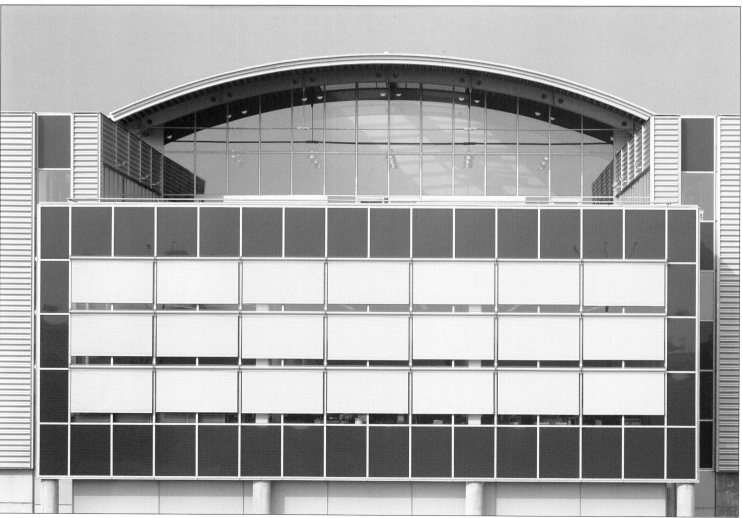

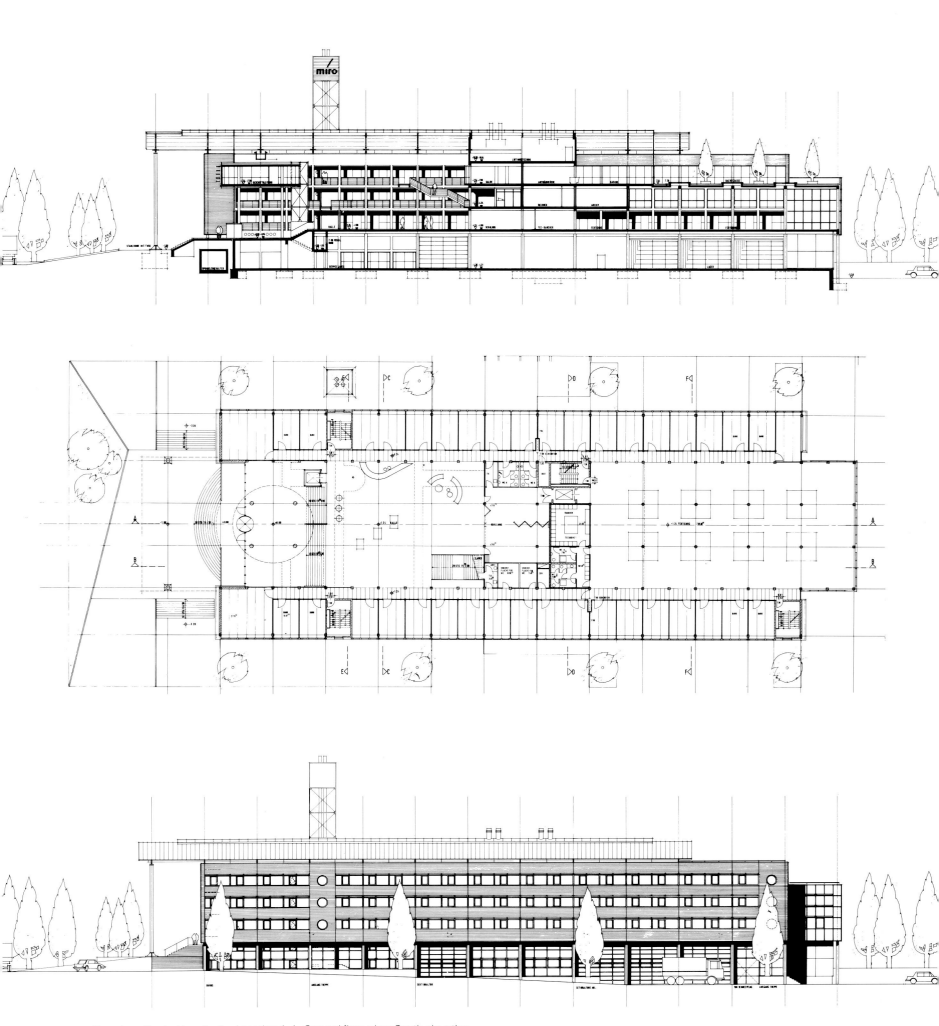

From top: Central longitudinal section A-A; Ground floor plan; South elevation

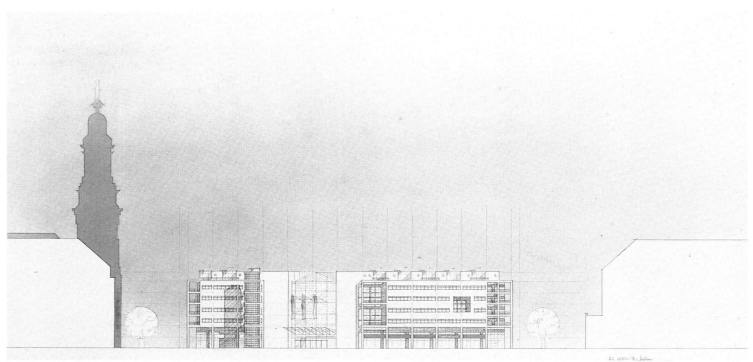

North elevation

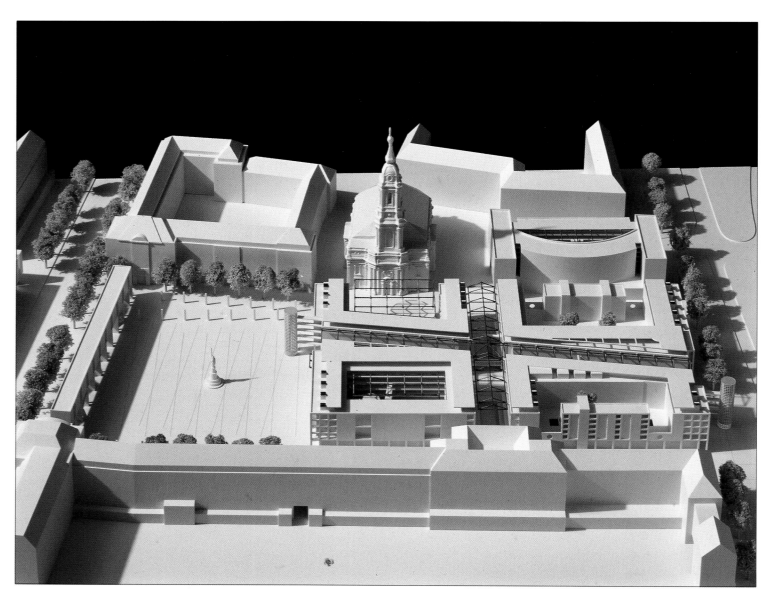

ALTMARKT
Dresden

Site plan

Competition: 1991 - First Prize
Design: Meinhard von Gerkan
Assistants: Hilke Büttner, Kai Voss

Morphologically, the proposed new building reflects the historical situation, with the complex of five buildings creating streets, alleys and squares analogous to the former street pattern.

The Kreuzkirche is enclosed to the south and east producing a dynamic and exciting sequence of squares that reconstitute the diagonal reference to the spacious Altmarkt.

The Schreibergasse lies almost where it used to; its intersection with the alley that crosses it has a glazed roof forming a covered junction. The openings lead to the neighbouring spaces.

Apart from a fountain in the centre, the open area of the new Altmarkt is structured only by its paving, which marks the different directions and spatial relations.

Otherwise, the Altmarkt is very clearly demarcated, but in order to separate it spatially from Ernst-Thälmann-Strasse, we propose a colonnaded building to serve as an open wall, physically and visually penetrable at ground level.

On the site between Pfarrgasse and Schulgasse a hotel building is proposed, again with a block-like structure.

It is the intention of the architects that the whole complex be restrained.

Unity and variety are held in strict balance, mainly by the double layering of the façade. The areas between the inner and outer layer of the façade are in almost all cases usable.

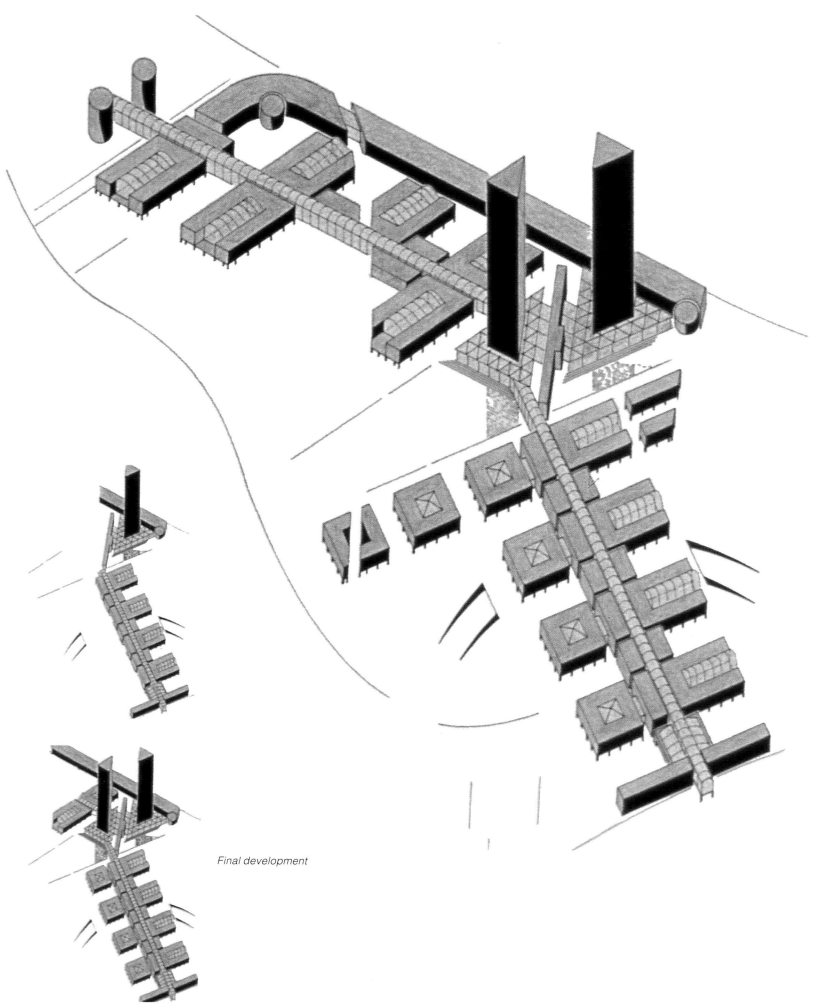

Final development

Top: Phase I; Bottom: Phase II

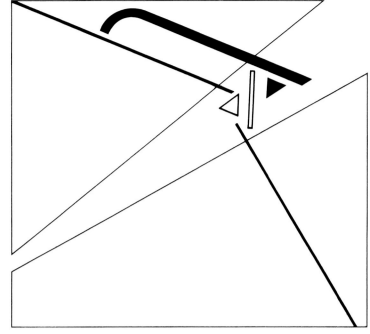

"STAR SITE"
Birmingham International
Business Exchange (1988)

Design: Meinhard von Gerkan
Assistant: Hans-Jörg Peter

Two glazed Galleria form a pedestrian axis on Level 1 linking the complex with the proposed new station and existing streets. The axes meet in a plaza which is also glazed and marked by two towers. The switching station will become a technology museum.

An 8-10 storey car park for 7500 cars is proposed along the M6 Motorway. It also acts as a noise protection barrier.

A large park at the centre of the plaza has water gardens, hills and trees and could also serve as a sculpture garden.

The whole complex is five to six storeys and brick is used throughout. Two triangular towers (150m to 170m) form a landmark and create tension.

A six-storey superstructure of mainly atrium buildings with glazed courtyards connects directly with the Galleria floor.

The main road follows the unattractive river bed, partially underground.

All buildings have a direct road link; cars are housed in the multi-storey car park or at ground level or directly under each building. A service road with parking runs under the Galleria.

The line of the Grand Union Canal creates intentional disturbances, and various small canals are proposed.

Level 1 is mainly for shopping. Offices are located on the floors above, with flats and maisonettes at roof level. The two towers are mainly offices; a hotel could be accommodated on the upper floors. More museum facilities could also be provided.

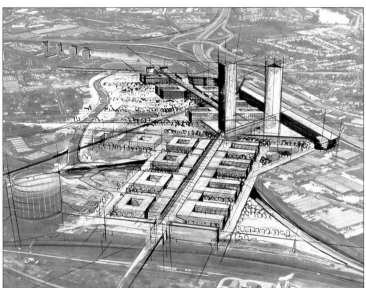

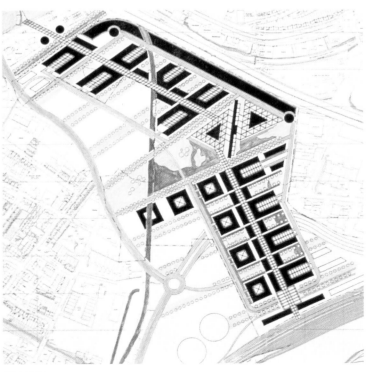

Site plan

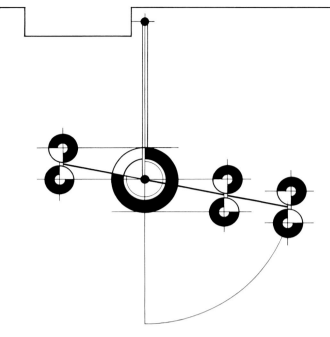

AIRPORT CENTER
Hamburg Airport

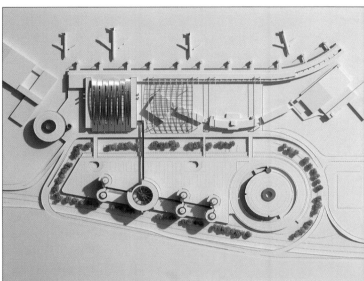

Project study:1990
Design: Meinhard von Gerkan,
Karsten Brauer

This study has succeeded in proving that additional facilities can be provided on the land side of Hamburg airport.

The airport hotel provides the main junction. The glazed south-east façade of its ten-storey hall faces the new terminal. The mix of activities and the bustling life in its domed hall, which is permanently flooded with light, will make the hotel foyer the main focal point of the Airport Center.

The office complex consists of three separate buildings, each of them in the form of a double cylinder.

A circular structure was chosen for the hotel and for the office buildings, picking up the design of the two multi-storey car parks, and continuing it in a coherent whole, thus creating an urban design that deliberately counterbalances the architectural structure of the departure halls, and gives the entire complex an unconventional and highly individual form.

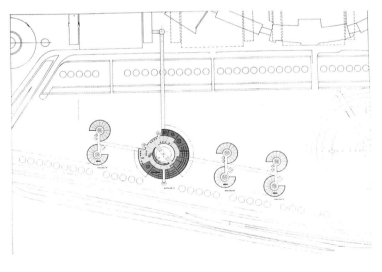

Typical user floor; Longitudinal section

WAREHOUSE CITY - KEHRWIEDERSPITZE
Hamburg

Competition: 1990 - Second Prize
Design: Volkwin Marg
Assistants: Hakki Akyol, Martin Bleckmann, Jutta Hartmann-Pohl, Christian Tibi
Revised design: 1990
Assistants: Martin Bleckmann, Jutta Hartmann-Pohl, Andreas Leuschner, Reiner Schröder

Shifting flows in world trade require new groupings of geographical trading centres with synergy effects. These will be arranged in Hamburg's western warehouse centre permitting linear growth and intercommunication through a common services centre.

Urban renewal will create a new architectural complex in which the ten-year old warehouse centre, postwar architecture and future buildings will create a harmonious dialogue.

The historic building at Kehrwieder-fleet will be restored and the island site of Kehrwiederspitze, a reminder of the original fortifications, rebuilt to form the bridgehead of the warehouse city.

The solid block-like structures of warehouses K and A will be preserved.

The same materials (masonry, open-work steel and patinated copper sheeting) will be used but the contrasting interplay of massive solid forms and openwork means that for the new buildings preference will be given to the transparency of glass and steel.

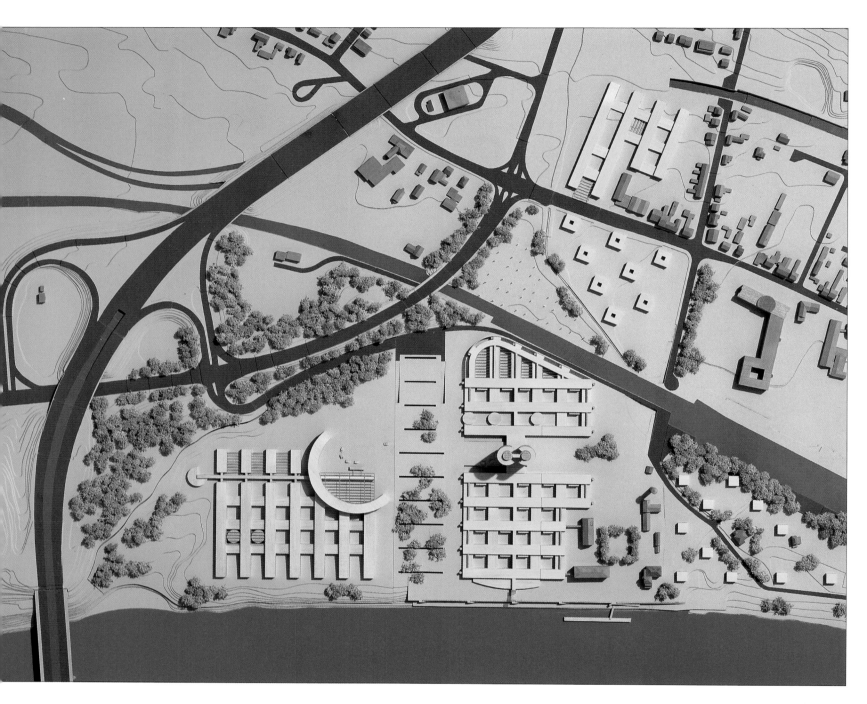

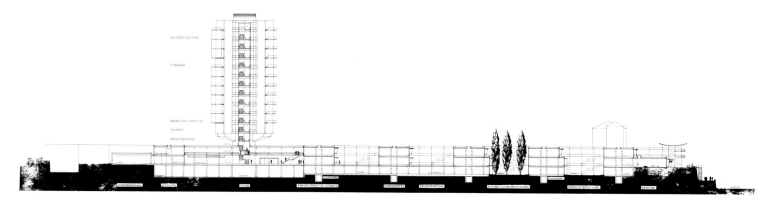

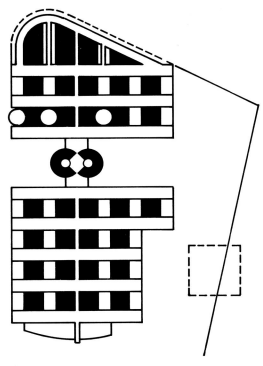

THE "CEMENT FACTORY"
Bonn

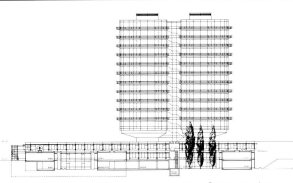

Opposite: Bank elevation; Longitudinal section. Above: Cross section

Competition: 1990 - 3rd Prize
Design: Meinhard von Gerkan
Assistants: Hilke Büttner, Kai Voss

The existing features of the competition site are the determining factors of the design. The two outstanding topological and architectural features of the cement factory are the pair of towering cylindrical silos and the flat buildings.

These two features have dominated the site for years and given it its character. They are to remain the determining forms of the new building, but with a change of use ensuring that the topological character of the site is retained and the architecture has historical continuity despite the change in use.

A fifteen-storey tower block is proposed in place of the two silos. The great circular shape of the flat building acquires the status of a ministerial building. All the other buildings are spread out like a carpet with a maximum height of only two storeys in order to create interconnecting green areas accessible to the public.

A network structure is proposed, with the buildings set into the site one storey below ground. A central axis, at right angles to the Rhine, links the entrance hall below the tower block with all office areas and, at the south-west end, leads directly to the canteen on the riverbank.

Parking is provided in a two-storey underground car park. The green of the park is continued above the garage. The slit-like incisions in which the fire escapes are set reveals their underground location.

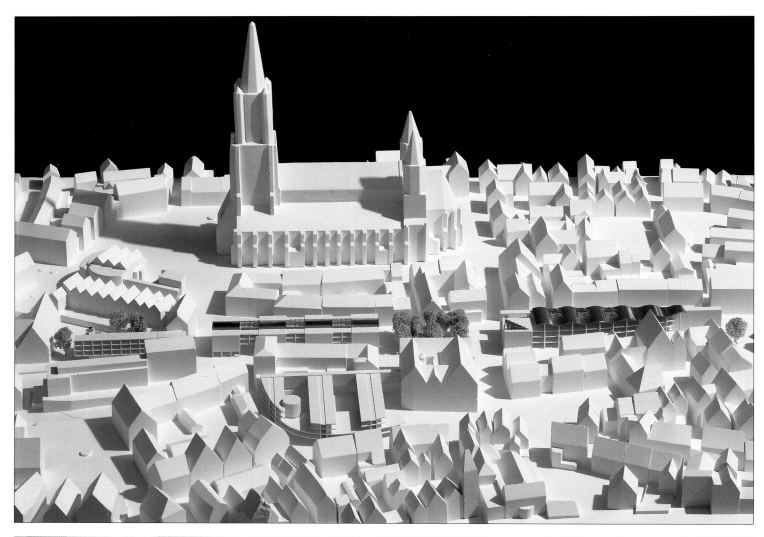

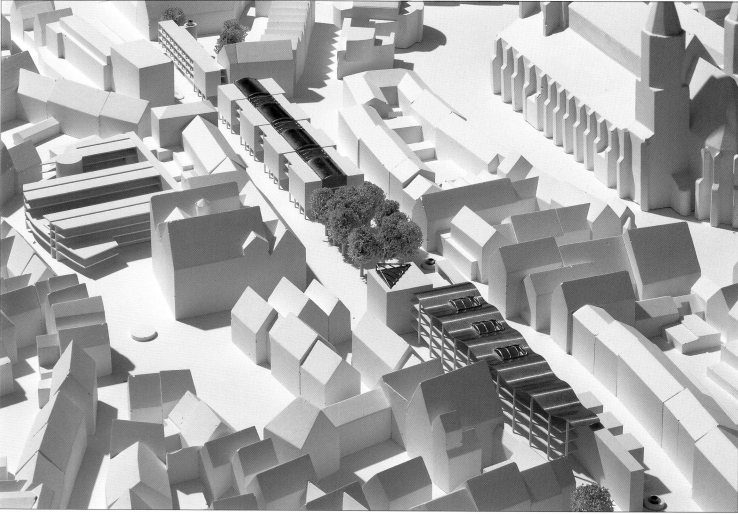

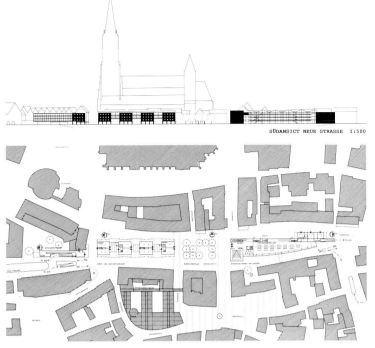

SÜDANSICT NEUE STRASSE 1:500

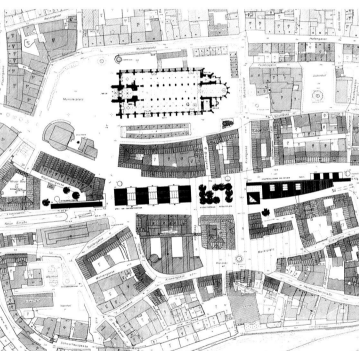

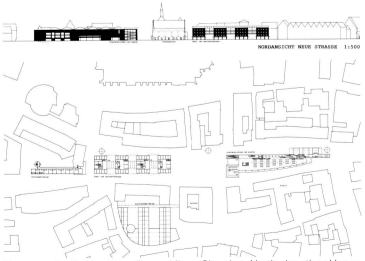

NORDANSICHT NEUE STRASSE 1:500

From top: South elevation; Ground floor; Site plan; North elevation; Upper floor

NEW STREET
Ulm

Ideas Competition:1990 -Second Prize
Design: Meinhard von Gerkan
Assistants: Kai Voss, Volkmar Sievers

New architecture must be carefully inserted into the urban fabric if suitable streets and squares are to be created, if the vitality of the inner city is to be reactivated and if people are to be induced to linger in the city centre. Intervention in the form of wide traffic-bearing roads was a major stage in the history of urban planning - albeit a mistaken one according to today's thinking - but the new objectives of urban renewal should not be concealed either structurally or formally.

The aim, therefore, is to achieve a taut structure, which will be incorporated in the old city like a new spine running parallel to the longitudinal axis of Ulm cathedral. There will be no attempt to deny that this is a modern scheme, or that it is part of an overall design.

The height and size of the buildings, and their outline on the streetscene, will certainly be related to the pleasing proportions of the historic buildings, although the architecture will make use of the formal means of today's architectural language to achieve this aim.

The scheme and the envisaged urban renewal should appear as a unified whole. Although individual buildings with their different uses will be characterised by variety, all the buildings should have the same basic identity.

219

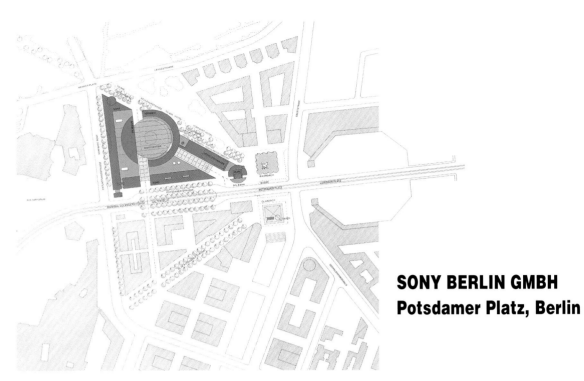

SONY BERLIN GMBH
Potsdamer Platz, Berlin

Competition: Award, 1992
Design: Meinhard von Gerkan
Assistants: Kai Voss,
Jens Kalkbrenner

The aim of the design concept was to create an urban area to enhance metropolitan life in a place with a very special quality of life. Although the triangular shape of the building site may appear disadvantageous, it will meet all the requirements if the concept is adapted to the particular conditions of the site and creates a form with a unique and unmistakeable identity.

The triangular site has urban areas of a completely different character on each of its three sides. To the south and east, are the new Potsdamer Strasse and the Potsdamer Platz with their bustling life, pulsating traffic, bus stops, public transport, shops, restaurants, malls and office buildings. To the north-east are the parklike greens of the Tiergarten, functioning as a place of relaxation, and to the west is the Kulturforum with the Philharmonie, Staatsbibliothek and several museums.

Three aspects of urban life - business and shopping, rest and relaxation, and cultural activities - are linked together by the design, both spatially and architecturally, with the Sony site as the main focus.

The circular inner space, 55m in diameter, will provide a setting for all urban activities.

An almost completely transparent glass roof protects dozens of shops, boutiques, restaurants and cafés on two

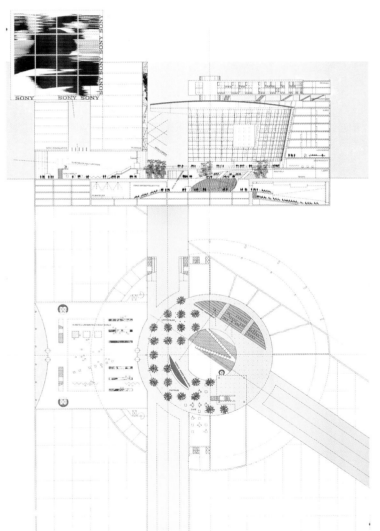

From top: Site plan; Elevation section; Sony Forum ground floor

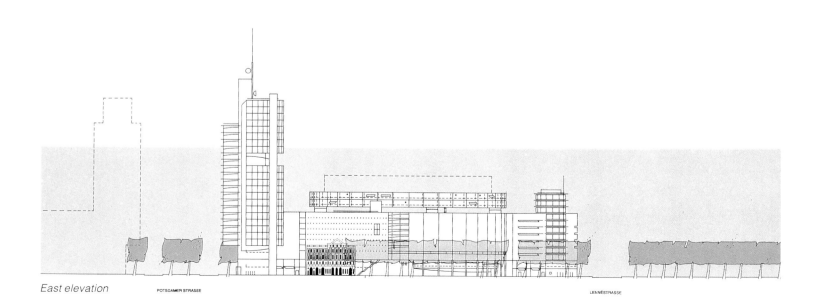

East elevation

POTSDAMER STRASSE

LENNÉSTRASSE

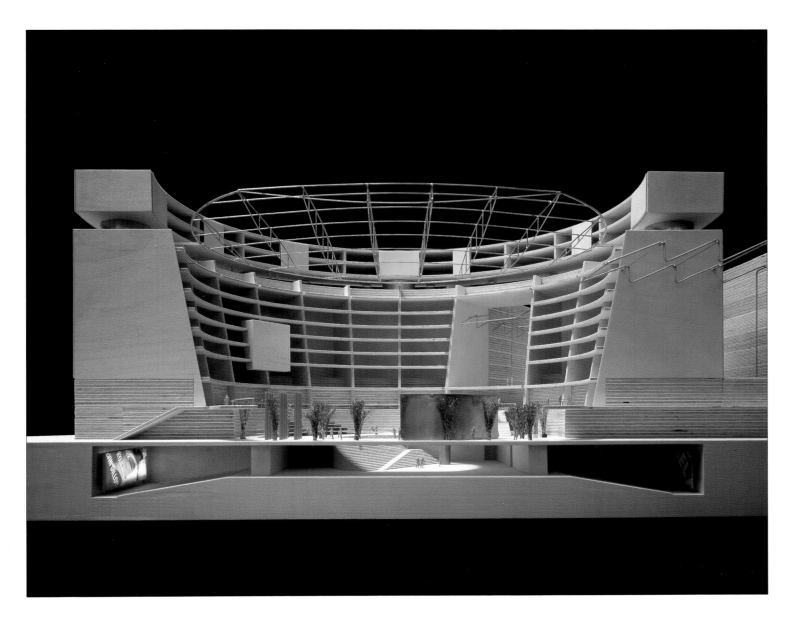

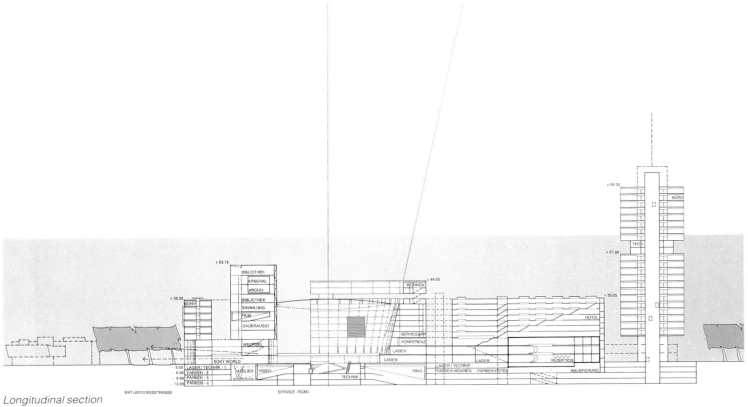

Longitudinal section

levels. Tables and chairs extend onto
the piazza and, on the first floor, onto
the surrounding gallery. But there are
also seats under 4m-6m high bamboos,
their transparent green providing a
pleasant ambience for relaxation.

The west of the piazza faces the
Filmhaus and the hall containing Sony
World, which is transparent and three
floors high, a continuous public space
that creates a pedestrian connection
with the Kulturforum.

But the main attraction of the piazza is
the convertible megascreen 80m wide
and 40m high. This screen will be the
largest visual display unit in the world.
Here Sony can present the latest
developments in audio-visual technology. Several performances can be
presented simultaneously, including
news and publicity.

The Filmhaus can use this "façade"
entirely or partly for displaying its own
experimental work.

The concept of the megascreen has
not yet been completely thought
through but it should be seen as a sti-
mulus that will enable Sony, the market
leader in the entertainment industry, to
test new media on an urban scale.

The megascreen is not only a two-
dimensional area, but a structure with
spatial depth so that work on new
installations can be carried out on the
scaffolding. For example, it is conceiv-
able that a stage can be integrated into
the screen permitting the performers to
frame their live performances with a
cinematic production. Because of the
size of the megascreen only parts of it
are needed for daily events, news and
publicity; other parts can be re-
equipped or technically converted.

Next to the vertical wall of the megascreen, the adjoining walls form a
cylinder that is open at the top. Within
this circular structure all facilities merge
- shops, restaurants, conference rooms,
apartments, and rented office space.

It is proposed that most of the housing be located on the three upper floors
of the circle. Access is on a promenade
on the ninth floor, which can be reached
from a main access point on Bellevue-
strasse. This "aerial floor", with its
views over the surrounding city and
the piazza, will be a special attraction.

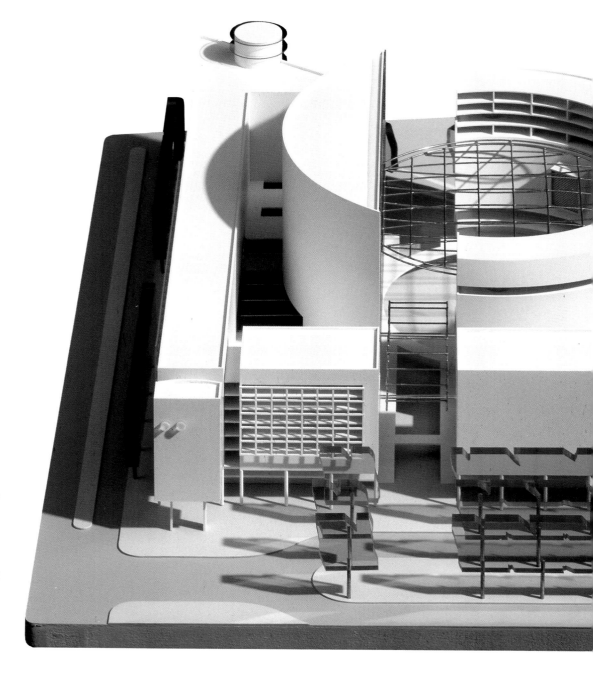

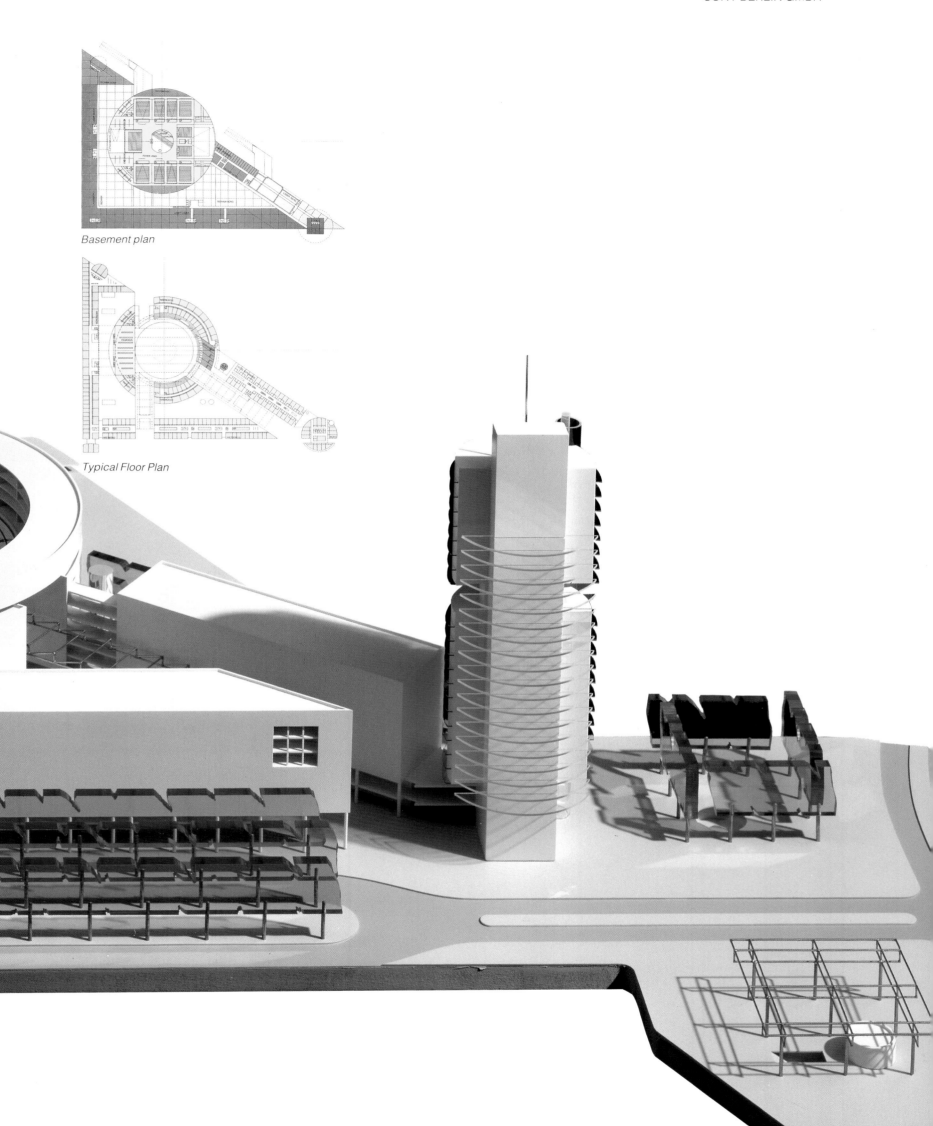

Basement plan

Typical Floor Plan

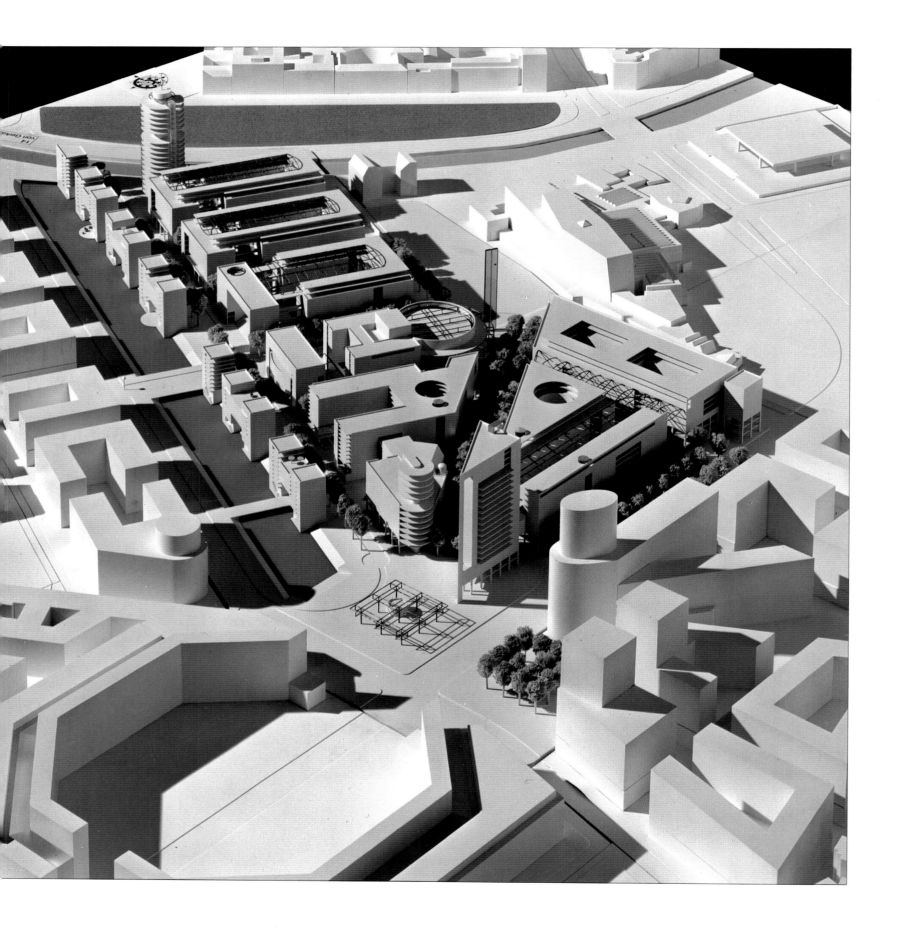

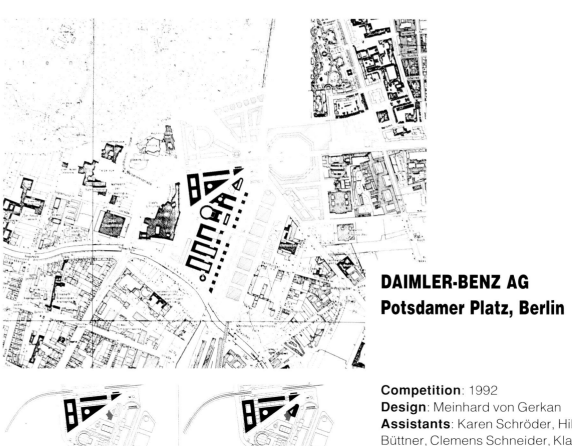

DAIMLER-BENZ AG
Potsdamer Platz, Berlin

Competition: 1992
Design: Meinhard von Gerkan
Assistants: Karen Schröder, Hilke Büttner, Clemens Schneider, Klaus Lenz

A balance between the structural unity of the urban framework and the variety of individual buildings and complexes is an essential condition for the recreation of the European city.

The design abstains from individualising single buildings as solitary monuments. The block-like cohesion of the complex as a whole and its typological relations will be the dominant features. Only very few exceptions are permitted: the two towers and the theatre with its cylindrical foyer that will allow the life of the theatre to flow out into the public space of the Alte Potsdamer Strasse.

The design of the individual buildings and their façades aims at optimal life and variety, with individual styles emerging within a general canon.

The façades have not yet been designed in detail. The following principles were followed:

- Integration of interior and exterior. Glazed inner courts, passages, entrance halls, etc. so that the outside space flows into the interior.

- Double façades to create transitional zones between interior and exterior not only for sound insulation and air-conditioning, but also to let life inside flow out into the public street.

- The design features the contrast of block-like solid stone surfaces on the one hand, and openwork, transparent façade structures on the other.

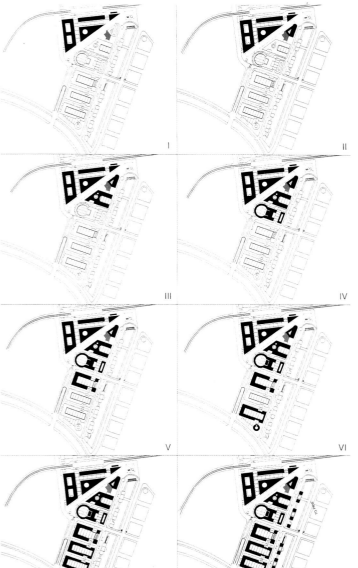

From top: Site plan, Phases of development

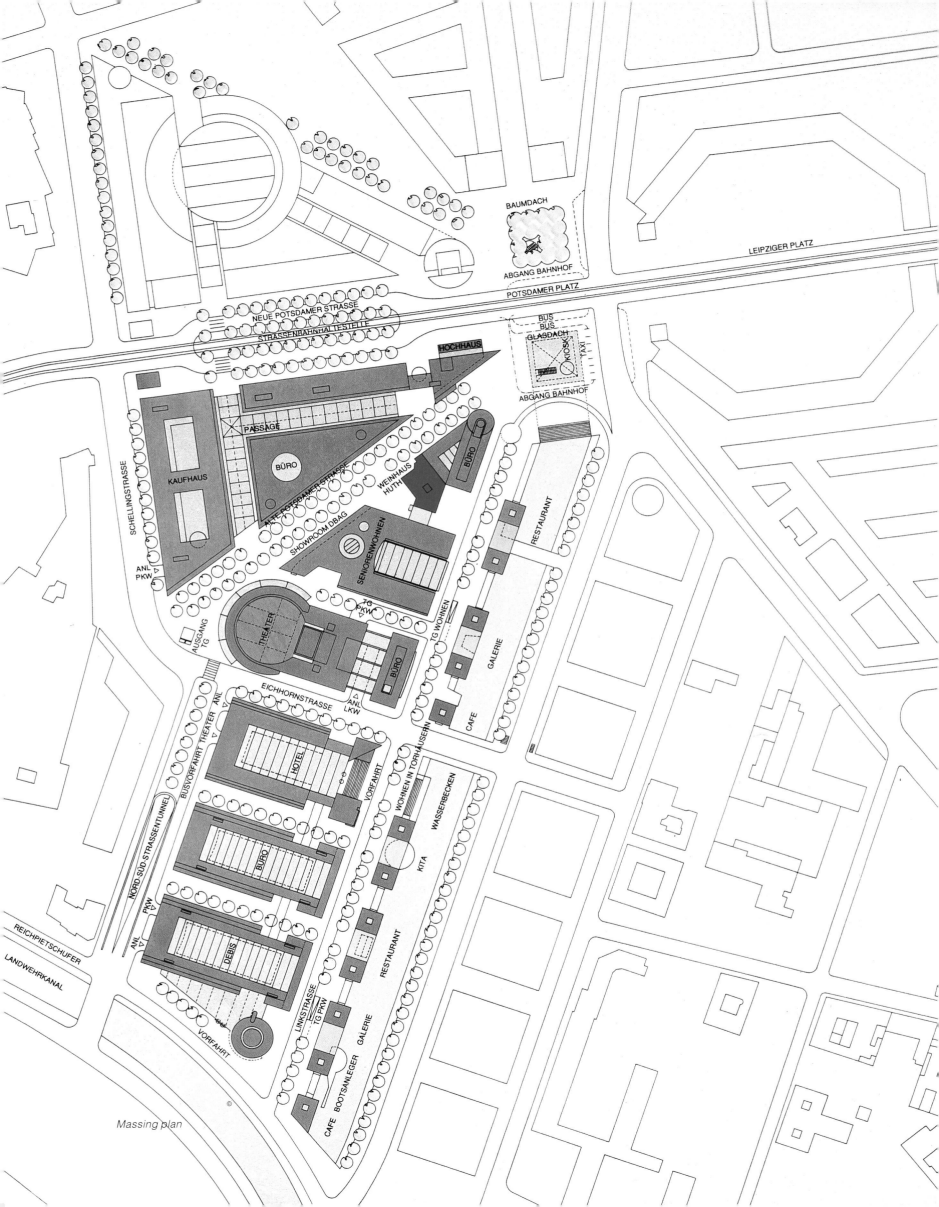

BAUMDACH

LEIPZIGER PLATZ

ABGANG BAHNHOF

POTSDAMER PLATZ

NEUE POTSDAMER STRASSE

STRASSENBAHNHALTESTELLE

BUS
BUS
GLASDACH
KIOSK
TAXI

ABGANG BAHNHOF

HOCHHAUS

SCHELLINGSTRASSE

PASSAGE

BÜRO

KAUFHAUS

ALTE POTSDAMER STRASSE

WEINHAUS HUTH

BÜRO

RESTAURANT

SHOWROOM DBAG

ANL PKW

SENIORENWOHNEN

GALERIE

TG PKW

AUSGANG TG

TG WOHNEN

THEATER

BÜRO

CAFE

ANL LKW

EICHHORNSTRASSE

BUSVORFAHRT THEATER

ANL

HOTEL

VORFAHRT

WOHNEN IN TORHÄUSERN

NORD-SÜD-STRASSENTUNNEL

BÜRO

WASSERBECKEN

KITA

REICHPIETSCHUFER

ANL PKW

LANDWEHRKANAL

DEBIS

RESTAURANT

VORFAHRT

LINKSTRASSE

TG PKW

GALERIE

CAFE

BOOTSANLEGER

Massing plan

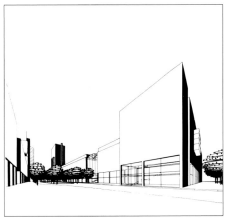

Neue Potsdamer Strasse - View from the Kulturforum

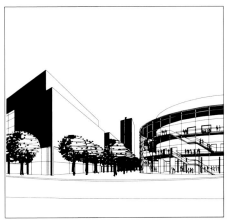

Alte Potsdamer Strasse - Theatre

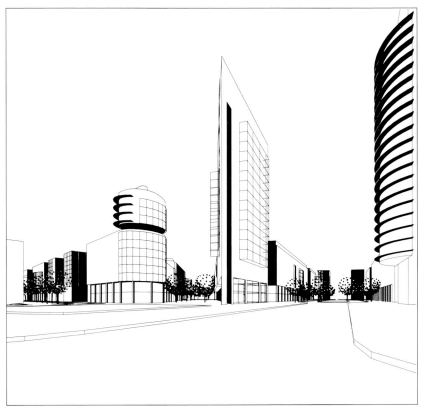

View from Potsdamer Platz

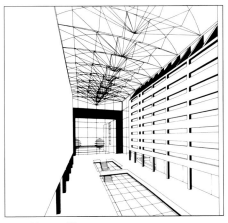

Hotel foyer - View

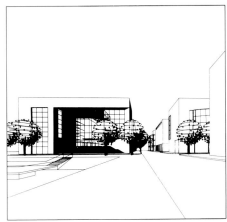

Hotel - Eichhornstrasse

Waterside view

PASSENGER TERMINAL
Stuttgart Airport (1980-1991)

Competition: 1980 (First Prize)
Design: Meinhard von Gerkan
Karsten Brauer, Klaus Staratzke
Assistants: Arturo Buchholz-Berger,
Michael Dittmer, Otto Dorn, Marion
Ebeling, Edeltraut Grimmer,
Gabriele Hagemeister, Rudolf Henning,
Berthold Kiel, Antje Lucks,
Marion Mews, Hans-Heinrich Möller,
Klaus-Heinrich Petersen

The massing at the new terminal is
reduced to two elementary forms: a long
section on a triangular cross section
and a rectangular hall on a trapezoid
cross section. These geometric shapes
provide the dominant focal points that
put some order into the heterogeneous
environment of the present airport.

The roof rises from the road access
side towards the runways, in an indirect
symbolic expression of the concepts
"gate" and "flying". More directly, the
construction of the terminal roof is.
based on the structure of a tree, thus
providing an unmistakeable and individual feature for Stuttgart Airport.

The skeletal structure is built like a
stem branching into flower. The weight
of the roof is borne by a column grid with
free spans of 4m to 5m into the
"branches", each of which carries four
spans. Twelve "branches" in tubular
profiles combine to make a trunk which
is set in a foundation. This skeleton
forms the dominant feature of the
design of the terminal building.

Where the aircraft park in line, the
departure lounges and routes between
the road and flight sides are arranged in

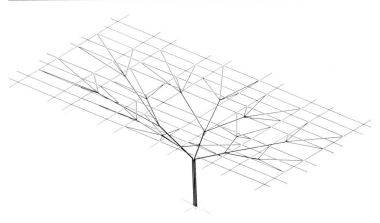

Tree structure

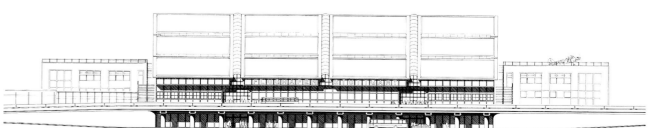

L to R: South and North elevations

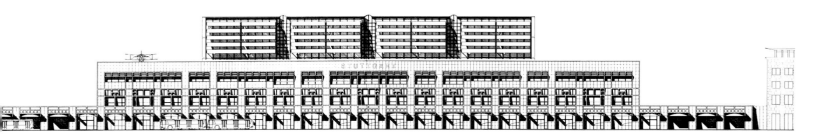

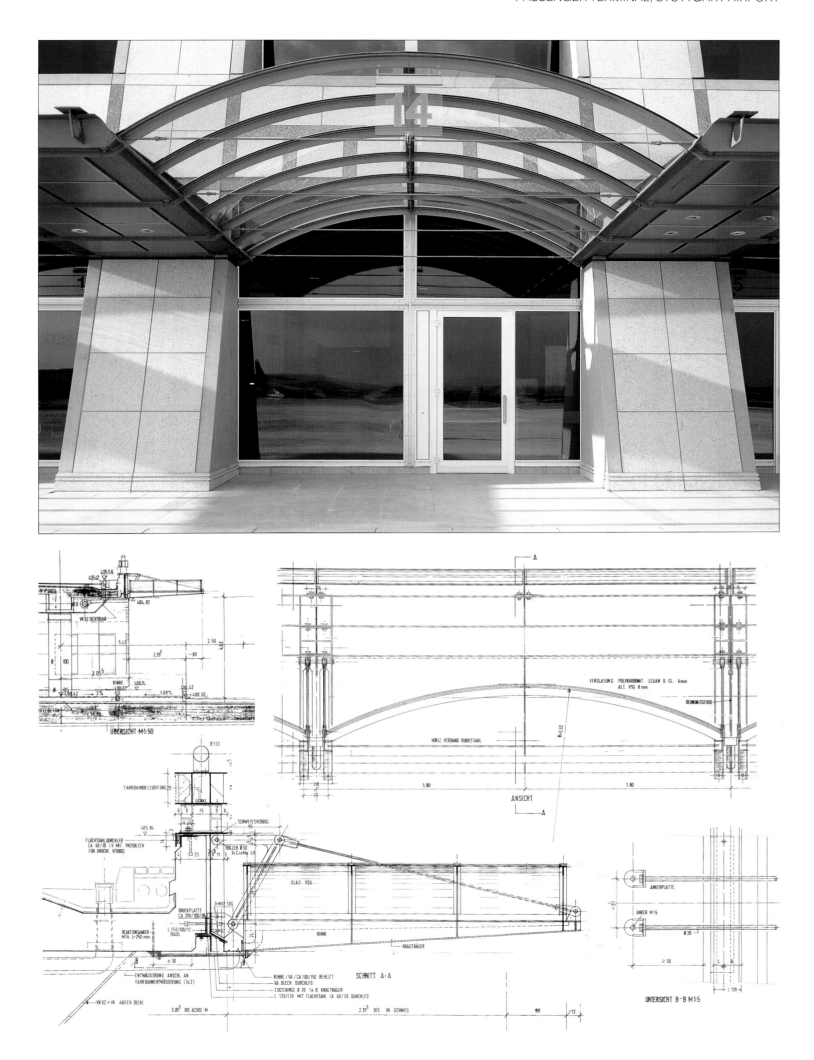

Opposite: Working drawing of the north façade

a long building. Its base has a cross section resembling a dike because of the difference in height of the terrain on either side. So the building perches as if on the ridge of a hill, and it also acts as a noise barrier between the runways and the surrounding area. The sloping surfaces of the façade integrate the building mass topographically into the surrounding area, and the large terminal hall, which is covered only by the tree-structure of the roof, is open on all sides like a covered open space, with a dominant symbolic shape.

At the front, the two elements of the building overlap and intersect. The spine of the long building ends in the hall in terraces, which project in arching semi-circles in the centre. The visitor who goes up to these terraces finds restaurants, the VIP lounge and conference rooms, and the observation terrace lies on the "ridge" of the spine.

The base of the building is clad in natural stone, and so rustication is an essential feature. The windows are recessed and stand vertical in the oblique plane, creating a strong plastic effect over the monolithic base, with the openwork steel construction rising above it. The wall of the terminal building faces south and is fully glazed; it has blinds with rotating wing-like sections, which operate automatically to provide different degrees of shading.

The great hall in the form of an oblique glass cube over the dike cross section of the base with a roof supported by a steel tree-like structure was an essential element of the competition design nearly ten years ago. Not only the side walls of the hall, but also the roof itself were to be one large area of glass to give maximum daylight in the hall. The change from daylight to dark, the differences in the degree of daylight depending on the time of year and the weather, would also create the ambience in the building.

In the competition model, the idea evolved of making the rising oblique shape of the roof in two layers of glass. The warmth of the sunlight as it entered would be trapped by the top layer and either transported to the lower layer through thermal circulation or fed into the technical system inside the building in order to create energy.

The idea of a large glass hall could not be realised, and another solution had to be found for the implementation of the basic idea of the design - the hall

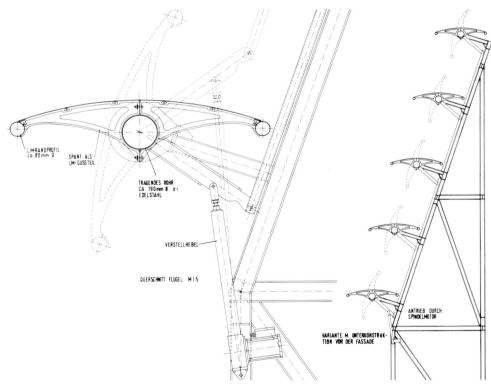

South façade structure

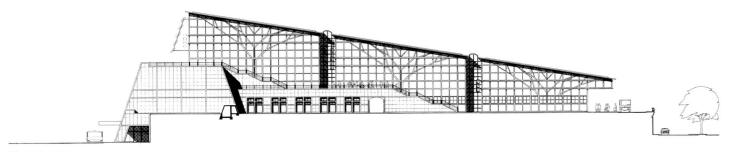

Side elevation

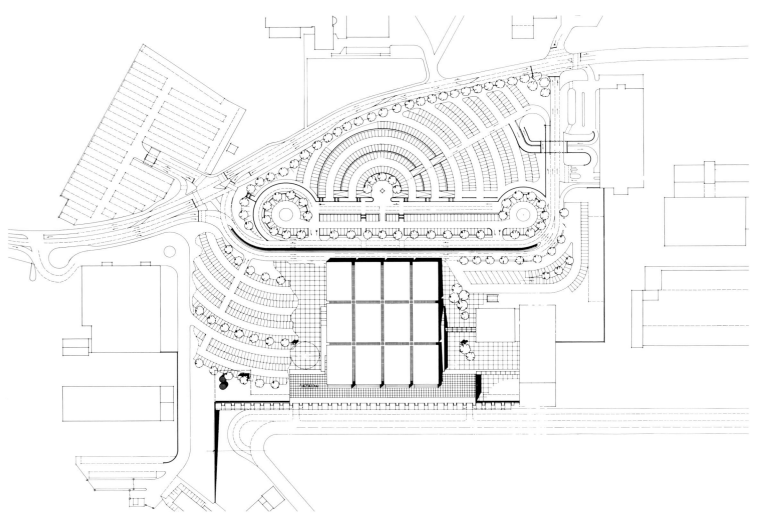

Site plan

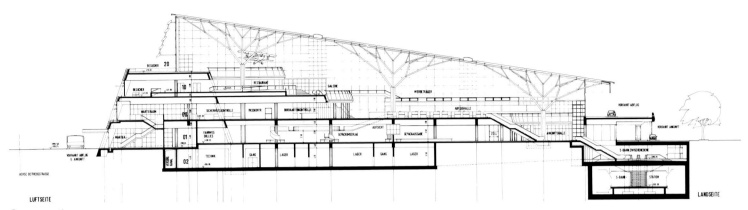

Cross section

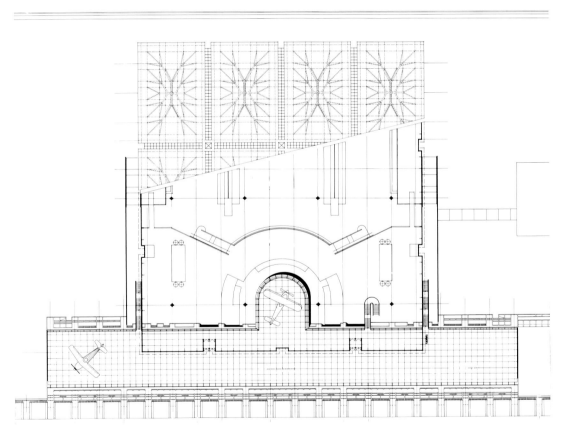

Terrace level

as a large, light space. The Airport Authority laid great emphasis on blinds for the large glazed sides of the hall to provide both partial and full shade.

In keeping with the supporting structure, the surface of the roof is divided into 124 fields by the tree trunks. Where they rest on the "tips of the branches" these fields form closed areas. Between them are band-like strips with glass toplights; these articulate the roof surface, and also let some daylight into the hall through the roof. Using a retro-reflecting light prism system developed by Bartenbach, the arithmetical share of the heat entering was sufficiently minimised for this amount of glazing to be acceptable.

To put it simply, this prism system is based on the fact that the sun's rays that enter, in relation to the main angle at which they enter, are reflected by the edges of small triangular prisms, allowing only diffuse light to reach the interior. The direction of the arrangement of the prisms within the glass bands creates a structure that is not clear to the layman at first glance, although the view of the sky against the light is ensured by a refracting angle.

The roof rises like a tilted desk from the road side to the runway side. It covers a rectangular area of 82.8m by 93.6m. The twelve supports stand at intervals of 21.6m and 32.4 m.

The roof itself consists of a grid, the underside of which is perceived in the hall as a structured ceiling. The rectangular interspaces are coffered. The roof surface is divided into twelve rectangular fields, and the dividing bands have glass toplights. This makes clear the structural and formal relation of the roof with its tree-like supports. The "tree supports" are analogous to the structure of a natural tree: they fan out like branches into supports made of round tubes, with a trunk, branches and twigs. The junctions between these industrial tubular profiles of different diameters are made of moulded parts formed individually by craftsmen.

In order to absorb any distortion that may result from varying loads on the support system, the points where the roof rests on the supporting grid are jointed to the trees. One special effect of the tree supports is that they can take a large part of the emergent horizontal load and deflect it.

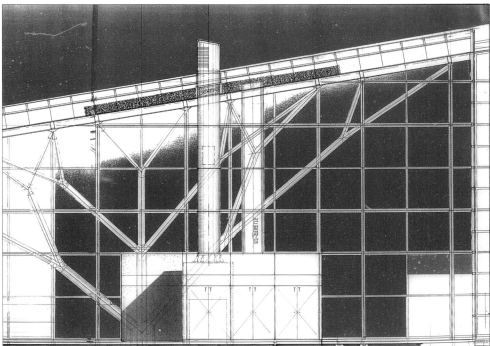

Middle: Detail drawing of the tree supports

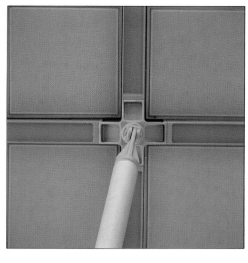

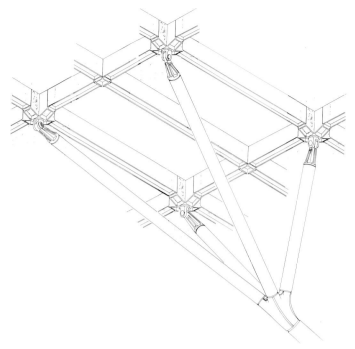

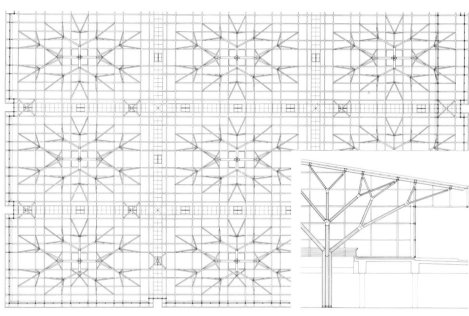

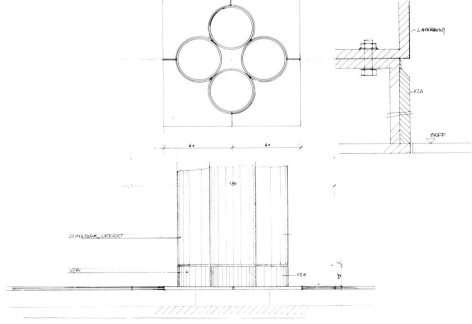

Elevation and cross section of the "treetrunk"

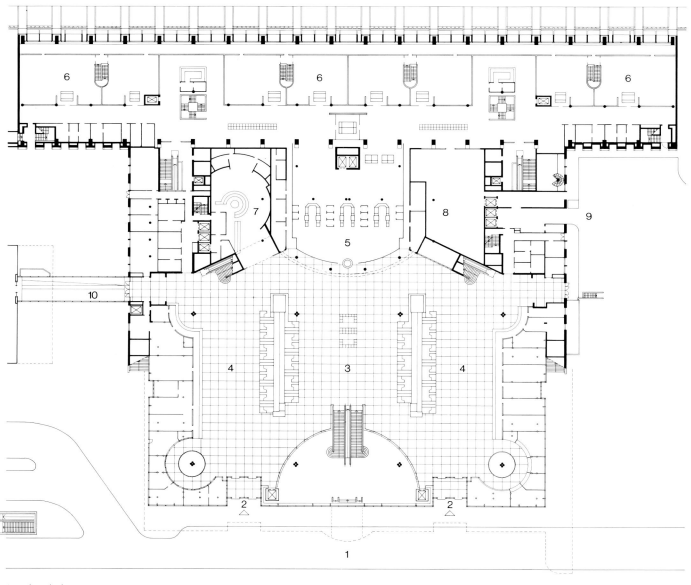

Departure level plan

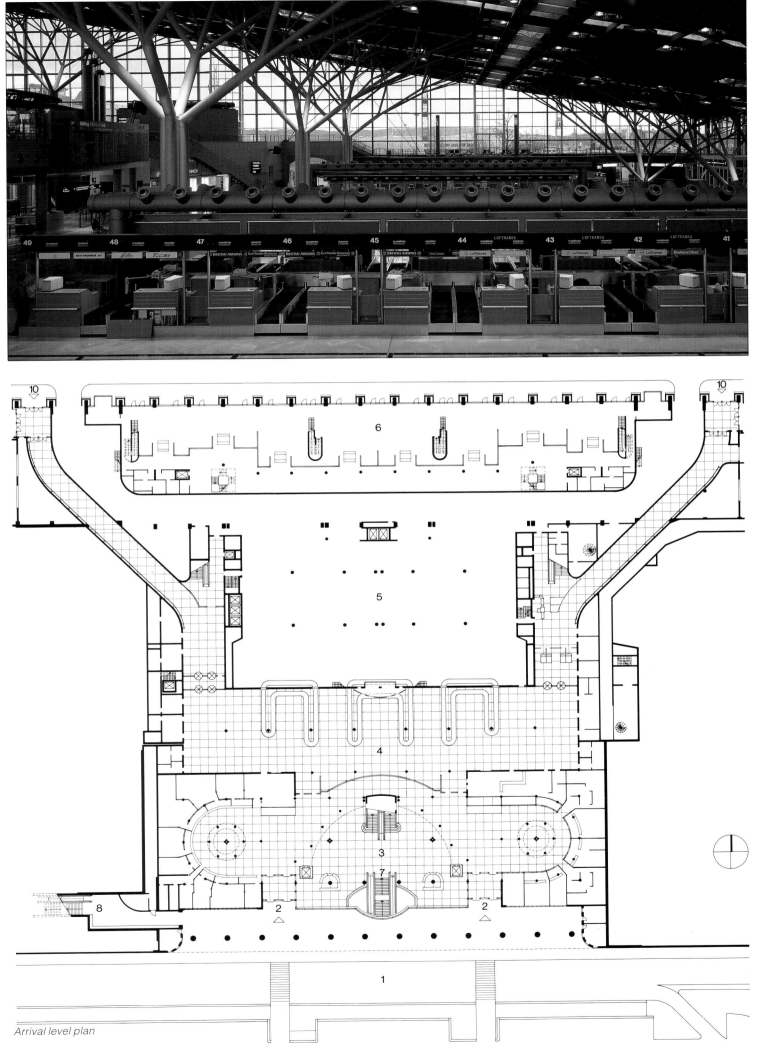

Arrival level plan

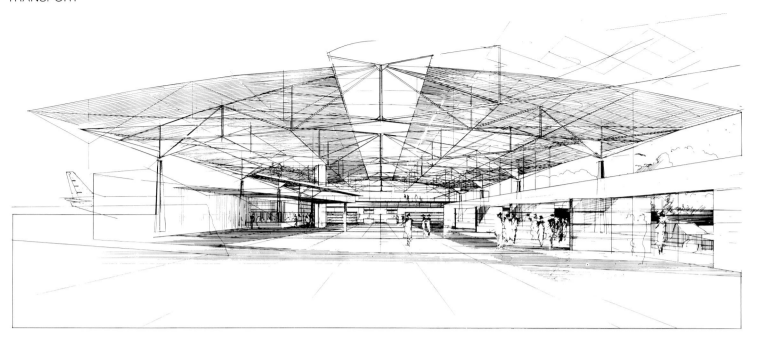

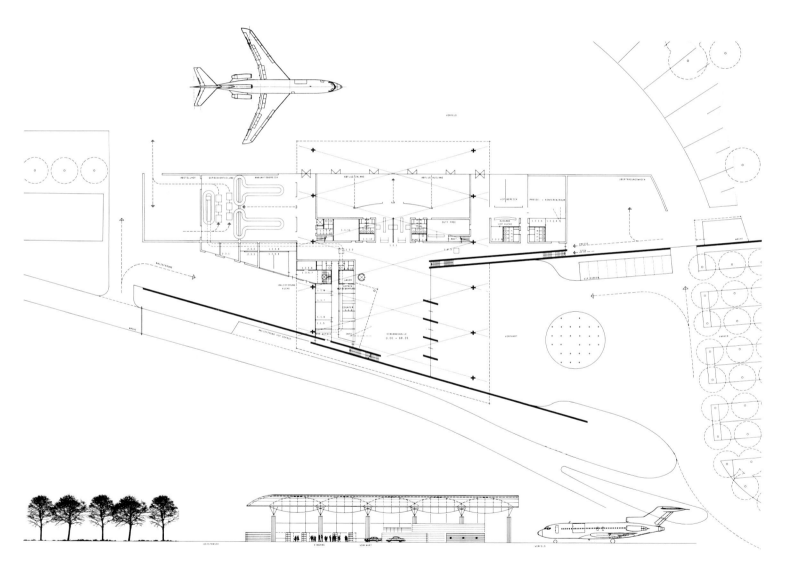

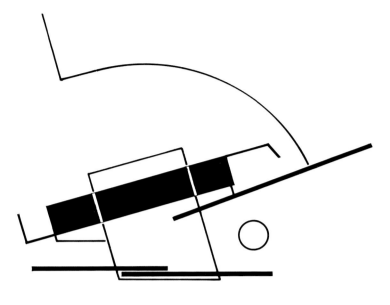

VIP LOUNGE
Cologne-Wahn Airport

Design: Meinhard von Gerkan
Assistant: Volkmar Sievers

The main design feature is a large hall with an arched roof supported by steel girders trussed with sag rods arranged in a rhomboid shape. Long cross walls, which extend beyond the main body of the building, form the boundaries between the public and the controlled areas, and also comprise on the land side the welcoming feature of the entrance to the building with its access for motor vehicles.

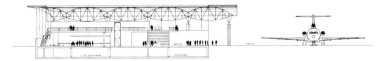

Cross section; Opposite from top: View into the hall; Main floor plan; Entrance elevation; Front elevation

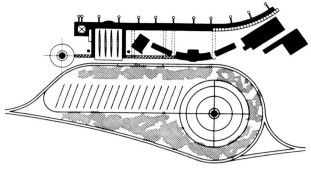

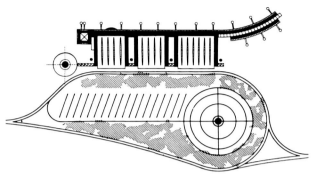

PASSENGER TERMINAL
Hamburg Airport (1986-1993)

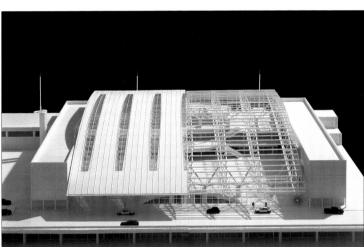

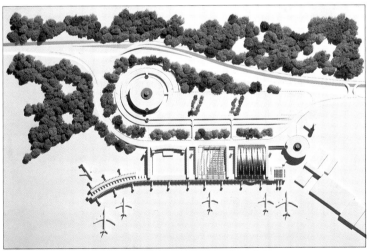

From top: The stepped building; Maximum possible use

Competition: 1986 - First Prize
Design: Meinhard von Gerkan,
Karsten Brauer
Assistants: Jürgen Hillmer, Karl-Heinz
Follert, Christel Timm-Schwartz, Klaus
Hoyer, Franz Merkel, Eunice Jenye,
Ahmed Alkuru, Damir Perisic, Evgenia
Werner, Thorsten Hinz, Wolf Tegge,
Sabine Müller, Renata Dipper, Gisbert
von Stülpnagel, Berthold Kiel, Peter
Autzen, Christian Kleiner, Uwe
Schümann, Uwe Welp, Rüdiger Franke,
Christian Kleine, Sabrina Pieper,
Thomas Bieling, Georg Ritschl, Hans-
Hermann Krafft, Marion Mews, Tilman
Fulda, Gisela Rhone-Venzke, Thomas
Rinne, Sabine von Gerkan

The connecting "spine" of the complex
is the departure gate, which swings out
to the west at the northern end.

It enables the charter hall to be
retained; it ensures that buildings can
be added on the east side later, thus
providing three additional locations
close to the terminal; and it counterbalances the long, asymmetrical bay on
the land side.

The parts of the building at right
angles to the departure gate form
structural caesuras, their architectural
features giving them coherence. The
principle of order has been obeyed
without predetermining future development of the site.

The architectural principle for the
design is to integrate "old" and "new",
and to establish long-term organisation,
while allowing sufficient scope for
future development.

257

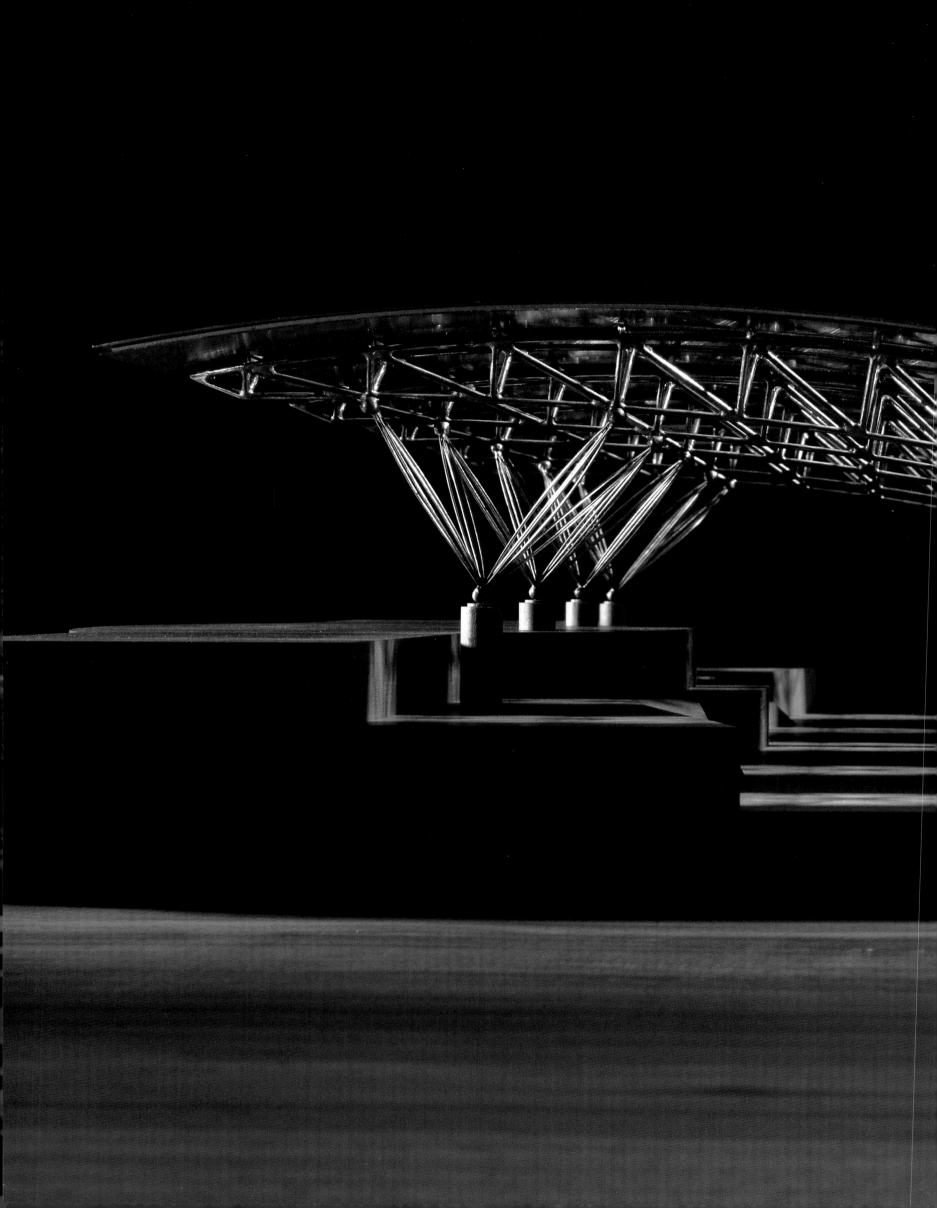

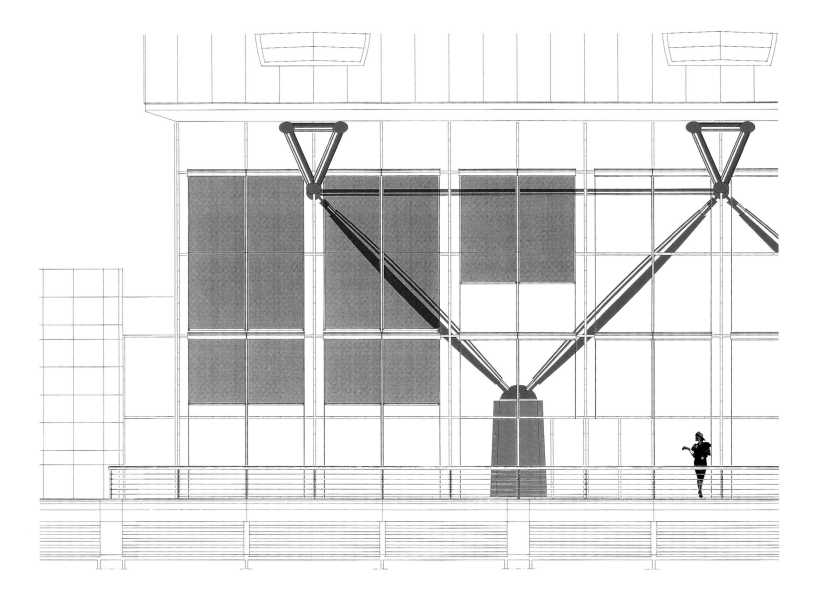

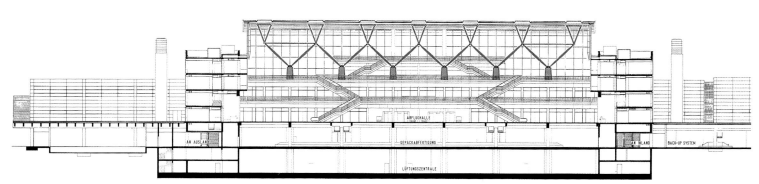

From top: Detail of cross section; Cross section

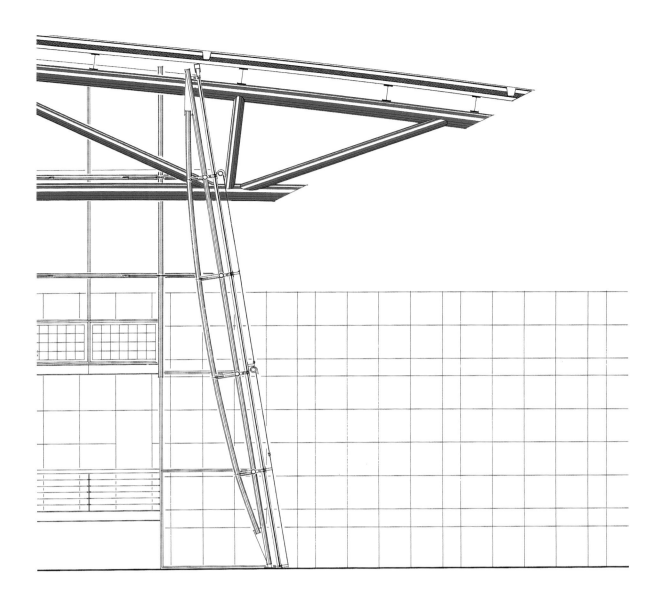

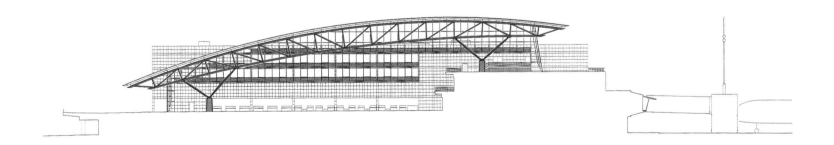

*From top: Detail of longitudinal section;
Longitudinal section*

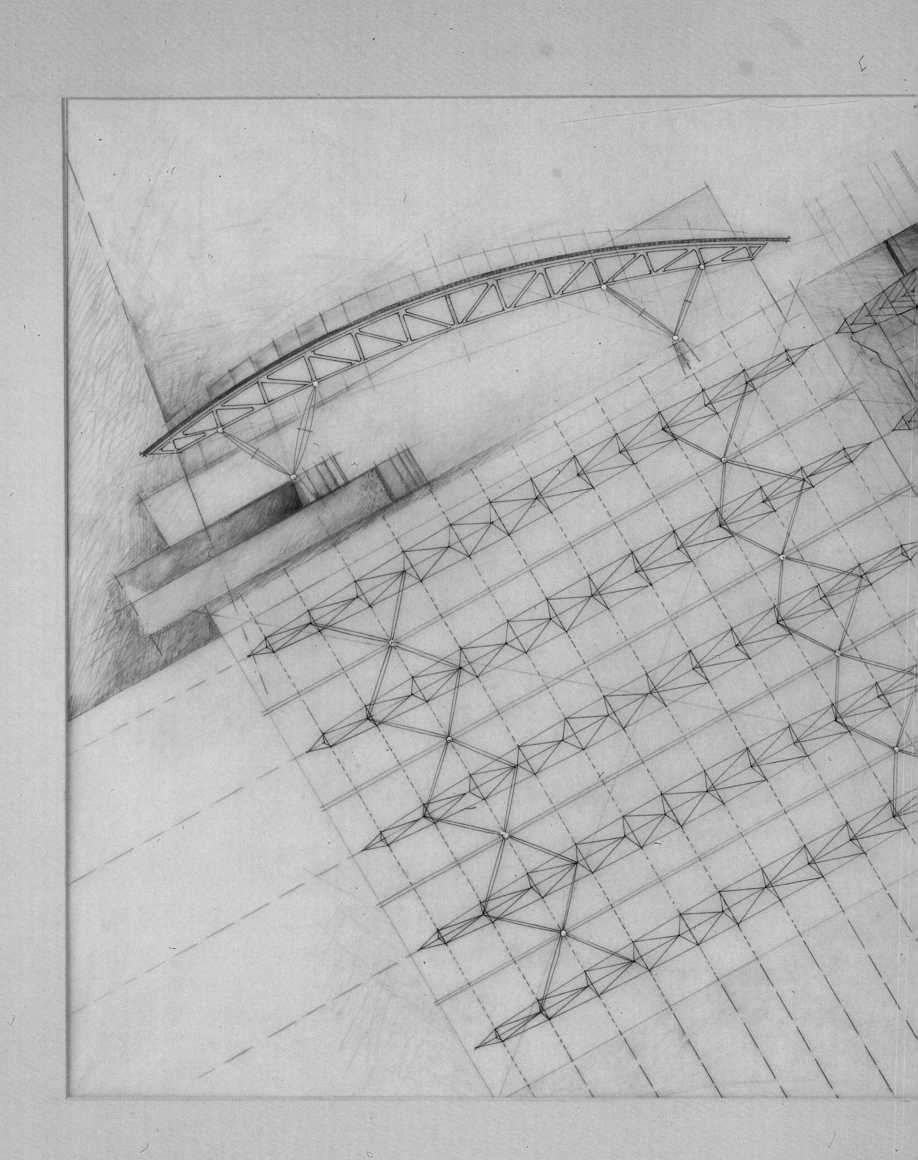

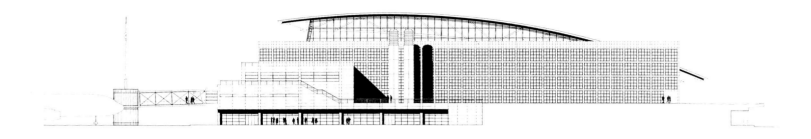

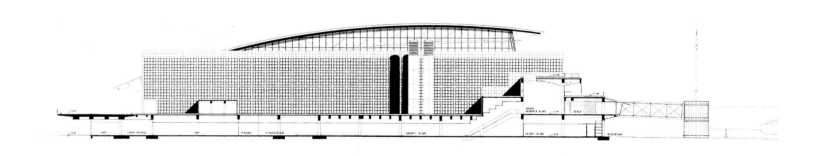

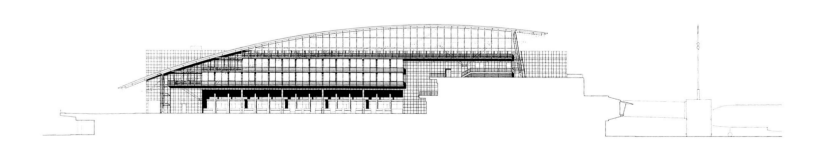

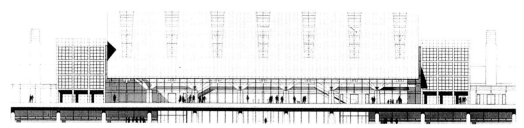

From top: South elevation; North elevation;
Section through the hall; East elevation - land side

The new terminal is conceived as a wide hall flooded with light. The large curved roof encloses the departure floor and the floors that graduate upwards in one large spatial continuum. In shape and construction, the roof is similar to an aircraft flight deck. The seven curved girders, which are triangular in cross section, rest on twelve spatially articulated support heads. This dynamic steel structure is in deliberate contrast with the monolithic blocks of the building.

The roof spans an area of 75m x 101m. Its weight is directed downwards over pairs of diagonally straddled girders onto twelve concrete supports. Despite the large 62m span of the arch, the roof is a light, economical construction. The girders form a spatial lattice pattern with a cross section close to the ratio of their moment of flexion.

With the great static height of about 4.5m in the centre between the lower and upper girders, the cross sections of the tubular profiles are extremely well utilised. Glass toplights ensure the desired quality of daylight in the hall, and the girders, which are visible from below, form a pattern against the light. In order to ensure maximum architectural impact, the steel has not been clad and will be painted. The roof cover above the purlins consists of trapezoid metal sheets.

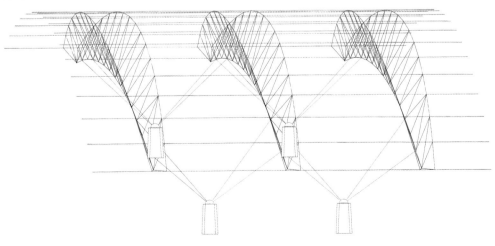

Bottom: Details of the structure of the truss and its supports

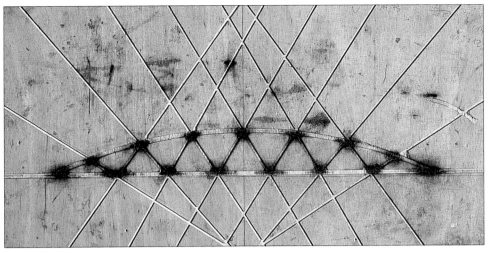

PYONGYANG INTERNATIONAL AIRPORT
North Korea

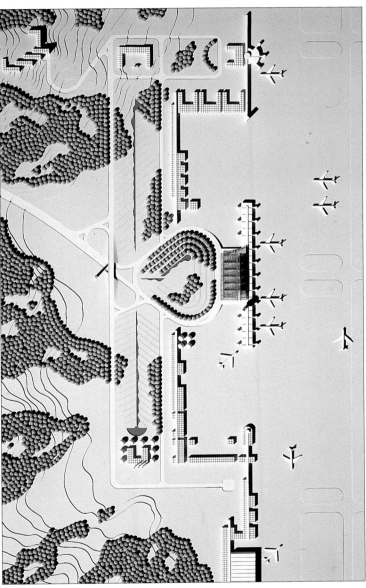

Design A: 1985
Design: Meinhard von Gerkan,
Karsten Brauer
Assistants: Thomas Bieling, Tuyen
Tran-Viet, Uwe Welp

The design is based on the motif of the traditional Korean roof. However, this is not cited literally but is transformed into the language of modern architecture.

Two great bowls of unequal size, each supported on the other, swing up 35m high above the cross-bar on the road side. They form the central feature of the passenger terminal. With their striking silhouette visible from a distance, they are typical of this country while also giving a dynamic quality to the spatial experience of the interior.

The supporting structure of straddled beams and girders forms a fish-scale pattern. It is located above the roof, with the bowls suspended beneath it. The vertical resting points push through the surface of the roof, while linear incisions in the roof surface let daylight into the hall beneath.

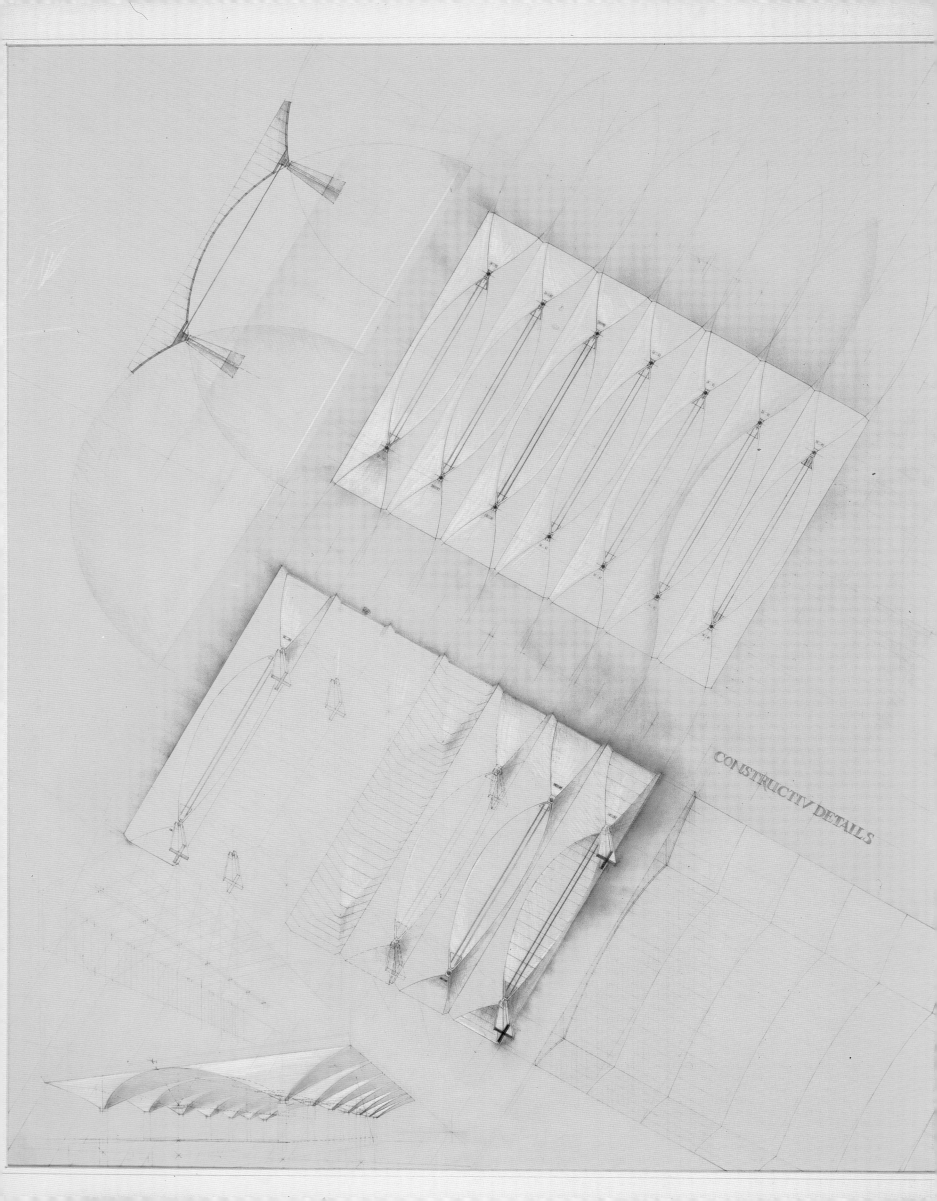

CONSTRUCTIV DETAILS

PYONGYANG INTERNATIONAL AIRPORT
North Korea

Design D: 1986
Design: Meinhard von Gerkan,
Karsten Brauer
Assistants: Thomas Bieling, Tuyen
Tran-Viet

This alternative study was made because our Korean clients did not like the
original design.

The centrepiece of the complex is a
light hall in which the check-in desks are
arranged on three different levels.

This hall is roofed by a huge convertible construction, which greets the
arriving visitors on the road side like a
monumental gateway.

Within the main hall the three levels
are staggered and linked by broad
stairways.

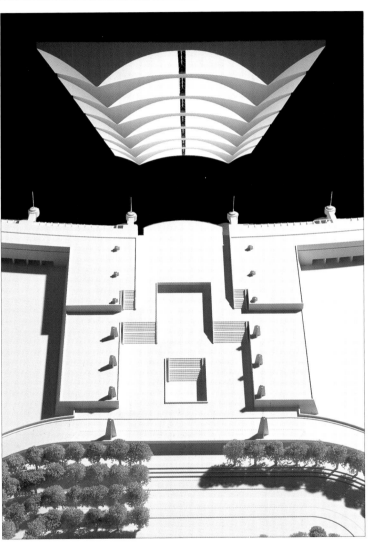

Top: The great roof arches

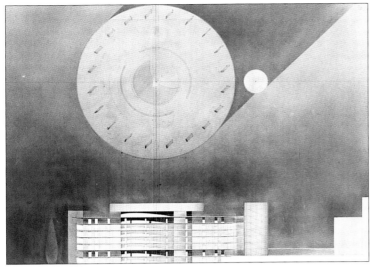

MULTI-STOREY CAR PARK
Hamburg Airport

Building commenced: 1989-1990
Design: Meinhard von Gerkan
Project partner: Klaus Staratzke
Assistants: Klaus Hoyer, Uwe Pörksen
*German Architects Prize for 1991 -
Commended*

Because of its position and form, the car park acts as a key junction and turning point between the various types of building and areas of use at the airport.

It is an integral part of the new departure terminal. It will have nine parking levels with a total of about 800 parking spaces arranged around a ring-shaped access driveway. The levels are reached via two spindle-shaped ramps in the middle of the circle, taking ascending and descending vehicles in opposite directions. Each level can be regulated by the traffic control system. On the ramps and the parking floors traffic is one-way, and the only intersections are at the entrances and exits.

Pedestrian access is on the north side, opposite the future terminal and uses a separate tower stairway with lifts. The tower is linked to the multi-storey car park by light bridges. The second stairway is on the opposite, southern side of the car park. Above the top parking level is another storey, circular in shape and set back, which contains the cooling equipment for the terminal.

Besides the dominant geometrical shape, another essential formal element in the design of the car park is the splitting up of the various levels by a "screen" consisting of a steel grid placed in front of part of them. This

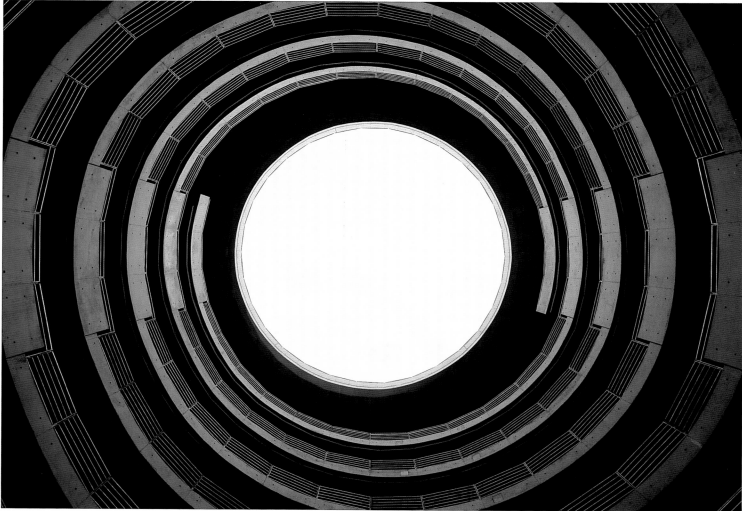

permits an outside view and ensures ventilation while providing accentuated articulation when seen from a distance.

The grid has been omitted on the entrance and exit levels and on the top two parking levels to make the whole building lighter and to emphasise the principle of the structure. The recessed technical storey with the cooling equipment has a similar façade in order to conceal the technical equipment from outside and to provide articulation for its large cylindrical shape.

The whole building is in reinforced concrete, with plate-shaped parking decks about 61m in diameter.

The roof is flat and tapers from 45cm to 26cm. The downward thrust is taken by an external ring of twenty supports 50cm x 120cm in diameter. The building is strengthened inside by a cylindrical wall 45cm thick. The ramps are cantilevered on the inside of the reinforced concrete cylinder and have a thickness of 45cm tapering to 25cm.

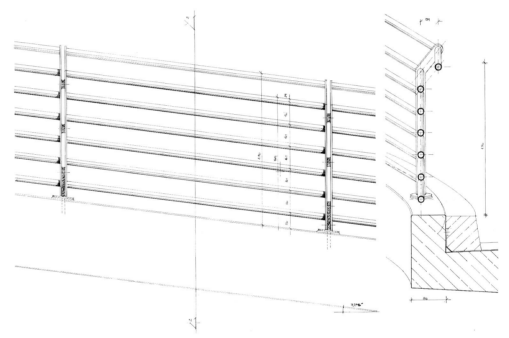

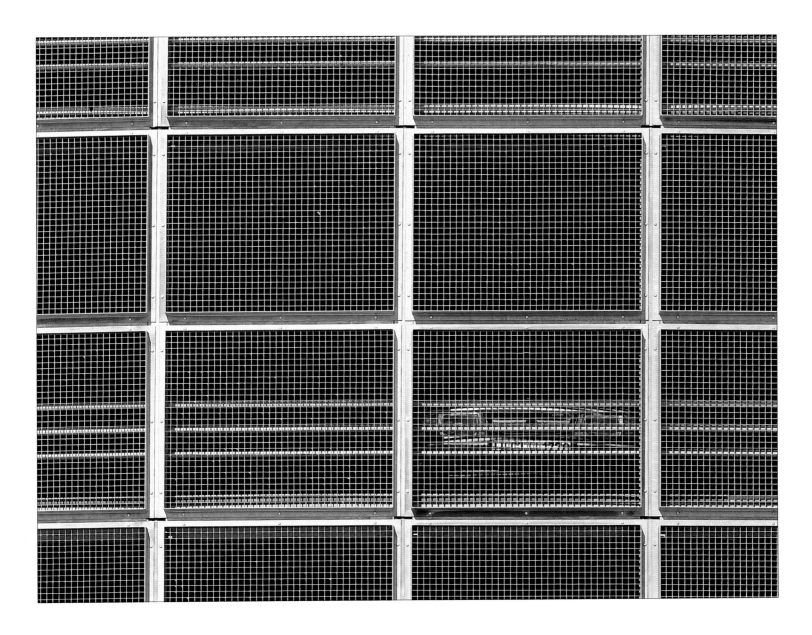

Section

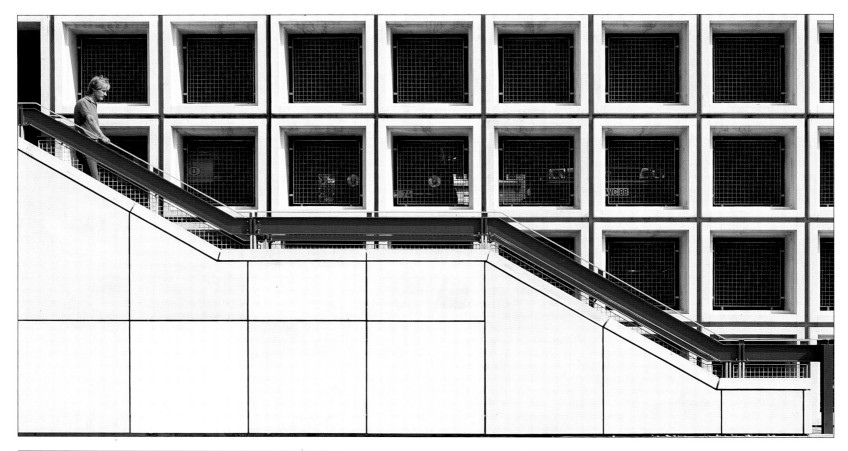

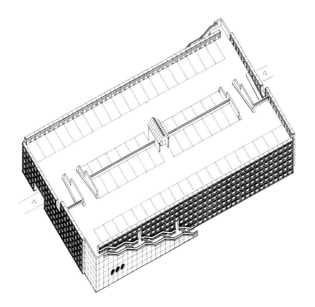

MULTI-STOREY CAR PARK, MAIN POST OFFICE ADMINISTRATION
Braunschweig (1984-1986)

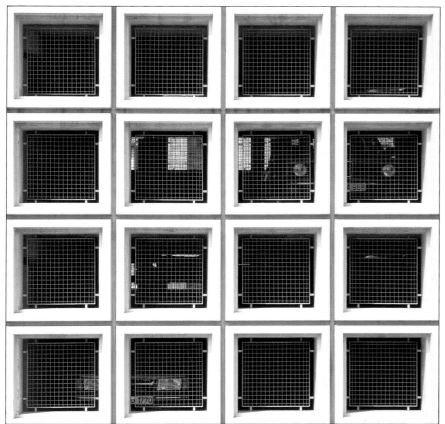

Design: Meinhard von Gerkan
Project Director: Bernhard Albers
Assistants: Knut Maass, Antje Lucks

The multi-storey car park has space for 240 vehicles arranged in the D-Humy system, which offers easy access and an economical use of parking space. In order to ensure good ventilation on the parking levels, the façade is largely open, but will appear solid. To achieve this, a modular honeycomb system has been developed based on combs 0.65m in depth. Their great plasticity and symmetry will give the optical effect of an unbroken façade.

The sides of each square of the honeycomb are twice the basic unit of 0.65m, that is 1.3m; two of these lengths, that is 2.6m, make up the height of each storey and the width of the parking space for each vehicle. In contrast with the patterned surface of the façade, the outer stairs rise up in a diagonal across the building, providing direct access to each storey. The gabled façades reflect the recessed parking levels.

The great depth of the prefabricated concrete parts has a dual aesthetic aim: to give the building lightness and transparency, despite its solid form; and to create shadows sloping inwards and the effect of deep coffers when seen from the side so that the building will not look like a set of shelves for cars with associations of an unattractive interior.

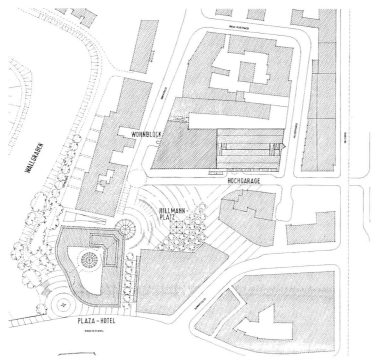

HILLMANN GARAGE
Bremen (1983-1984)

Design: Meinhard von Gerkan
Project partner: Klaus Staratzke
Assistants: Peter Sembritzki, Klaus Lübbert, Tuyen Tran-Viet

The garage has a total of 529 parking spaces, arranged on seven levels in the D-Humy system. Part of the ground floor is reserved for commercial vehicles.

The contrast between solid and broken façades and the arrangement of an access stairway diagonally across the main façade are intended to avoid the monotony of uniform subdivisions, without denying that this is a multi-storey car park. The identity of the building should reflect its function.

The entire façade is walled in three different kinds of brick. For large areas, two monochrome colours were mixed randomly. The differences in colour are only slight, which has given the wall some life without a spotted effect.

The supports, floor and base are made of dark fired klinker. The walls have open incisions ensuring natural ventilation but with no outside view. Brick was chosen because it is traditional in northern Germany and it is the predominant building material in the district around Bremen. The colour was chosen to match Bremen's main railway station, which is nearby. For a multi-storey car park, which is unlikely to be well maintained although subject to heavy wear and tear, brick is a very suitable material because it is particularly durable and does not show the dirt.

Top: Site plan; Bottom: Parking levels arranged in the D-Humy system

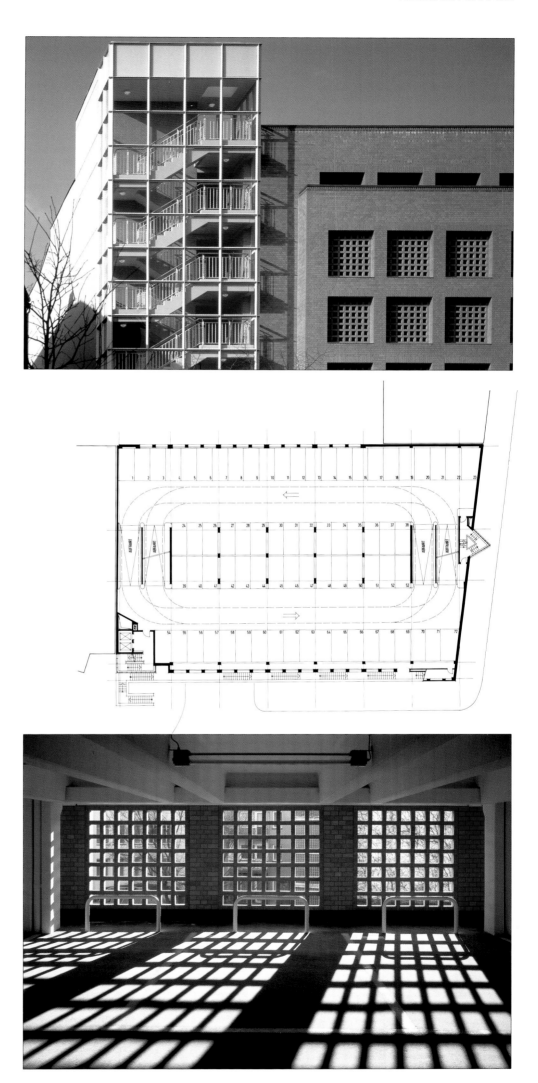

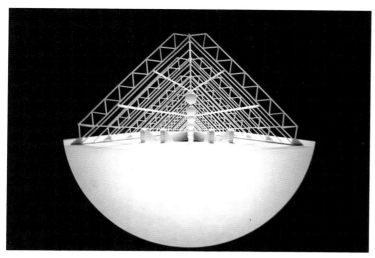

CITY RAIL STOP
Main Railway Station
Bielefeld (1983-1991)

Design: Meinhard von Gerkan
with Hans-Heinrich Möller

The main feature of the design of the station is the use of light.

Platforms: The skilful placing of the platform lights, which were developed specifically for this railway station, ensures that the platforms are brightly lit. The roof and the tracks remain dark. This creates linear areas of light that offer a new quality of spatial experience through the sequence of light and dark. The access area: An area 30m wide and 35m long, without roof supports, was required. For structural reasons the height could only be 2.85m. This is too low for the area but the use of indirect lighting raises the height visually.

The reflection of the lighting in a mirrored roof above the lights gives the impression that the source of light is floating above the roof.

Roof clouds and wall waves: The roof cloud floats over the high frontage of the access area linking it with the platform level, thus giving the area its own dynamic and plasticity. This motif is applied to the wall areas, too, where it also serves to identify the platform levels. The main access area: The need to make the city rail stop visible from the railway station gave rise to the idea of a ramp-like connection between the road and the stop. The transparency of the building, the opening up of the lower ground level and the glass prism above ground with a view directly onto it, make the stop clearly visible from a distance - architecture illustrating function.

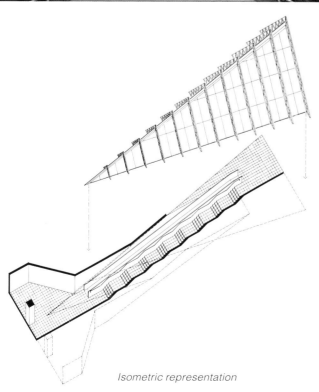

Isometric representation

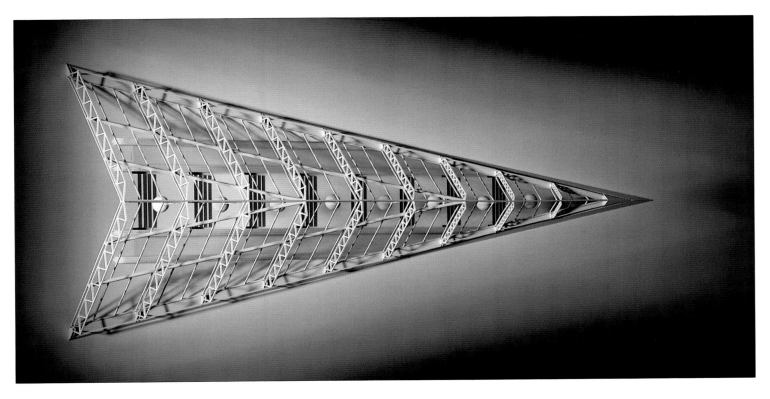

CAFÉ ANDERSEN
Hamburg (1990-1991)

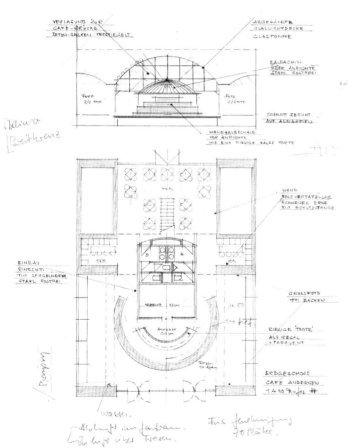

Design: Meinhard von Gerkan
Project Partner: Klaus Staratzke
Assistants: Peter Sembritzki
Oliver Brück

The aim here was to avoid both red plush nostalgia and the chic of the fashionable ice-cream parlour, and to create an atmosphere of clarity and simplicity utilising the features of the existing building to develop a unique spatial entity.

However, the new café was to be not only original and highly individual, it was also to express durability through clarity and simplicity of function, colour and materials. The vaulted ceiling, in industrial prefabricated metal profiles, gives the room generous proportions and a dominant feature. The light is projected from industrial spotlights against the metal surface, from which it is reflected to give the room brilliant illumination. Neither the interior design nor the cakes and pastries have anything to hide.

The sales area is dominated by the circular counter, which enables customers to see the cakes from all sides. The subsidiary rooms, including the cloakrooms, are arranged like a metal wagon along the central axis of the room; a baldaquin arches from here over the sales area. A straight staircase leads to a new gallery, its recesses providing the more cosy corners of the café.

The entrance façade was developed from the existing concrete structure.

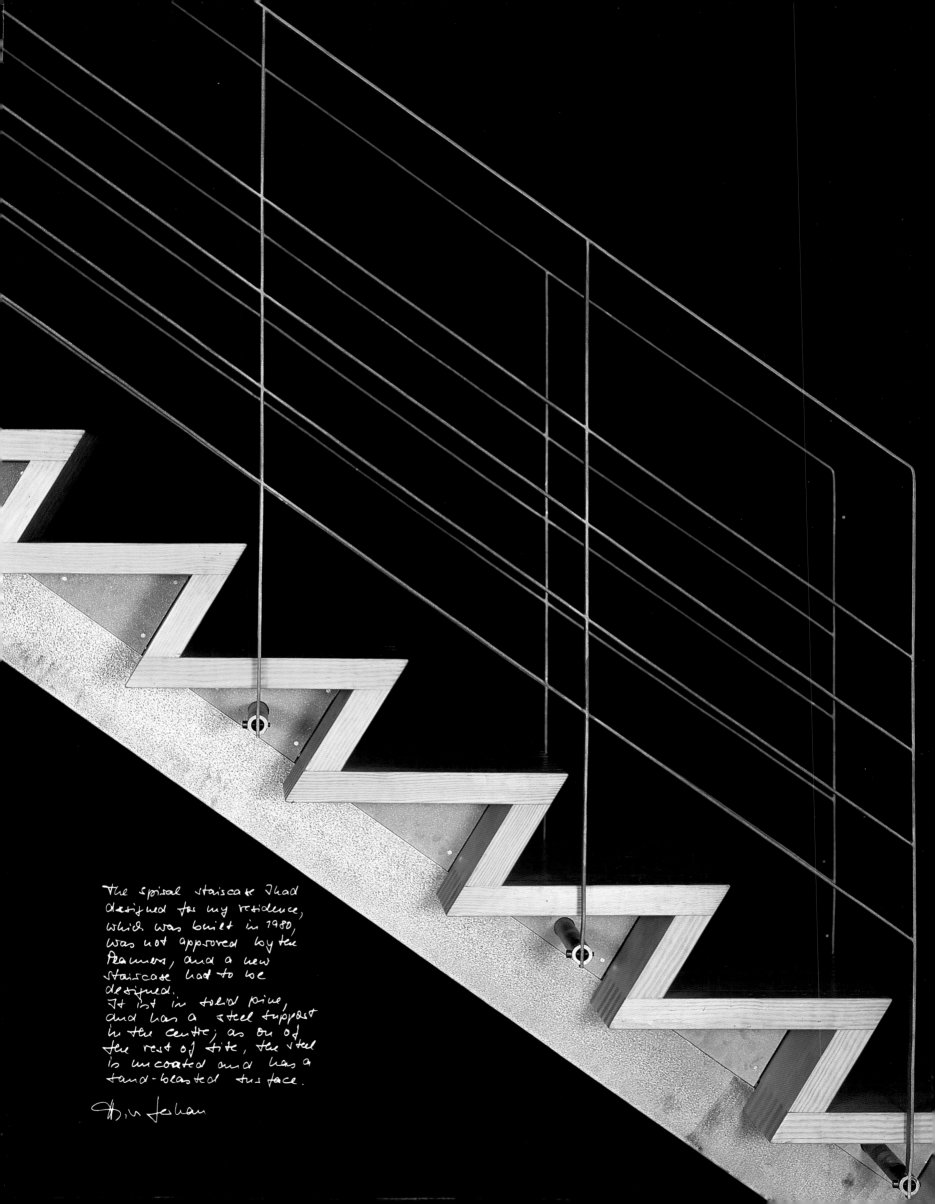

The spiral staircase I had
designed for my residence,
which was built in 1980,
was not approved by the
Planners, and a new
staircase had to be
designed.
It is in solid pine,
and has a steel support
in the centre; as on of
the rest of site, the steel
is uncoated and has a
sand-blasted surface.

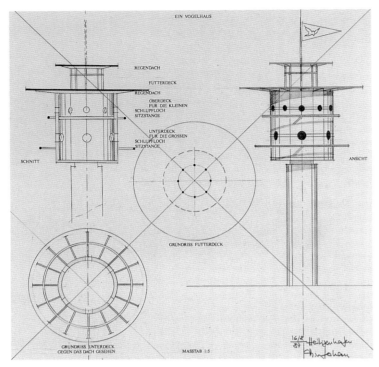

A BIRD HOUSE
(1987)

Design: Meinhard von Gerkan

How would an architect design a bird house, if he were asked to do so? The German radio and television magazine "Hör zu" wanted to know, and I was happy to oblige. Just the job to relax with on a summer evening, free of constraints and restrictions, in the bird sanctuary on the Baltic coast.

My projecting top curves like a sickle and offers shade from the sun and shelter from the rain to the birds perched on the rods running round underneath. The upper platform is a meeting place, and the tiny hut on the roof contains dry food.

The upper storey is for the little birds, the lower one for the bigger birds. Building anything like this on a larger scale would be just an architect's dream.

PROJECTS AND AWARDS

PROJECTS UNDER CONSTRUCTION

1993 Algiers Airport
- Schleswig Holstein Commercial School
- Augustinum Kühlhaus Neumühlen College, Hamburg
- Passenger Terminal, Hamburg Airport
- Fleetinsel, Hamburg
- District Court, Braunschweig
- Employment Exchange, Oldenburg
- Post Office 2, Hanover
- Conversion of the District Court, Flensburg
- EAM, Kassel
- Refurbishment of the old building, Lazarus Hospital, Berlin
- Multi-storey Car Park P2, Berlin-Tegel Airport
- Galeria Duisburg
- Deutsche Revision, Frankfurt am Main
- Concert and Conference Hall, Lübeck
- Brodschrangen, Hamburg
- Schaarmarkt, Hamburg
- Graskeller "Hypobank", Hamburg
- Germano-Japanese Centre, Hamburg

PROJECTS AT THE PLANNING STAGE

1993 Vocational School (second phase), Flensburg
- Harburger Quarre, Hamburg
- Harburger Hof, Hamburg
- Neuer Wall, Hamburg
- Adult Education Centre and State Library, Heilbronn
- Hansetor Bahrenfeld, Hamburg
- "City-Center", Mülheim
- Bahnhofsplatz, Koblenz
- Stuttgart Airport (second phase)
- Hillmanneck, Bremen
- Bahnhofsgalerie, Wilhelmshaven
- Platz der Republik, Frankfurt/Oder
- Astoria Hotel, Leipzig
- District Court, Hamburg-Nord
- Sternhäuser, Norderstedt
- Rehaklinik, Usedom
- Hotel Ku'damm Eck, Berlin
- Leipzig Trade Fair
- EBL Offices, Leipzig
- Kehrwiederspitze, Hamburg
- Bei St Annen, Hamburg
- Fontenay Apartment Block, Hamburg
- Friedrichshain Complex, Berlin

COMPLETED PROJECTS

1967 Stormarnhalle, Bad Oldesloe

1969 Max-Planck Institute, Lindau/Harz
- Köhnemann House, Hamburg

1970 An der Alster Residential Development, Hamburg
- Sports Centre, Diekirch/Luxemburg

1972 Apartment Block, Alstertal, Hamburg

1974 Shell AG Headquarters, Hamburg
- Airport, Berlin-Tegel

1975 Aral AG Headquarters, Bochum
- School Centre, Friedrichstadt
- Plant and Operations Building, Berlin-Tegel
- Noise Insulation Hangar, Berlin-Tegel
- Vehicle Hangar, Berlin-Tegel
- Grit Store, Berlin-Tegel

1976 Oldenburg Tax Office. Oldenburg
- District Vocational School, Bad Oldesloe
- College Sports Facilities, Kiel

1977 Psychiatric Institution, Rickling

1978 Town Houses, Hamburg Bau 78
- Terrace Houses, Hamburg Bau 78
- Taxi Circuit, Berlin-Tegel Airport
- Technical School, Hamburg-Bergedorf

1979 Redevelopment of the "Fabrik", Hamburg
- Kohlhöfen Residential District, Hamburg

1980 Hanse Viertel, Hamburg
- European Patent Office, Munich
- Taima and Sulayyil, 2 new developments in the desert, Saudi Arabia
- MAK Offices, Kiel-Friedrichsort
- Mechanical Workshops and Heating Installation, Psychiatric Institution, Rickling
- Biochemical Institute, Braunschweig University
- Ramada Renaissance Hotel, Hamburg
- House "G", Hamburg-Blankenese
- Residential Unit, Psychiatric Institution, Rickling

1982 Extension to the Otto-Versand Headquarters, Hamburg
- Community Hall, Ritterstrasse, Stade
- "Black Box" Schaulandt, Electronics Shopping Precinct, Hamburg

1983 Ministry of the Interior, Kiel
- Home for the Disabled, Südring, Hamburg
- Hohe Bleichen Accounts Office, Hamburg
- Multi-Storey Car Park, Poststrasse, Hamburg
- DAL Offices, Mainz

1984 Lufthansa Administrative Offices, Hamburg
- Hillmann Garage, Bremen
- Residential and Commercial Building, Marktarkaden, Bad Schwartau

- Energy-Saving Building, IBA/Berlin
- 6 Townhouses, IBA/Berlin
- Indoor Tennis Courts, Bad Schwartau
- Police Station, Panckstrasse, Berlin

1985 Plaza Hotel, Bremen
- COCOLOCO, Building and Boutique, Hanse Viertel, Hamburg
- Thetmarshof and Falkenhorst Psychiatric Hospitals, Rickling

1986 OPD Multi-storey Car Park, Braunschweig
- Redevelopment of the Michaelsen Landhaus as a Doll Museum, Hamburg
- Technical and Vocational School, Flensburg
- Hamburg Office, Bonn

1987 Residential and Commercial Building, Grindelallee 100, Hamburg

1988 Residential Development, Fischmarkt, Hamburg
- Rheumatism Clinic, Bad Meinberg
- EKZ Conversion, Hamburger Strasse, Hamburg
- Residence, Saalgasse, Frankfurt

1989 Judiciary Building, Flensburg
- Elbterrassen, Hamburg

1990 Main Post Office Building, Braunschweig
- Training Centre for the Hamburg Electricity Authority, Hamburg
- Moorbek Rondeel, Norderstedt
- Multi-storey Car Park, Hamburg Airport
- Clinic, Bernauer Strasse, IBA, Berlin
- Town Hall, Bielefeld
- On Board Service, Berlin-Tegel Airport

1991 Passenger Terminal, Stuttgart Airport
- Sports Arena, Flensburg
- Café Andersen, Hamburg
- Lufthansa Offices (second phase), Hamburg
- City Rail Stop, Bielefeld
- Sheraton Hotel, Ankara
- Shopping Centre, Ankara
- Saargalerie, Saarbrücken
- Matzen Office and Commercial Building, Buchholz
- City Centre, Schenefeld
- Hillmann Building, Bremen
- Miro Data Systems, Braunschweig

1992 Architect's House (vG), Elbchaussee, Hamburg
- Jumbo Shed No. 7 for Lufthansa, Hamburg
- Zurich House, Hamburg
- Salamander Building, Berlin
- Extension to DAL offices, Mainz

COMPETITIONS

First Prize/Place

1964 Sports and Conference Hall,
Hamburg (1)
– Indoor and Open Air Swimming Pools,
Braunschweig (1)

1965 Indoor and Open Air Swimming Pools,
SPD
– Max-Planck Institute, Lindau/Harz (1)
– Oldenburg Tax Office, Oldenburg
– Sports Centre,
Diekirch/Luxemburg(1)
– Berlin-Tegel Airport
– Stormarnhalle, Bad Oldesloe (1)

1966 District Indoor Swimming Pool,
Cologne (1)
– College Sports Facilities, Kiel (1)

1970 Shell AG Headquarters, Hamburg
– District Vocational School, Bad
Oldesloe (1)

1971 European Patent Office, Munich
– General Purpose Building III,
Hamburg University
– Residential Development,
Gellerstrasse, Hamburg (2)
– Shopping Centre, Alstertal,
Hamburg (1)

1972 ARAL AG Headquarters, Bochum
– School Centre, Friedrichstadt

1974 Vocational School Centre, Hamburg-
Bergedorf
– Provincial Insurance Headquarters,
Kiel (3)

1975 Deutscher Ring, Hamburg
– Munich II Airport (2) (3)

1976 District Administration,
Recklinghausen
– Moscow Airport
– Community Centre, Stade

1977 Algiers Airport
– Otto Versand Headquarters,
Hamburg
– MAK Headquarters, Kiel (1)
– Police Station, Panckstrasse, Berlin

1978 National Library, Teheran (1)
– Joachimsthaler Platz, Berlin (1)
– Ministry of Transport, Bonn

1979 Combined Town Hall and Indoor
Swimming Pool, Berlin-Spandau
– Sports Facilities and Swimming Pool,
Mannheim-Herzogenried (3)
– Biochemical Institute,
– Braunschweig (1)
– Chemical Institute, Braunschweig

1980 Vereinsbank, Hamburg (1) (3)
– District Administration, Meppen (2)
– Academy of Fine Arts, Hamburg
– Römerberg, Frankfurt
– Fleetinsel, Hamburg
– Lazarus Hospital, Berlin (1) (2) (3)
– Vocational School Centre,
Flensburg (1)
– Lufthansa Hangar, Hamburg
Fuhlsbüttel
– Stuttgart Airport
– Johanneum Sports Hall, Lübeck

1981 Town Hall, Bielefeld
– Kravag Offices, Hamburg (2) (3)
– Plaza Hotel, Bremen
– DAL Offices, Mainz (1)
– Residential Development,
Bad Schwartau
– Judiciary Offices, Braunschweig
– Refurbishment Kieler Castle

1982 "Rose Complex" in the Rheumatism
Clinic, Bad Meinberg

1983 Grüner & Jahr Publishing House,
Hamburg

1984 Corner Development, Quickborn
– District Court, Flensburg

1985 Museum and Library, Münster

1986 Townhall, Husum
– Hamburg Airport
– Bäckerstrasse, Halstenbek (2)(3)
– Employment Exchange, Oldenburg

1987 New spatial lay-out, Bertelsmann

1988 Zurich House, Hamburg
– Federal Ministry for the Environment,
Bonn
– Salamander Building, Berlin
– Störgang, Itzehoe
– EAM Kassel
– Bahnhofsplatz, Koblenz

1989 Housing Development, Falkenstein
– Bertelsmann Foundation, Gütersloh

1990 Concert and Conference Hall, Lübeck
– Deutsche Revision, Frankfurt
– Adult Education Centre and Library,
Heilbronn
– Housing Development, Hamburg-
Nienstedten
– Technology Centre, Münster

1991 Germano-Japanese Centre, Hamburg
– Hansetor Bahrenfeld, Hamburg
– EKZ, Langehorn Markt, Hamburg
– Zeppelinstein Office Complex,
Bad Homburg
– City Centre Development,
Frankfurt/Oder
– Altmarkt, Dresden (2nd phase)

1992 Leipzig Trade Fair
– Neuköln Forum, Berlin
– City Centre, Grünau Berlin
Mollstrasse, Hans-Beimler-Strasse
ECE
– Auditorium, Oldenburg
– Siemens Nixdorf, Munich
– District Court, Hamburg Nord
– Wünsche House, Feenteich,
Hamburg
– Telecom, Suhl (1)
– Hotel Bansin, Baltic Sea (1)

Second Prize/Place

1965 Niebüll District Headquarters Building

1966 Jungfernstieg, Hamburg (1) (3)
– Munich Olympics, Project B
– Church Centre, Hamburg-Ohlsdorf
– School Centre, Heide
– Main Post Office, Bremen
– Main Tax Office, City-Nord, Hamburg
– Sports Ground, Bremen University

1972 Government Building, Lüneburg

1975 Town Planning, Billwerder-Allermöhe
– Ministry of the Interior, Kiel
– Town Planning Uni-Ost, Bremen
– Service Hangar, Munich II Airport

1977 Hamburg-Bau 78

1980 Gasworks, Munich
– Volkswagen Factory Offices,
Wolfsburg
– Oldenburg Townhall, Oldenburg

1981 Chemistry Building, Braunschweig
University
– Employment Exchange, Kiel
– Max-Planck Quantum Optics, Munich
– Clinic II, Nürnberg Süd (1)

1982 "Orangery", Castle Park, Fulda

1983 Daimler Benz AG, Stuttgart

1984 German National Museum, Nürnberg
– Secondary School and Sports Hall,
Schleswig-Holstein

1985 Natural History Museum, Balje

1986 Post Offices, Hamburg
– Kummellstrasse, Hamburg
– Technik III, Kassel University
– Harbour Design, Heiligenhafen

1987 Radio Towers
– Virchow Institute, Berlin

1988 Town Hall, Celle
– Multi-storey Car Park, Paderborn
– New Orangery, Herten

1989 Leisure Pool, Wyk auf Föhr
Königsgalerie, Kassel

1990 Cologne Airport
– Kehrwiederspitze, Hamburg
– New Street, Ulm
– Acropolis Museum, Athens

1991 Altmarkt, Dresden
– Krefeld Süd
– Industrial Zone, Münster Harbour
– Herne Marina
– Süderelbe Harbour Station, Hamburg

1992 Olympia 2000 - Cycling Arena and
Swimming Pool, Berlin
– Sound insulation, Schwaben Market

Third Prize/Place

1965 Wolfsburg Theatre (1)

1966 Sports Hall, Bottrup (1)

1969 Engineering Academy, Buxtehude

1970 Steilshoop Community Centre,
Hamburg
– School and Training Centre, Niebüll

1971 Development of the western City
Centre, Hamburg

1973 Headquarters Colonia Insurance
Company, City Nord, Hamburg

1977 Post Office Savings Bank, City Nord,
Hamburg

1978 EKZ Extension, Alstertal, Hamburg
– Mannheim Townhall

1979 Sports Centre, Berlin Free University,
Düppel Nord

1980 College, Bremerhaven (1)

1985 Town Planning Competition, Münster

1986 Federal Art Gallery, Bonn

1987 Police Headquarters, Berlin

1988 TU and HDK Libraries, Berlin

1989 Concert Hall, Dortmund
– International Marine Court, Hamburg

1990 Television Museum, Mainz
– "Cement Factory", Bonn
– Münster State Hall, Münster
1991 Station, Spandau

Fourth Prize/Place

1963 Civic Centre, Kassel

1969 Spa Treatment Centre,
Westerland/Sylt
– Comprehensive School, Steilshoop

1971 Federal Chancellor's Department,
Bonn

1975 Townhall Extension, Itzehoe

1979 FU Sports Centre, Berlin-Dahlem
– Church Records Office, Hanover
– Sports Hall, Bielefeld

1981 Federal Telecommunications Ministry,
Bonn

1983 Maria-Trost Hospital, Berlin

1986 History Museum, Bonn

1987 Employment Exchange, Flensburg

1988 Schering Berlin

1989 Deutsche Bundesbank, Frankfurt
– Documenta Exhibition Hall, Kassel
– University Library, Kiel

Fifth Prize/Place

1966 School and Sports Centre, Brake

1980 Federal Ministry of Employment and
Social Affairs, Bonn

1985 Göttingen Library

1987 City Hall, Wiesloch

1989 Art Gallery and Extension to the
Townhall, Wolfsburg
– Town Planning, Kiel University
– Zurich House, Frankfurt

1990 Ericusspitze, Hamburg

Commended

1963 Residenzplatz, Würzburg
– Löwenwall, Braunschweig

1965 Town Planning, Hamburg-Niendorf
– Indoor and Open Air Swimming Pool
SPD

1966 Pinakothek, Munich (1)
– Town Planning, Kiel (special commendation) (1)

1967 Olympic Buildings, Munich, Project B
– Open Air Swimming Pool, Bad
Bramstedt

1968 Comprehensive School, Weinheim
– Alsterufer Residential Development,
Hamburg

1969 Comprehensive School,
Mümmelmannsberg, Hamburg

1970 Aldeby School Centre, Flensburg
– EPA Munich, 1st Phase
– High School, Bargteheide (1)

1971 Shopping Centre, Hamburg-
Lohbrügge
– Town Planning, Tornesch (1)
– Swimming Pool Complex, Bad
Oldesloe

1972 Convalescent Home, Helgoland

1977 Bauer Verlag, Hamburg
– Axel-Springer-Verlag, Hamburg
(special commendation)

1979 Computer Centre, Deutsche Bank,
Hamburg (1)
– Town Hall, Neumünster

1980 Town Planning, Valentinskamp,
Hamburg
– Römerberg Frankfurt - Compulsory
submission
– "Wohnen im Tiergarten", IBA Berlin

1981 Sorting Office, Munich

1982 German Library, Frankfurt
– Daimler-Benz AG, Stuttgart
– Hamburg Savings Bank

1983 Technikerkrankenkasse, Hamburg

1987 Second Phase of the State Library,
Münster
– Pfalz Theatre, Kaiserslautern

1991 "Rosenstein" and "Nordbahnhof",
Stuttgart
– Museum of the 20th Century,
Nürnberg
– Sony Berlin GmbH, Potsdamer Platz,
Berlin

(1) Project worked on in partnership with
other architects

(2) Competitions in which no first prize was
awarded and so the project was in
fact placed first

(3) Competitions in which several equal
places were awarded

PHOTOGRAPHIC CREDITS

CHRISTIAN BARTENBACH, Munich
142, 242

HANS CHRISTIAN BRINKSCHMIDT,
Hamburg
23

RICHARD BRYANT, Kingston-on-
Thames
24 bottom, 26, 30, 31 bottom, 32, 33,
34, 66, 70, 80, 81, 82/83, 124/125, 129
bottom, 230, 232-233, 234-235, 238,
244 top, 246-247, 252-253 top, 286,
288 top, 290, 291 top, 291 bottom

DAIMLER BENZ AG, Berlin
226

H.G. ESCH, Cologne
64, 72

BERNT FEDERAU, Hamburg
17 top, left and right

KLAUS FRAHM, Börnsen
2, 4, 22, 36, 38, 37 middle, 120, 121,
122, 127 bottom, 128, 129, 136, 137,
138, 139, 143, 157 bottom, 158, 159,
190, 191, 192/193, 194, 195 , 196/197,
198, 199 , 266/267

WOLF-DIETER GERICKE, Stuttgart
3, 8, 236 top, 237 top, 239, 243 top, 244
bottom, 245, 248, 249-250-251, 253
bottom

HEINRICH HEIDERSBERGER,
Wolfenbüttel
15 bottom

E. HEITKAMP GmbH, Niederlassung
Hamburg
273 bottom

ROLF KOEHLER, Berlin
12 second from bottom

WALTRAUD KRAUSE, Munich
9 top

LANDESBILDSTELLE, Berlin
17 second from top

HEINER LEISKA, Hamburg
Front cover, 9 bottom, 11 top, 11 second from top, 11 bottom, 14, 16 second
from top, 17 bottom, 18, 20, 21, 24 top,
27, 31 top, 35, 37 top, 39, 41, 42, 44/45,
46, 52, 53, 54/55, 56/57, 58, 59, 60, 61,
62, 63, 67, 71, 73,84, 85, 86, 87, 88, 90,
91, 92, 93, 94, 95, 96, 97, 98, 100, 106/
107, 109, 110, 111, 112, 113, 123 top,
126, 134, 132, 135 top, 135 top, 144/
145, 146, 147,148, 149 middle, 150,
152, 153, 154, 162, 163, 164, 165, 166,
172, 173, 174, 175, 177, 184, 186, 187,
200, 201, 202, 203, 204, 205, 206, 209,
210, 211, 212, 213, 214/215, 216, 217,
218, 220-221, 222-223, 224-225, 231
top, 236 bottom, 237 bottom, 243
middle, 243 bottom, 255, 257, 258/259,
260, 261, 262/263, 265 bottom, 268,
269, 270, 271, 272, 273 top, 274, 275,
276/277, 278, 279, 280, 281, 282, 283,
284, 285, 287 top, 288 bottom, 289
bottom, 294, 295

MANFRED SCHULZE-ALEX, Hamburg
140, 227-228

WILFRIED TÄUBNER, Kürten
10 top

VAP, Hamburg
167

GERT von BASSEWITZ, Hamburg
11 third from top, 156, 157 top, 160, 161

von GERKAN, MARG & PARTNERS,
Hamburg
65, 102, 108, 123 middle, 123 bottom,
127 top, 149 bottom, 231 middle

MICHAEL WORTMANN, Hamburg
12-13, 68, 69, 74, 75 top, 76/77, 78, 79,
168/169, 170/171, 133, 135 bottom,
178, 179, 180, 181, 182, 183, 208, 256,
265 top, 265 middle, 287 middle, 289
top, 290 middle, 292, 293